Swift's Tory Politics

F.P. LOCK

DUCKWORTH

Published in 1983
Gerald Duckworth & Co. Ltd.
The Old Piano Factory
43 Gloucester Crescent, London NW1

ISBN 0 7156 1755 9 (cased)

British Library Cataloguing in Publication Data

Lock, F.P.
    Swift's tory politics.
    1. Swift, Jonathan–Criticism and interpretations
    2. Politics in literature
    I. Title
    828'.509   PR3728.P/

    ISBN 0-7156-1755-9

Photoset in North Wales by
Derek Doyle & Associates, Mold, Clwyd
and printed in Great Britain by
Redwood Burn Ltd. Trowbridge, Wilts.

SWIFT'S TORY POLITICS

Contents

Note on References

The following abbreviations are used to refer to the standard editions of Swift's works:

Corr. Correspondence. Ed. Harold Williams. 5 vols. Oxford, 1963-5.
JS Journal to Stella. Ed. Harold Williams. 2 vols. Oxford, 1948.
Poems Poems. Ed. Harold Williams. 2nd ed. 3 vols. Oxford, 1958.
PW Prose Writings. Ed. Herbert Davis. 14 vols. Oxford, 1939-68.

References by volume and page numbers are given in the text, as (*PW* xi.132), except that line numbers are given for particular passages from poems. There are editions of a number of important political works with useful introductions and commentaries; I refer to them where appropriate, but I have preferred to quote from and give references to the above editions as most readers will have easier access to them.

In the notes, the place of publication of books is London except where otherwise specified, short references are used for second and subsequent citations of the same work within the same chapter, and the following additional abbreviations are used:

BIHR	*Bulletin of the Institute of Historical Research*
POAS	*Poems on Affairs of State,* vi-vii, ed. Frank H. Ellis (New Haven, 1970-5)
PQ	*Philological Quarterly*
Somers Tracts	*A Collection of Scarce and Valuable Tracts,* ed. Walter Scott, xii-xiii (1814-15)

Preface

This is a 'tory' interpretation of Swift, arguing that he was by no means the political liberal, the unequivocal champion of 'liberty' that some of his modern admirers would like him to have been. If Swift is read out of context, he can indeed sound deceptively liberal and libertarian. But taken as a whole and in context, his writings reveal a deeply conservative, even reactionary, political thinker. Central to my argument is Swift's attitude to the Revolution of 1688. But there is so little evidence about this from the 1690s that I have found it best to approach the question by looking first at Swift's writings as a tory journalist between 1710 and 1714, the most fully documented and the most exciting years of his political life. Swift believed in the government he was writing for. His tory pamphlets are very largely the expression of his own cherished political ideas, attitudes, and values. His views on the political issues of 1710-14 were coloured by, and lead back to, his attitude to the Revolution. It was a grudging, qualified acceptance; a reluctant, balance-sheet approval. He deviated neither into wholehearted acceptance nor into overt rejection of the Revolution settlement, even though many tories after 1714 drifted either towards the whigs or towards the Jacobites. This distinctive attitude characterises all Swift's political writings which touch on the subject, and is a major theme in this book. The same consistency over a long period of time can be seen in his fundamental political values (order, hierarchy, and stability), which were those of a 'natural' tory of his day. These values had been threatened by the Revolution and its aftermath, and Swift held to them all the more firmly when (after 1714) they appeared to be threatened by the very establishment that ought to have protected them. I have discussed such major texts as *The Drapier's Letters* and *Gulliver's Travels*, but there is more to Swift's politics than they reveal and I have tried to stimulate interest in some of the less widely read tracts and pamphlets.

I am grateful to the Henry E. Huntington Library for a research fellowship which enabled me to work on this book for some months in its congenial surroundings and with its great resources for the study of Swift at my disposal. I should also like to thank Claude Rawson, whose invitation to contribute an essay on 'Swift and English politics' to his forthcoming *The Character of Swift's Satire: A Revised Focus* provided a stimulus to write about Swift's political journalism. I have occasionally drawn on that essay here.

F.P.L.

CHAPTER ONE

The Four Last Years

Several reasons can be advanced to account for the extraordinary flourishing of political literature and journalism in the reign of Queen Anne, especially in the 'four last years' between the trial of Dr Sacheverell in 1710 and the death of the queen in 1714. Popular participation in politics, and national educational standards, both reached new heights around 1640, but these trends were sharply reversed after the Restoration in 1660. Elections became infrequent, there was a determined attempt to restrict the franchise, and educational levels may even have fallen. These conditions, so unfavourable to political writing, were themselves reversed after the Revolution of 1688. More people became involved more often in national politics. The electorate grew to around 300,000 voters by 1715. General elections were held more frequently, and there were more contested elections in the constituencies. There was renewed interest in the education of the poor, although few people can have intended that charity-school children would take any part in politics. There were, however, important and divisive political issues that appealed to all sections of the community, so that interest (if not direct participation) in politics was almost universal. After 1715 these post-Revolution trends were again reversed, so that between about 1700 and 1715 probably a higher proportion of Englishmen enjoyed the franchise, had opportunities to exercise it, and cared about the working of politics than would again be the case before the mid-nineteenth century. It was to this enlarged electorate and politically conscious nation that the writers and journalists of Queen Anne's reign appealed. National politics was primarily a struggle between the two great parties, the whigs and the tories. Most voters remained loyal to their party, but the outcome of elections would be determined by shifts in popular support from one party to the other. The press was a very important means of influencing both the steady and the volatile elements of public opinion. In 1695 pre-publication censorship of the press had been allowed to lapse. This did not lead to the immediate creation of rival propaganda machines, for the parties were slow to realise how the press could be used in a systematic way. By 1710, however, rudimentary but effective organisations had developed, so that a pamphlet or paper written on one side of a question was practically assured of a reply from the other. Stringent libel laws remained available to the government of the day, but they were hard to enforce and convictions were difficult to obtain. Some of the most objectionable publications were prosecuted by way of example, but it proved impossible for governments to exercise the general restraint on the press that had existed before 1695 and that was still usual in Europe. The result was a large increase in the volume of printed political comment, and especially in the amount of outspoken criticism of the government and its policies that was perforce tolerated. Sales and circulation figures suggest that there may have been an audience of about 80,000 regular readers of political news and comment. Britain was the wonder of Europe in the freedom of political writing and in the size of its politically aware and active nation.

During the course of Queen Anne's reign an increasingly bitter struggle was waged between the two major parties. Between 1702 and 1708 mixed ministries, with important posts divided between whigs and tories, were the rule, but co-operation between the parties proved so difficult that from 1708 governments were composed primarily (though never exclusively) of members of one of the parties. Although most writers, including the most partisan, pretended to deplore the existence and excesses of the parties, this was little more than an inherited and obsolete rhetoric, and parties were the most important single factor in politics. The two parties were divided from each other by fundamentally opposite constitutional ideas, religious attitudes, and foreign policies. There were also divisions within parties that could, at times, play as crucial a role as the opposition between parties. The substance of political conflict was thus as favourable to the growth of a political press as the conditions that involved so many people in it. The period of Swift's continuous involvement in English politics, 1710-14, was unequalled before the reign of George III for the volume and virulence of its paper controversies. Swift was not the only major writer to take part in them. Defoe was a prolific contributor, while Addison, Steele, and Arbuthnot made important though less frequent contributions. Numerous lesser figures, gentlemen as well as hacks, played parts of varying importance. Some of Swift's best writing, both public and private, belongs to these years. Yet it is easy to see why his writings on English politics should be less widely read than his Irish pamphlets of the 1720s, especially *The Drapier's Letters* and *A Modest Proposal*. The English pamphlets require a greater knowledge of their political context for a proper understanding, while the Irish ones address issues that are far more appealing to the modern sensibility. The result has often been a distorted picture of Swift's politics that overemphasises the champion of 'liberty' at the expense of the spokesman for authority. To redress this imbalance it is necessary to begin with a close look at Swift's writings on behalf of the tory government of 1710-14 and the literary-political conditions in which they were written.[1]

i

By modern standards, early eighteenth-century newspapers were tiny in size and circulation, although it seemed to many contemporaries that their numbers and popularity were a public nuisance. The format of the typical newspaper was a single folio half-sheet, printed in double columns on both sides and containing about 3000 words of news. Newspapers were expensive at 1d (or 1½d after the imposition of the stamp duty in 1712), but anyone who could afford the 1d required to enjoy a coffee-house could read the papers there for no extra charge. The usual frequency was two or three issues per week. The *Daily Courant* was the only regular daily newspaper, although during their limited runs the *Spectator* and the *Guardian* were both published daily. Throughout Queen Anne's reign the newspapers were dominated by foreign news. Much less space was given to

---

[1] My approach to the study and interpretation of Swift's involvement in English politics has been particularly influenced by the following works of historical scholarship: Keith Feiling, *A History of the Tory Party, 1640-1714* (Oxford, 1924); J.H. Plumb, *The Growth of Political Stability in England, 1675-1725* (1967); Geoffrey Holmes, *British Politics in the Age of Anne* (1967); and J.P. Kenyon, *Revolution Principles: The Politics of Party, 1689-1720* (Cambridge, 1977). For biographical information about Swift himself I have drawn freely on Irvin Ehrenpreis, *Swift: The Man, his Works, and the Age* (2 vols, 1962-7).

domestic events and there was hardly any editorial commentary; a paper showed its political bias through the selection and presentation of news items. The prominence given to an item, or the tone in which it was reported, would often indicate the paper's editorial attitude. In 1704 a careful estimate of the circulation of newspapers, drawn up to support a proposal to tax them, gave the total weekly output as 43,000, with sales of individual papers varying from 400 to 6000 per issue. The most popular papers were the official government *London Gazette* (6000 copies, twice weekly); the strongly tory *Post Boy*, edited by Abel Roper (3000 copies, three issues per week); and the *Post Man* (3800-4000 copies, three per week), edited by the Huguenot refugee Jacques Fonvive, which enjoyed a reputation for accuracy and impartiality. There were more whig papers than tory ones, but they had individually smaller circulations (the *Daily Courant* 800, Defoe's *Review* only 400).[2] The proposal for a tax was not adopted in 1704, but when a tax of ½d per half-sheet was imposed in 1712 there was a substantial initial fall in the circulation of newspapers, with several papers ceasing publication, followed by a much slower recovery. Figures based on the purchase of the stamped paper on which newspapers (from 1 August 1712) had to be printed show that in the first weeks after the imposition of the tax between 67,000 and 78,000 papers per week were being produced (compared with 44,000 in 1704). By mid-1713 this figure had been reduced to about 46,000.[3] The revenue raised was so small in relation to the government's overall budget that the tax should be seen as primarily an attempt to impose an indirect censorship on political news.[4] A more drastic measure might have worked, but the appetite for news was by 1712 too great for a small tax to dampen it. The newspapers survived and expanded.

One reason for the ineffectiveness of the stamp tax in checking the printing of news was that each copy of a paper was read by several readers, so that the extra cost of the tax was spread very

[2] These circulation figures (derived from the 1704 tax proposal) are taken from James R. Sutherland, 'The circulation of newspapers and literary periodicals, 1700-30', *The Library*, xv (1934), 110-24.

[3] These figures are taken from Henry L. Snyder, 'The circulation of newspapers in the reign of Queen Anne', *The Library*, xxxiii (1968), 206-35.

[4] In *Robert Harley and the Press* (Cambridge, 1979), J.A. Downie contends that the tax was 'primarily a revenue-raising device' (p. 158). But the sum raised in the first year was only £6000, and all the evidence points to the government's real aim being a reduction in the volume of printed news and political comment.

thinly. Coffee-houses, for example, where the provision of the newspapers was a major customer-drawing attraction, would easily absorb the extra cost. It has been estimated that each copy would have been read by as many as ten or twenty readers.[5] Swift, in the *Drapier's Letters*, thought that his pamphlet would reach everyone if one copy were printed for every twelve potential readers (*PW* x.3). Many people, however, would have read several papers, so that it is difficult to calculate the size of the political reading public from the circulation figures. No partisan paper reached a circulation higher than about 4000 copies, which the tory *Evening Post* enjoyed in 1712. If each copy reached ten readers, that would indicate a 'tory' audience of about 40,000. If the 'whig' audience was about the same, a total newspaper reading public of about 80,000 would be suggested. The evidence of the *London Gazette* (which, although controlled by the government of the day, was read by both parties for its foreign and official news) is consistent with this figure. Its sales were about 7500 in 1705-7, declining to about 5400 in 1710. Such figures would have allowed it to reach most newspaper readers in 1707; the falling off would easily be accounted for by the declining importance of war news after 1708, or by the more partisan turn that politics took after that date. If there were about 80,000 newspaper readers, this would compare with a figure of about 40,000 for those who had received higher education.[6] It seems unlikely that newspapers were read, except on unusual occasions, by many people who had not received some years of secondary education. The importance of these figures (which are inevitably very approximate) for the study of Swift's politics is that they help define the size and nature of the political reading public. Many more people would glance at a newspaper than would read an *Examiner* essay, and fewer still would be likely to read through a whole political pamphlet. Genuinely popular participation in politics was commonly confined to rioting (as at the time of the trial of Dr Sacheverell) or enjoyment of the good things that flowed at election times.

Swift certainly did not despise the influence and effects that reports in the newspapers might have. There are scattered

[5] Sutherland, 'The circulation of newspapers', p. 124. I regard the lower figure as more plausible.

[6] The estimate of those having received higher education is based on figures in Lawrence Stone, 'The educational revolution in England, 1560-1640', *Past and Present*, xxviii (1964), 41-80, principally the figure of 820 annual entrants into higher education for the decade 1690-99 (p. 54).

references both to his writing paragraphs for insertion and to his altering reports or keeping them from being published at all. During his period of residence in London in 1710-14 it is likely that he was more continuously involved with the government and tory papers than the surviving evidence indicates. As early as 1708, when his then friend Richard Steele was editor of the *London Gazette*, we find Swift toning down the too-positive prediction of a battle (*Corr*.i.96). Under the tory government, he was able to use his influence to have first William King (the lawyer and wit) and then his friend Charles Ford appointed gazetteers (*Corr*.i.286, *JS* ii.543), and to secure for Ben Tooke a grant for the printing of the *Gazette* (*JS* i.316). When the *London Gazette* was being edited and printed by his friends, it would be natural to suppose that Swift took at least an occasional interest in the paper, more probably influencing the selection of news printed than actually writing anything for it. Swift did contribute several items to Abel Roper's *Post Boy*, and at least one to the *Evening Post* (*PW* vi.196-200). These few items are known from Swift's acknowledgement of his authorship elsewhere; it is likely that he wrote or revised further items that cannot now be identified. In April 1711 Swift ensured that an injurious report about archbishop King was kept out of the *Post Boy* (*JS* i.237; *Corr*.i.219-20); in March 1712 he wrote that 'Roper is my humble Slave' (*JS* ii.519).

Regular political commentary was available, if not in the newspapers, in the periodical papers specifically devoted to it. They did not reach so wide an audience as the newspapers, for none ever achieved the circulation figures of the more popular papers. Nor, of course, being largely topical and partisan, did they rival the great essay journals, the usually apolitical *Tatler*, *Spectator*, and *Guardian*. In the early part of Queen Anne's reign the most important were John Tutchin's extreme whig *Observator*, Charles Leslie's crypto-Jacobite *Rehearsal*, and Defoe's moderate-whig *Review*. The *Observator* had a circulation of about 1000, the *Review* only about 400, the *Rehearsal* probably even less. All three are frequently referred to in contemporary sources, and it would be easy to conclude that they enjoyed an influence much greater than their small circulation figures would suggest. But the preponderence of hostile references (a typical one is Swift's in *Examiner* No. 15, 16 November 1710; *PW* iii.13-14) may suggest rather that they were visible targets, notorious rather than (beyond a small committed readership) influential. A whig journalist who wanted to brand all the tories as extremists and Jacobites would find plenty of material for the purpose in the *Rehearsal*. Like the newspapers, these papers were addressed to a regular readership of the party faithful. Their brevity allowed them to reach a wider audience than the typical pamphlet; they were well suited to being read aloud in a group and discussed. Much the same conditions applied in the more deeply-divided political world of the latter part of the reign. The *Examiner* reached a circulation of about 2000, which was about the same figure as the popular *Spectator* maintained after it doubled its price to 2d on the imposition of the stamp duty (the *Examiner*, in line with most papers, cost 1½d).

With the newspapers limiting themselves to news, and the essay papers constrained in length by their newspaper format, the staple form for the publication of extended political comment and argument was the pamphlet. The typical pamphlet was addressed to a single topical issue, was about 10,000 words long, appeared as an unbound octavo of about 48 pages, and sold for 6d. The usual range of size was between 16 pages (2d) and 96 pages (1s). Any text shorter than 16 pages would usually be published in a form like the newspapers for 1d; few pamphleteers wanted to risk tiring their readers by going much over 100 pages. Longer works intended to appeal to pamphlet-readers would be broken up into parts (as was Francis Hare's lengthy reply to Swift's *Conduct of the Allies*). The essence of a pamphlet was its brevity and its topicality, qualities conducive to immediate popular success but hardly to survival. There are few pamphlets of the day, apart from Swift's, that still attract readers; and his pamphlets cannot be properly understood if only his are read.

We know that the partisan papers had regular circulations of up to about 4000 copies, and that they were read by possibly ten times that number of readers. Figures for pamphlets are more difficult to arrive at, and it is naturally only for the exceptionally successful that figures were recorded. With the ordinary pamphlet, we sometimes know how many were printed, but not how many were sold. Fortunately, the printing and publishing history of one of the most popular and interesting, Swift's own *Conduct of the Allies*, can be followed in detail through the *Journal to Stella*. The *Conduct* was a standard length, 96 pages, and sold for 1s; it was thus twice as long and expensive as the average pamphlet. Its success exceeded expectation, for the first edition (published on 27 November 1711) was printed with 1712 on the title page, as was usual for books and pamphlets printed towards the end of a year. A second edition was not expected to be needed immediately. In the event, the first edition of 1000 copies sold out in two days. A second edition was sold in 'five hours'; by 3 December half of a third edition was already sold, and by 5 December a fourth edition was already in the press. Swift comments that this was 'reckoned very extraordinary, considering 'tis a dear twelve-penny book, and not bought up in numbers by the party to give away, as the Whigs do, but purely upon its own strength' (*JS* ii.430). The size of these editions is not known, but each was probably between 1000 and 1500 copies. This was the usual size of an edition for most books, except for those (like almanacs) which were very cheap and had assured immediate sales. These first four editions were printed from the same setting of type (with some small corrections), and with the proportionately very high cost of paper the publisher would not have wanted to risk overprinting.[7] It was not only the whigs, of course, who bought up pamphlets in quantity for subsidised or free distribution. On 6 December Swift reports that the printer 'is going to print the pamphlet in small, a fifth edition, to be taken off by friends and sent into the country' (*JS* ii.431). This fifth edition, printed in a smaller type, was compressed into only 48 pages. With paper the largest single cost factor, this meant that it could be sold retail for 6d; although, as Swift says, most of the edition was probably 'taken off by friends' at wholesale rates. On 28 January Swift reported further that a sixth edition of 3000 copies had been sold, and that a seventh was in prospect; total sales were now 11,000. A seventh edition was duly printed, but sales had by then slowed down, for an eighth was not called for until 1713. The *Conduct of the Allies* was a spectacular success. Swift regarded the sale of 11,000 copies as 'a most prodigious run' (*JS* ii.474), and the figure would later impress Dr Johnson as remarkable for its time. Even if we did not have Swift's sales figures, the number of replies that the pamphlet provoked is evidence of its contemporary impact.

    Two important inferences can be made from Swift's figures. The first is that, after the sale of the first four editions (perhaps

----

[7] For bibliographical descriptions of the early editions, see H. Teerink, *A Bibliography of the Writings of Jonathan Swift*, 2nd ed., rev. Arthur H. Scouten (Philadlephia, 1963), pp. 281-2. For normal edition quantities, see Philip Gaskell, *A New Introduction to Bibliography* (Oxford, 1972), pp. 160-2. Gaskell notes that, in the hand-press period, no appreciable reduction in unit costs was achieved by editions much larger than 1500.

5000 copies in all) the publisher regarded the limits of the market for a shilling pamphlet as having been reached. Further extension of the readership required a cheaper price, achieved by a smaller format (the equivalent of a modern reprint in paperback). Secondly, such reprinting could roughly double the circulation, to rather more than 11,000 (depending on the size of the seventh edition, and how many copies of it sold immediately). That, very roughly, halving the price would double the circulation of a pamphlet is confirmed by a remark of Thomas Burnet's, who was angry with his publisher for not reprinting one of his pamphlets in smaller format: 'twice the number will buy a three penny thing than would a six penny one.'[8] The publisher's decision may, in this case, have been a perfectly sound one, taking into account the cost of resetting in smaller type. If we take the size of the immediate sale of Swift's *Conduct* as 5000, it will be seen that, at ten readers per copy, the whole of the normal tory reading public (suggested above as about 40,000) would have been reached. The sale of about 12,000 reached by the cheaper printings must have taken the pamphlet well beyond the normal confines of the tories; such a figure implies that the pamphlet was very generally read, by readers on both sides of the political divide and by many who did not normally read political pamphlets at all.

Political pamphlets appeared in great numbers, especially in times of political tension. The annual output during Queen Anne's reign was certainly several hundred. Most of these can have made little impact on the political public at large, and probably few people made any attempt to keep up with them all. A reasonable guide to the more successful ones is provided by looking for those which reached a second edition, or which evoked a reply. A pamphlet that reached a fourth edition and provoked replies would be among the very small number that we can be sure would have been read by, or would at least have come to the attention of, the main body of informed public opinion.[9]

---

[8] *The Letters of Thomas Burnet to George Duckett, 1712-1722*, ed. David Nichol Smith (Oxford, 1914), p. 21.

[9] There is a need for studies of the 1710-14 pamphlet debates on the sophisticated model provided by Mark Goldie, 'The Revolution of 1689 and the structure of political argument: an essay and an annotated bibliography of pamphlets on the allegiance controversy', *Bulletin of Research in the Humanities*, lxxxiii (1980), 473-564. James O. Richards, *Party Propaganda under Queen Anne* (Athens, Georgia, 1972), is based on only about 110 pamphlets in all. F.F. Madan, *A Critical Bibliography of Dr Henry Sacheverell*, ed. W.A.

Not all of Swift's pamphlets achieved this distinction. The figure
of not much more than 11,000 copies for the circulation of the
Conduct of the Allies, however pleased Swift was with it, looks
small when set against the really spectacular figures of 80,000
copies of the pirated editions alone that Defoe claimed for his
True-Born Englishman (1701), or the 100,000 copies of a modern
estimate for the total sales of Henry Sacheverell's sermon *The
Perils of False Brethren* (1709).[10] While both these pamphlets
undoubtedly made a very considerable contemporary impact,
there are good reasons for doubting that so many copies could
have been printed or sold. Defoe had no way of knowing how
many copies of the pirated editions were printed. He claims that
there were about twenty editions, including the authorised ones
(not all of these can now be found), which suggests a figure much
closer to 20,000 copies than to 80,000. Since some of the editions
sold for only 1d, sales could have reached 20,000, for this is
roughly the readership of one of the popular almanacs. Some
editions of Sacheverell's sermon, too, were sold for 1d, but it is
very doubtful whether there was a large enough reading public to
support sales of 100,000 copies even at 1d. The population of
England and Wales was about five million in 1700, of which
about 750,000 were adult males with minimal literacy.[11] Yet only
about 40,000 had received higher education. The general
impression that a reading of contemporary pamphlets gives,
combined with such indicators as that Latin is not usually
translated but Greek rarely used, suggests that the readership at

---

Speck (Lawrence, Kansas, 1978), does not attempt the kind of analysis provided
by Goldie but provides excellent material for such an analysis.

[10] For Defoe's estimate of the numbers printed of his *True-Born Englishman*,
see *POAS*, vi.763. Of the twenty-one editions claimed by Defoe, only nine or ten
are recorded in D.F. Foxon, *English Verse, 1701-1750* (Cambridge, 1975), i.173-4.
The need for a substantial scaling-down of Defoe's figure is also suggested by his
exaggerated estimate of 'above two Hundred Thousand single Papers publish'd
every Week' in 1711 (preface to vol. vii of the *Review*). The earliest figures from
the stamp-tax returns in 1712 suggest a total between 67,000 and 78,000; Snyder,
'The circulation of newspapers', p. 215. The figure of 100,000 for Sacheverell's
sermon is given by Geoffrey Holmes, *The Trial of Dr Sacheverell* (1973), p. 75.
The major piece of evidence is the statement by the publisher, Henry Clements,
that 'betwixt 35,000 and 40,000 of those sermons in 8vo' were printed (quoted in
Holmes, *Sacheverell*, p. 74). I believe that a scribal error has made these figures
ten times too large. The problem is too complicated for full discussion here, but I
hope to make it the subject of a separate study.

[11] The estimate of adult male literacy is based on the graph in David Cressy,
*Literacy and the Social Order: Reading and Writing in Tudor and Stuart
England* (Cambridge, 1980), p. 176.

which the pamphleteers aimed went beyond, but not much beyond, the university-educated. I have already suggested that the readership of the newspapers comprised about 80,000 people, and a slightly lower figure would probably be about right for the regular readers of pamphlets. Thus at ten readers per copy, a partisan pamphlet which went through four editions of about 1000 copies each would reach the whole of its potential audience; this is consistent with the initial sales of the 1s editions of *The Conduct of the Allies*. On occasion, men who were not regular readers of pamphlets might be sufficiently moved or interested by a particular issue or crisis to read one. Defoe and Sacheverell may have penetrated somewhat further into this occasional readership than Swift, since the *Conduct* was never reprinted at 1d, but sales figures of 80,000 or 100,000 are so out of line with other evidence and estimates that they must be exaggerated. In any case, the political writer would aim his pamphlet at what he took to be the usual audience, not at the potentially larger readership which he was most unlikely ever to reach.

Almost all political pamphlets were published anonymously, and the authorship of many remains unknown or uncertain. But few really important and influential pamphlets were written by unknown or occasional authors; a notable exception is *Faults on Both Sides* (1710) by Simon Clement.[12] The success of this attempt to persuade the public that the policies of Robert Harley were synonymous with moderation was all the more remarkable from an otherwise unknown pamphleteer. The speed with which a pamphlet would be required to achieve maximum topical impact would usually give the practised writer with good connections with the book trade a major advantage over the occasional contributor to the debate. The speed with which Defoe, well-informed on almost every conceivable topic of political controversy, could produce a pamphlet is remarkable. Defoe was a professional in the sense that he wrote for a living. Swift was an amateur in the strict sense, since he did not accept money for writing his pamphlets, but with his main efforts devoted to political writing he too was really a professional. Apart from his own writings, Swift may have taken some part in organising tory propaganda. Arthur Maynwaring certainly played such a part for the whigs between 1710 and his death in

---

[12] The dominant part played in the allegiance controversy by authors 'with longstanding reputations as controversialists' is noted by Mark Goldie, 'The Revolution of 1689', p. 479. For Clement, see Henry L. Snyder, 'The authorship of *Faults on Both Sides* (1710)', *PQ*, lvi (1977), 266-72.

1712, writing occasionally but more often supervising and correcting the work of underlings like Francis Hare, Marlborough's chaplain.[13] In the cut and thrust of political pamphleteering, professionalism was a necessity, but self-respecting writers were sensitive about maintaining their status as gentlemen. At least three reasons can therefore be advanced for the acceptance of the almost universal convention of anonymity. Before 1695, except for rare and brief periods (such as at the time of the Popish Plot, and at the Revolution) pre-publication censorship had been strictly enforced in England. This meant that pamphlets critical of the government had usually been clandestine, published not only without any author's name but often with no imprint or a fictitious one. In theory at least, gentlemanly modesty did not allow avowed writing for publication. In practice, this idea was largely obsolete by 1700, but it lingered on in the various subterfuges that had been designed to allow authors to print their works without incurring the charge of vanity. Anonymous publication was one of these, for it could plausibly be pretended to be unauthorised. Many authors, of course, felt a genuine reluctance to acknowledge their work before the public's verdict was known, especially with their first works. Political pamphleteers had a further reason for anonymity: they needed to establish their disinterestedness. Whether defending or attacking the government, the pamphleteer would assert his independence and patriotism. The credibility of a pro-government pamphlet would be lost if its author was known to be a ministerial pensioner; the arguments against the government would be read with less patience if they were known to come from a notorious malcontent.

Fear of prosecution was probably the least important of these reasons. Even under the pre-1695 licensing system, licensed political pamphlets were normally anonymous; and after 1695 most pamphlets carried a genuine publisher's imprint. Even when they did not, it was usually possible for the government to find out who had printed a particular pamphlet if it really wanted to.[14] Prosecutions intended to obtain convictions were

[13] For a full account of his activities, see Henry L. Snyder, 'Arthur Maynwaring and the whig press, 1710-1712', *Literatur als Kritik des Lebens*, ed. Rudolf Haas and others (Heidelberg, 1975), pp. 120-36. Downie, *Robert Harley and the Press*, claims that Swift 'gradually assumed control of the tory propaganda machine' (p. 131), but the evidence is scanty.

[14] The fullest study is still Laurence Hanson, *Government and the Press, 1695-*

rare, and usually indicated that the government had lost patience with some frequent offender. Convictions were hard to obtain, not because the law was lenient or defective (it was extremely stringent), but because juries were reluctant to convict, the freedom of the press having become a national shibboleth, and technical acquittals often nullified the strongest evidence. The government's preferred method (followed by whigs and tories alike in office) was the arrest and harassment of printers and publishers. Arrest and temporary detention were serious matters to the small printer, especially, who could ill afford to leave his business to itself for long. Printers who took such risks would expect appropriate reimbursement from an author or (more usually) the political interest he represented. When George Ridpath was prosecuted by the tory government in 1713, whig sympathisers collected a subscription for him.[15]

For writers like Swift, Addison, and Maynwaring, sensitive to their status as gentlemen and consciously superior to hacks like Defoe and Oldmixon, anonymity was a natural choice rather than an imposed constraint. Swift, certainly, carried the desire for anonymity to a point where it may seem pathological, but it was normal among the class of classically-educated writers. Just as Swift never acknowledged authorship of *A Tale of a Tub*, John Locke entered some of his own works as anonymous in his own library catalogue and admitted being their author only in the codicil to his will.[16] The most important exception to the rule of anonymity was the sermon, which was usually published with the name of the preacher, the place and date of delivery, the occasion and the audience, and the author's position in the church, all on the title-page.[17] Even here, it was usual for the

1763 (Oxford, 1936). Additional evidence is presented in Donald Thomas, 'Press prosecutions in the eighteenth and nineteenth Centuries: the evidence of the King's Bench indictments', *The Library*, xxxii (1977), 315-32. The kind of private intelligence available to the government is illustrated in Henry L. Snyder, 'The reports of a press spy for Robert Harley', *The Library*, xxii (1967), 326-45.

[15] Peter Wentworth to Lord Strafford, 26 December 1712; *Wentworth Papers, 1705-39*, ed. James J. Cartwright (1883), p. 310.

[16] John Harrison and Peter Laslett, *The Library of John Locke* (2nd ed., Oxford, 1971), p. 43; Maurice Cranston, *John Locke: A Biography* (1957), pp. 459-60.

[17] Many sermons were in effect political pamphlets; they are very prominent in White Kennett, *The Wisdom of Looking Backward* (1715), a compendium of the pamphlet literature of 1710-14. The sermons of the mainly tory country clergy (which were rarely printed) reached a large audience that seldom or never read a political pamphlet.

preacher to be requested to publish, and such requests were part of the ritual of preaching on official occasions. All authors in the Queen Anne period, whether gentlemen or hacks, shared the need to appear to their readers in a guise of impartiality. There was in fact very little genuinely independent or disinterested publication (who would write it, and for whom?), and even the printers and publishers had often a particular political affiliation; but everyone felt the need to pretend to impartiality. The extent to which politics was polarised is seen in the way words acquired party overtones; 'moderation' was a whig code-word, it did not mean what it said. The pretence might wear thin, but the convention was respected. Writers who broke it were liable to be regarded either as lunatics (like John Dunton) or as monsters of self-importance (like Richard Steele). When in 1715 the bumptious Thomas Burnet put his name on the title-page of his pro-government pamphlet, *The Necessity of Impeaching the Late Ministry*, it was regarded as a blatant act of self-advertisement.

Pamphlets and periodicals were the mainstays of political controversy, but they were supplemented both by more ephemeral and by more substantial matter. Ballads, lampoons, and other such single-sheet pieces were usually hawked about the streets for 1d or $\frac{1}{2}$d by the ballad-sellers; political papers were often distributed free. Such ephemera, calculated primarily to influence popular opinion and feeling, could also appeal to the more sophisticated. Swift wrote several such pieces, perhaps as much because he enjoyed writing them as because he thought them important. Yet indirectly even such pieces could have a significant effect, for the professional politicians could not afford to ignore the susceptibilities of public sentiment. The popular pro-Sacheverell feeling had done much to help destroy the whig-dominated government in 1710, and popular opinion on such topics as France, popery, and the Pretender was a factor that the tory government had to content with in its period of office. At the opposite end of the scale from the ballads, there were also published large-scale treatises on historical, religious, or political subjects which might accidentally (by the timing of their appearance) serve a polemical purpose, or which might have been intended to serve as part of the contemporary debate. Perhaps the best known examples are the books that William Wake and Edmund Gibson wrote as a result of the controversy about the rights of the anglican convocation. Solidly researched works addressed to a small learned audience, they nevertheless made available evidence and arguments that were useful in the pamphleteering of the day.[18]

Not all politicians in Anne's reign regarded printed propaganda as either important or influential. Both Marlborough and Godolphin, for example, looked on it with indifference or contempt.[19] Such attitudes were characteristic of a generation that had served its political apprenticeship at the court of Charles II, where (except at times of unusual crisis, such as the Popish Plot) intrigue and court favour counted for more than public opinion. By contrast, the generation of politicians who came into prominence after the Revolution were much more aware of the power of the press. Robert Harley was pre-eminent in this respect. It is suggestive that Harley, who made more extensive use of the press than any other contemporary and who showed a more continuous interest in propaganda, won his way to government office not through influence or royal favour but through having made a nuisance of himself in the parliamentary opposition. He needed, from the outset of his career, to be able to influence and manipulate opinion, to be able to win the support of the independent backbenchers in the House of Commons. In the campaign to impeach the four lords in 1701 (the occasion of Swift's first political pamphlet), Harley saw the press exploited against him, and public opinion turned against the Commons in favour of the four lords. The lesson was not lost on him. When he became Secretary of State in 1704 he took some steps towards the development of a pro-government press. When he became effective head of the government in 1710 he was at even greater pains to ensure that the government's policies should be properly

---

[18] The convocation controversy can be studied from both sides in Norman Sykes, *William Wake*, Archbishop of Canterbury, 1657-1737 (Cambridge, 1957), i.80-157; and G.V. Bennett, *The Tory Crisis in Church and State, 1688-1730: The Career of Francis Atterbury, Bishop of Rochester* (Oxford, 1975), especially pp. 44-80. When Henry Sacheverell, in *The Perils of False Brethren* (1709), made a slighting reference to archbishop Grindal (qto ed., reprinted Exeter, 1974, p. 35), the whig church-historian John Strype immediately produced a small pamphlet in defence of Grindal, and used the occasion to launch a subscription for his scholarly *History of the Life and Acts of Edmund Grindal* (1710).

[19] On 9 May 1706 Marlborough wrote to his wife: 'I do not know who the author of the review is; but I do not love to see my name in print, for I am persuaded that an honest man must be justified by his own actions, and not by the pen of a writer, though he should be a zealous friend' (*Private Correspondence of Sarah, Duchess of Marlborough*, 1838, i.22). Admittedly Marlborough was not always as philosophical as this, especially when the writer was far from a 'zealous friend'. John Oldmixon, *The Life and Posthumous Works of Arthur Maynwaring* (1715), records Godolphin's contempt for the press (p. 158).

represented in the press, and one of the writers that he secured to do this was Swift. Although public opinion and the pamphleteering designed to influence it probably reached a peak in the reign of Queen Anne, the government did not stop spending money on the press after 1714. With fewer elections to worry about, and more patronage at his disposal, Robert Walpole had less need of the press than Harley had had, yet he made sure that government views and policies were explained and defended in newspapers and pamphlets. It was largely the accident that he failed to employ the more notable writers that has transmitted a poor image of him to posterity, as Harley's fortunate employment of Swift has earned him a posthumous reputation (among literary students) rather better than he deserves.[20]

The period from 1701 to 1715 was marked by some very sudden and substantial shifts in public opinion. External events were sometimes responsible. In 1704, news of the spectacular success of the battle of Blenheim undermined the case of the tories who were arguing for a sea-based war strategy and gave the whig war policy a great boost in popularity. In 1708 the attempted Jacobite invasion again gave the whigs a much-needed popular issue to exploit against their opponents. External events could sometimes bring into the open such deep but dormant fears as the popular hysteria that the trial of Dr Sacheverell produced for the 'Church in Danger'. In 1713 the whigs failed to capitalise sufficiently on the supposed defects of the tory peace treaties to win the general election. But it was not long after the election that they found a much more potent charge against the ministry by accusing it of plotting to bring in the Pretender. It was much easier to excite and mobilise public opinion through its fear of the Pretender than through more mundane issues like the commercial treaties with France. It is abundantly clear that the press could exploit popular feelings, as Swift did in the *Conduct of the Allies*. To some extent an issue could be artificially manufactured out of such issues, as the whigs were able to create popular indignation about the failure of the French to demolish Dunkirk in 1713. Yet the power of the press had its limits. Even Swift could not neutralise the whig charges of Jacobitism against the government, and in 1714, conscious of his impotence in this new situation, he retired to the country to observe developments he could no longer influence.

---

[20] For Harley, see the often speculative account in Downie, *Robert Harley and the Press*; for Walpole, see Bertrand A. Goldgar, *Walpole and the Wits: the Relation of Politics to Literature, 1722-1742* (Lincoln, Nebraska, 1976).

Swift's inability actually to reverse popular opinion was symptomatic of what may seem a paradox, that the great bulk of contemporary political writing was addressed to an audience already in at least basic agreement with the author's assumptions and point of view. Swift's pamphlets, for example, are addressed to the tories; he hardly ever bothers to take into account whig susceptibilities, much less to try to convert them to his opinion. Yet there remains a very perceptible difference between the way in which Swift addressed his tory readers and the high-flying rhetoric of the more notorious tory extremists. Swift avoids the violence and virulence characteristic of Sacheverell. Like most contemporary pamphleteers, Swift adopts a moderate style even when what he is saying is actually hard-line tory extremism. The reasons for this strategy can be deduced from the voting patterns of contemporary electors.[21] The constituencies which were the most open to swings in public opinion were the counties, where the electoral qualification was the uniform forty-shilling freehold. For the most part, the counties were also the larger constituencies, ranging from Rutland with nearly a thousand voters polling in a typical election to Yorkshire with about ten thousand. Only a few of the borough electorates were larger than a thousand. Voting in all constituencies was open, and many poll books survive to show precisely how each elector voted. Where such poll books are extant for successive or nearly successive elections, they can be analysed to reveal voting patterns and trends. Such data (obtained through computer analysis) is available for Kent and Hampshire in Queen Anne's reign, two of the five counties whose voting records most nearly mirrored the national trend in each general election (the other three were Middlesex, Surrey, and Cheshire); and also for some less typical counties of varying characters (Bedfordshire, Buckinghamshire, Rutland, and Westmorland). While the picture that emerges from the study of these counties may be modified in detail by future research, several facts about voting

---

[21] These voting patterns can be deduced from the evidence of surviving poll books. The basic study is W.A. Speck, *Tory and Whig: The Struggle in the Constituencies, 1701-1715* (1970), which should be supplemented by W.A. Speck and W.A. Gray, 'Computer analysis of poll books: an initial report', *BIHR*, lxiii (1970), 105-12; and by W.A. Speck, W.A. Gray, and R. Hopkinson, 'Computer analysis of poll books: a further report', *BIHR*, lxviii (1975), 64-90. Geoffrey Holmes, *The Electorate and the National Will in the First Age of Party* (Lancaster, 1976) also has much valuable detail and comment on election results in the period.

behaviour seem firmly established. Each party could count on a
core of loyal supporters who would vote for its candidates in every
election, however unpopular nationally the party might be. But in
any particular election only a minority of those entitled to vote
might actually do so. Thus 3517 freeholders voted in the
Hampshire election of 1705, and 4753 in the 1710 election; but
only 1466 electors turned out on both occasions.[22] This turnover of
voters is much larger than could be accounted for by such causes
as death and mobility; on each occasion many freeholders entitled
to vote must have abstained. It is known that while most electors
remained loyal to their party, there was a proportion of 'floating'
voters who would change their allegiance from one election to
another. The proportion of such voters seems to have been
between ten and twenty per cent, with the lower figure being the
more usual. But what really decided the outcomes of elections was
neither the hard core of party loyalists not the floating voters, but
the willingness of the 'fair weather' supporter to attend the poll
and vote. Victory depended on getting out the 'occasional' voter.

The following table shows the votes cast in the Kent county
elections in 1713 and 1715:[23]

1713

Sir Edward Knatchbull (tory)	2823
Percival Hart (tory)	2797
Mildmay Fane (whig)	2185
Edward Watson (whig)	2175

1715

Mildmay Fane (whig)	3229
William Delaune (whig)	3171
Sir Edward Knatchbull (tory)	3084
Percival Hart (tory)	3014

The tories lost the 1715 election despite managing to increase
their vote. What turned the election in the favour of the whigs
was their superior ability in getting out the 'occasional' vote. Of
the 7540 freeholders who cast straight party votes (that is,
excluding the small number who at a single election divided

---

[22] These figures are from Speck and Gray, *BIHR*, lxiii.105-12.

[23] All figures for the Kent elections are taken from Norma Landau,
'Independence, deference, and voter participation: the behaviour of the
electorate in early eighteenth century Kent', *Historical Journal*, xxii (1974), 561-
83.

their votes between whig and tory candidates), 1419 voted tory in both elections and 1268 voted whig. Thus the tories could count on a slightly larger 'hard core' of support. But of those who voted in 1713 but not in 1715, 935 were tories and only 688 were whigs. Thus some hundreds of freeholders who might have been expected to support the losing side failed to vote when they could see the tide going against their party. Of the new voters in 1715, 1470 voted whig and 1397 voted tory, giving the whigs a very slight advantage in the search for 'new' voters (who may, of course, have voted in elections before 1713). Of the freeholders who switched their party allegiance, 278 voted whig in 1715 who had voted tory in 1713; but the tories only gained 85 votes that had gone to the whigs in 1713. The size of this shift to the whigs should be qualified by a geographical fact: that of the 278, no fewer than 148 lived in the six parishes most susceptible to political influence by the government of the day (Deptford, Greenwich, Woolwich, Gravesend, Gillingham, and Chatham). So that over half the apparently 'floating' vote can be attributed to patronage and influence rather than the simple operation of public opinion. The largest single factor in the whig victory was their greater success with the 'occasional' vote, which would of course comprise those electors who would be most easily influenced by public opinion and propaganda. If they were sufficiently committed to a party not to vote for its opponents, they might decide to abstain when their party would obviously lose, as many tory voters did in Kent in 1715. Conversely, the prospect of being in the majority would tend to bring such freeholders to the poll.

The way in which electors were more willing to support the party that was perceived to be in the ascendent is well illustrated by the evidence for the small county of Westmorland in 1701-2.[24] At the general election in December 1701 there was a turnout of 1169 electors and a small whig victory, in line with the national trend. At the 1702 election Westmorland again followed the direction of the country at large. Queen Anne's accession in March had given a boost to the tories, two of whom were elected in Westmorland in place of the whigs. The overall turnout was slightly down: 1007 in 1702 against 1169 in the previous December. Of the 492 freeholders who had cast straight tory

---

[24] Figures given are from R. Hopkinson, 'The electorate of Cumberland and Westmorland in the late seventeenth and early eighteenth centuries', *Northern History*, xv (1979), 96-116.

votes in December 1701, only 130 failed to vote in 1702; but of the 520 who had voted for the two whig candidates, a massive 316 failed to poll in 1702. There were 256 new tory voters, but only 91 new whig ones. Of the 1169 who had voted in December 1701, only 633 voted again in 1702, making the role of the 'new' voters (many of whom had no doubt voted in elections before December 1701) decisive. The greater success of the tories in getting out their vote must have been greatly helped by the fact that, with the queen's backing behind them, they were expected to win the election nationally.

The bid for the support of the 'occasional' and the 'floating' voter would not, of course, be confined to election times. Between elections there would be a need to cultivate political interests to ensure their support at election times. There would be annual elections in the towns; events of county importance like the quarter-sessions or even race meetings could be used as political forums; and the next general election would not be far off. There were eight general elections between 1701 and 1715; the eighth after 1715 was not until 1760. Whether he was writing for or between election times, the tasks of the propagandist would be much the same: to cheer the faithful; to encourage the 'occasional' voter by convincing him that the issues were important and his side was likely to win; to gain, if possible, a proportion of the 'floating' vote by presenting his as the party of conscience, national interest, and success; and to asperse the opponents, with a view to making the floating voter less likely to support them. To do all this in the same pamphlet might seem a daunting task. Even the most skilful and experienced propagandists were not uniformly successful, and of course the importance attached to the various possible groups to whom appeal might be made would vary according to the political situation. But the evidence of the pamphlets themselves amply bears out that the primary task was seen as confirming the faithful and encouraging the waverers, not converting the opponent. Only a small minority of the electorate would actually be regular readers of pamphlets. But they would be the most influential makers of opinion, and what they needed was a good supply of arguments and examples to use as ammunition in the various forums of debate: in parliament; in the coffee-houses; in local social gatherings; even in the pulpit, that great organ for disseminating tory opinion to a vast largely unreading public. Politics in Queen Anne's reign was highly polarised; few people had any doubts about which party they would normally support.

Yet they might have their doubts about a particular issue or policy, and a skilful propagandist would relate that particular to general party principles. Thus in 1713 a whig writer would try to explain how the delay in the demolition of Dunkirk tended to the introduction of popery and the Pretender; in 1710 a tory writer would seek to explain how the continuance of the whigs in office would infallibly have ended in the ruin of the church and the monarchy. In 1710 Harley told Swift that the *Examiner* was needed to 'keep up the spirit raised in the people' (*PW* viii.123), by which he meant that he intended to exploit the pro-Church and tory feelings (engendered by the trial of Dr Sacheverell) in favour of negotiating an early peace. Arthur Maynwaring told Oldmixon that the *Medley* was similarly needed to have 'kept up a Spirit in the *Whigs*', by which he meant allow them to put a brave face on things while public opinion was (temporarily, he hoped) against them.[25] Neither Harley nor Maynwaring, neither Swift nor Oldmixon, contemplated any attempt to convert their opponents to their own views; the function of propaganda was to 'keep up the spirit' of its own side.

It seems most unlikely that many people read both the *Examiner* and the *Medley*. A few, of course, would have professional reasons for doing so, and no doubt Oldmixon and Maynwaring, eager for errors to expose and debating points to score, were among the most avid readers of the *Examiner*. Swift was more contemptuous of the *Medley* than it could afford to be of him, for he had the advantage of being on the offensive. There was no real dialogue between the two sides. The floating vote that existed at the grass-roots level was probably much smaller among informed readers of pamphlets and periodicals. The rapidity with which essayists and pamphleteers answered each other should not be taken as readiness to engage in a dialogue; they were writing for their own side, and both, like the opposing armies after a doubtful battle, always claimed victory for themselves. Yet although there was no really 'centrist' political writing, it is possible to distinguish between writings aimed primarily at the party faithful and those that aimed more at an appeal (though from a party point of view) to the moderate and uncommitted. For example, in *The Management of the War, in a Letter to a Tory Member* (1711; by Francis Hare), which is mainly a defence of whig war policy, there is a list of a

---

[25] John Oldmixon, *Memoirs of the Press, Historical and Political, for Thirty Years Past* (1742), p. 12.

'Bundle' of tory pieces to which the *Management of the War* was offered as a reply. The six pamphlets mentioned (all of them published in 1710) are Henry St John's *Letter to the Examiner*; Simon Clement's *Faults on Both Sides*; Charles Davenant's *Sir Thomas Double at Court*; Defoe's *Essay upon Public Credit*; Abel Boyer's *Letter from a Foreign Minister*; and *The Secret History of Arlus and Odolphus*, of uncertain authorship.[26] Hare affects to admire the 'able Architect' (Harley) whom he supposes responsible for the pamphlets. Then he divides them according to 'the several sorts of Readers they are intended to impose on'. This one, he says, is written for the tories, another is aimed at the moderate men, another is for foreign observers; 'another is to gain the *Whigs*, or divide them at least.'[27] The last comment shows that Hare knew that none of the pamphlets was seriously written for the whigs, although they might try to foment divisions between the whig leadership and the 'fair-weather' rank and file. How far Harley was in reality the inspirer and co-ordinator of this barrage of pamphlets is unknown. But Hare was certainly correct in his analysis of the different audiences at which the various pamphlets were aimed, even though all were written on behalf of Harley's newly-installed government. The most extreme and intemperate is Davenant's *Sir Thomas Double at Court*, an angry piece that lashes out at all the iniquities of the whigs since the Revolution. Davenant mounts a full-scale attack on whig war-policy, particularly making a point that Swift will take up and expand, that the war has been paid for by the country gentlemen. Many of Davenant's points are made more briefly and more urbanely in St John's *Letter to the Examiner*; like Davenant, St John attacks the whigs and their policies in general. Both writers are clearly addressing the committed tory readership. The author of *The Secret History of Arlus and Odolphus*, on the other hand, says nothing about the current question of war or peace. Instead, he devotes most space to an allegorical history of Harley's fall from office in 1708, the blame

---

[26] I have given the authors as now known, though all the pamphlets were published anonymously. The *Letter to the Examiner* is reprinted in *PW* iii.221-7; *Faults on Both Sides* is reprinted in *Somers Tracts*, xii.678-707 (attributed to 'Richard Harley'); Defoe's *Essay upon Public Credit* is also reprinted in *Somers Tracts*, xiii.27-34 (attributed to Robert Harley). For Boyer's authorship of the *Letter from a Foreign Minister*, see Henry L. Snyder, 'Daniel Defoe, Arthur Maynwaring, Robert Walpole, and Abel Boyer: some considerations of authorship', *Huntington Library Quarterly*, xxxiii (1970), 133-53, especially pp. 147-50.

[27] Hare, *The Management of the War*, Part I (1711), pp. 3-4.

for which is laid on Godolphin, the Marlboroughs, and the Junto whigs. His main theme (again it is one on which Swift will elaborate) is the excessive power of the Marlborough-Godolphin connection. Indignation is directed at particular whigs (notably the Junto lords), but not at the whigs as a whole. The pamphlet might have found sympathetic readers among moderate whigs who were unhappy with the party's leadership, as well as among tories. *A Letter from a Foreign Minister* is likewise calculated to appeal to moderate opinion. Boyer attacks the Dutch for interposing on behalf of the old ministry, and suggests that the new government will secure better terms of peace for all the allies (the implication being that it will not favour the Dutch unreasonably at the expense of the other allies, as the whigs would have done). Boyer is careful to distinguish between the majority of moderate men in each party and their extremist wings; with a show of impartiality, he admits that just as not all whigs are republicans, not all tories are Jacobites. Like the *Secret History*, Boyer's *Letter* tries to detach moderate whigs from the party leadership by suggesting that a few great men have selfishly monopolised profit and power. When he gives brief characters of the newly appointed commissioners of the treasury, Boyer describes Harley as a non-partisan moderate. His political sanity has kept him from party madness: in 1696 he signed the association to defend William III but refused to vote for the attainder of Sir John Fenwick. Boyer predicts that the tories will win the forthcoming election, but he tries to allay whig fears by assuring electors that the new government is as committed as the old to maintaining the protestant succession, the public credit, and the toleration.

Simon Clement's *Faults on Both Sides* was the most successful of the six pamphlets listed by Hare; it went through the most editions and provoked the greatest numbers of replies. Its much-vaunted moderation is sometimes genuine, sometimes spurious. Thus Clement affects to appeal to the moderate men of both parties by charging the leaders on both sides with being self-interested; but it is only the whig leaders who are attacked in earnest. As in the *Secret History* and in Boyer's *Letter from a Foreign Minister*, the real object of attack is the combination of the Marlborough-Godolphin connection with the Junto. Moderate whigs are courted (though without doing anything to alienate the more moderate tories) by attacking the high-flying tory clergy (men like Francis Atterbury) and by a kind of theoretical old-whiggism that exposes how far the modern 'whig' leaders have in fact abandoned their 'old whig' ideas. Since the whig leaders are accused of turning tory (while it is placed to the credit of the 'tory' leaders that they now behave like good whigs), to be a true 'old whig' in 1710 is to support the Harley government. Nor does Clement neglect to appeal to the moderate tories, especially to those who were worried about the possible consequences of the explosion of high-church feelings in the wake of the Sacheverell affair. But the lack of any really distinctive tory themes suggests that Clement's primary aim was to mobilise support for Harley from among those whigs who were inclined to be independent of the Junto leadership. Defoe's *Essay upon Public Credit* is addressed first of all to the city of London, and perhaps secondarily was intended to reassure financial interests abroad. Defoe praises Godolphin's management of the treasury, but claims that Godolphin's presence at the treasury is not necessary for the support of public credit. 'I know no Persons or Parties in my Argument,' he says, and he sounds impartial; but since the current whig line was that the dismissal of Godolphin was sure to destroy credit, in fact Defoe's pretence of impartiality was a clear support of Harley. Thus between them the six pamphlets that Hare was concerned to refute appealed to a pretty broad spectrum of political opinion. No effort was wasted on those (principally the Junto whigs and their supporters) who would be sure to oppose the new government whatever happened. But attempts were made to conciliate all those from whom support might reasonably be expected. The summer and early autumn of 1710 was admittedly a very sensitive time politically. Until the composition of the new parliament was known, Harley could not be certain how far he might have to court the support of the more moderate whigs. At the same time, he could be certain of the support of the tories, at least in the early stages of the parliament. It seems unlikely that he would have approved the furious tone of Davenant's *Sir Thomas Double at Court*, nor probably was he entirely happy with the partisan programme sketched out in St John's *Letter to the Examiner*. The pamphlets that appealed for support to the moderates of both parties can be regarded as genuinely 'Harleyite', whether or not they were actually commissioned by the minister. But the moderation of these pamphlets was in large measure an illusion. They made different points in order to appeal to different prejudices and susceptibilities, but the main issue was the support of what (despite many empty professions to the contrary) was sure to be a tory government in policies that went directly against those of the outgoing whig-dominated administration. It was not often that such a complex structure of different rhetorical appeals was needed, but the configuration in 1710 serves to illustrate the complexity of the political rhetoric of the day. Swift usually wrote for the committed tories, but to broaden his possible appeal his rhetoric was commonly more moderate than the substance of his ideas. To understand his political writings, we need to keep in mind the conventions of contemporary rhetoric that tended to make a propagandist's language more moderate than his ideas, as well as the audience for which he was writing.

ii

Queen Anne had never been thoroughly reconciled to the whig-dominated ministry that had been forced on her in 1708 after the fall of Harley and the whig victory in the election held in the aftermath of the Jacobite invasion scare.[28] Nor did this government long remain popular in the country at large, especially after the failure of the peace negotiations in 1709, when it began to seem that the war would never end. The trial of Dr Sacheverell early in 1710, and the upsurge of popular feeling in support of the church that his trial produced, gave the queen her opportunity to rid herself of her de-tested whig tyrants. (Her freeing herself from their bondage is the subject, expressed through an allegory of the Swedish king Charles XII in exile at Bender, of *Examiner* No. 7, one of the series written before Swift took over the paper.) Aided and encouraged by Harley and his allies, the queen's first move was the appointment of the Duke of Shrewsbury as Lord Chamberlain in April. This was followed by the gradual reconstruction of the government, of which the most important steps were the dismissal of Sunderland (in June) as Secretary of State and of Godolphin (in August) as Lord Treasurer. Harley was appointed Chancellor of the Exchequer, and was recognised

[28] The most detailed narrative history is still George Macaulay Trevelyan, *England under Queen Anne* (3 vols, 1930-4), which is unsympathetic to tory aims and ideas. More recent research is reflected in Edward Gregg, *Queen Anne* (1980), though it is a biography and not a history of the reign. For a narrative of the period 1709-11 that puts Swift's journalism in its political context, see Michael Foot, *The Pen and the Sword* (1957).

as replacing Godolphin at the head of the ministry, although he did not become Lord Treasurer until 1711. In September 1710 parliament was dissolved, and in the ensuing general election a large majority of tories was returned. Harley had at this time two main policy aims: to break the power of the whig Junto, which in conjunction with Marlborough and Godolphin had dominated the government and the court; and to bring an end to the war. Initially at least he hoped to be able to achieve these aims with some bipartisan support, although the refusal of some important whigs (notably Cowper, the Lord Chancellor) to continue in office, and the large tory majority in the Commons, forced him in practice to head a mainly tory government. His further aims, beyond the negotiating of a peace settlement, are less clear, but he presumably intended to retain power and to preside over a moderate and popular peace-time government, something that had been unknown in England for many years.

In September 1710 Swift arrived in London. His official business was a mission (the second he had attempted) on behalf of the Church of Ireland, to secure the remission of some clerical taxes, the 'First Fruits' and 'Twentieth Parts', which had (in England) been remitted to form the fund that became known as 'Queen Anne's Bounty'. On his earlier mission, Swift had discovered that Godolphin was unwilling to extend this favour to the Irish church without some substantial concession, usually taken to be the Church's consent to the repeal of the Test Act which gave anglicans a monopoly of civil office. Swift was of course absolutely opposed to any such concession. In defence of the Test Act he had already written (in 1708?) his 'Argument against Abolishing Christianity' (*PW* ii.26-39), although this was not published until 1711. Swift arrived in London at a time of political uncertainty: Godolphin had been dismissed, but the election results and their large tory majority were still in the future. Most of his previous connections had been with the whigs, and at first he was unsure how these great changes would affect him and his mission (and also, of course, his search for personal preferment; in his early 40s, he was still only Vicar of Laracor). As late as 22 August he had hoped that Godolphin (the news of whose dismissal had not yet reached Swift in Dublin) might continue in office and aid his search for preferment (*Corr*.i.170). But soon after his arrival in London Swift must have realised that the political future lay elsewhere. After his disappointing experiences with potential patrons among the whig lords, he must have felt that neither he nor the church could do worse than under the old ministry. Swift had always been an avowed high-churchman, and this had always made him somewhat suspect to would-be whig patrons. Now personal factors helped to secure his pen for the tories. He went to see the dismissed Godolphin; his reception was 'altogether short, dry, and morose' (*Corr*.i.173). Harley, by contrast, sought him out and received him 'with the greatest Marks of Kindness and Esteem' (*Corr*.i.184). Swift repaid each in kind. He lampooned Godolphin in *The Virtues of Sid Hamet the Magician's Rod* (published early in October; *Poems*, 1.131-5), and the ex-minister would suffer more strokes of Swift's pen over the next few years. On 7 October Swift had dinner and his first long, private talk with the new minister; earlier in the day he had left with his printer his first piece of tory propaganda, a ballad on the Westminster election.[29] Harley flattered Swift with respect and confidence, promised the long-sought remission of the First Fruits, and engaged him to write for the government. How gratifying it was to be told that 'their great difficulty' was 'the want of some good pen' to defend the policies of the new government, and to be offered the job (*PW* viii.123).

Harley told Swift that his pen would be needed 'to keep up the spirit raised in the people, to assert the principles, and justify the proceedings of the new ministers' (*PW* viii.123). Swift's initial task, however, which absorbed most of his time and energy in the winter of 1710-11, was at least as much negative as positive. Between November 1710 and June 1711 he wrote a series of over thirty weekly *Examiner* papers with the twin aims of discrediting the old ministry and recommending the new. In these papers he develops a collective image of the discarded whigs as a set of corrupt and self-seeking politicians who have enriched themselves and their friends at the public expense. He promises to reveal their infinite and detestable enormities in detail, but in practice he confines himself to mainly general and unprovable (hence also not easily disproved) charges. In this way Swift tried to gratify the desires of the government's backbench supporters for investigations into past maladministration, substantive enquiries into which were in practice not very easy and which the government itself was not very anxious to prosecute. Not all of Swift's papers are negative; sometimes he dwells on the new government's policies and achievements, as in No. 42 (24 May

[29] The Westminster ballad (which is not in *Poems*) will be found in *POAS*, vii.480-6.

1711), where he praises the plan to build fifty new churches in London.

When Swift had his crucial interview with Harley on 7 October, ten issues of the weekly *Examiner* had already been published, and he did not take over until No. 14 (2 November). The paper's original subtitle had read 'Remarks upon Papers and Occurences', and the first six issues were actually critiques of, or replies to, specific pieces of whig journalism. With No. 7 (14 September) it became less dependent on the opposition for material, but until Swift took over it remained unfocused and miscellaneous in its targets and techniques. The essays range in level and tone from the humorous ridicule of Steele's journalism in No. 5 (31 August) to a serious statement of the case for the doctrines of passive obedience and non-resistence in the original No. 13 (26 October; this paper, usually attributed to Francis Atterbury, was omitted when the *Examiner* was reprinted in volume form). Swift's hand is evident at once in his first paper, No. 14 (2 November; No. 13 in the reprints, the renumbering of which has been here followed for subsequent references), from which point the paper has a more coherent policy and a more commanding tone. Instead of condescending to notice, much less to answer, the trash that poured from the whig press, Swift seized the initiative and left it to the whigs to answer him. His principal opponent, the *Medley* (which had begun publication on 5 October 1710, replacing the short-lived *Whig-Examiner*) was a competent and often witty paper, particularly notable for Maynwaring's skilful parallels drawn from Cicero.[30] It operated, however, under the serious disadvantage of being committed to answer the *Examiner*, so that it could seldom choose its own ground. Swift does not totally ignore the *Medley*. Towards the end of his series, in No. 41 (17 May 1711), he refers to 'a Paper called the *Medley*' (as though its very existence would come as news to his readers) which he 'never thought convenient to take Notice of, because it would have diverted my Design, which I

---

[30] No. 11 (11 December 1710) is neatly adapted from *De Provinciis Consularibus*, a speech against Caesar's recall from Gaul; suppressing all Cicero's egotistical references to himself, Maynwaring transforms the passage into a straightforward panegyric from an avowed enemy. In No. 15 (8 January 1711) he uses a passage from *De Domo suo* to associate the pretended 'church' party with immorality and irreligion. In No. 17 (22 January) the *Pro Sestio* is adapted to make the tories look like Cicero's 'populares' and the whigs like the true 'optimates'. I have used the collected edition of the *Medleys for the Year 1711* (1712).

intended to be of Publick Use' (*PW* iii.153). Swift had no need to answer the *Medley*, for the classes of people he was writing for did not read it; his task was to articulate the prejudices of his own tory constituency.[31]

The difficulties which Swift would have faced, had his been the answerer's task, can be seen in one of his least effective pamphlets, published in August 1711 as 'By the Author of the *Examiner*' in an attempt to draw on that paper's prestige. It related to a stale controversy going back to 1708, just before Harley's dismissal from the office of Secretary of State. A clerk in his department, William Gregg, was discovered to have been sending state secrets to France. A committee of whig lords, appointed to examine Gregg, was accused (by its tory critics) of trying to bribe Gregg to accuse Harley of complicity in his guilt. Such an accusation would have been extremely damaging to Harley, and of great use to the whigs in further discrediting him and preventing his possible return to political power and prominence. Gregg, however, refused to incriminate Harley and maintained his master's innocence until his death (Gregg was tried, found guilty, and hanged). In 1711, at the time of Guiscard's attempt to assassinate Harley, tory propagandists raked up this old story in order to draw parallels between the attempts of Guiscard and the whig lords. Swift made the comparison in the *Examiner* (No. 32, 15 March, and No. 33, 22 March; *PW* iii.108, 116). Oldmixon tried to combat the charges against the whig lords in the *Medley*, and in July 1711 he published a separate pamphlet on the subject, *A Letter to the Seven Lords of the Committee Appointed to Examine Gregg* (reprinted in *PW* iii.245-58). Guiscard's assassination attempt on Harley had made a deep impression on Swift, as is evident from the letter in which he described it to archbishop King (*Corr*.i.213-16). That was in March; in August Swift still felt sufficiently concerned to publish a pamphlet in reply to Oldmixon's, *Some Remarks upon a Pamphlet Called 'A Letter to the Seven Lords'* (*PW* iii.187-205). This has a very effective opening. Largely through his assured and peremptory tone, Swift convicts Oldmixon of the inconsistency of affecting to despise an opponent he finds it necessary to answer. At the same time (though we hardly notice it) this is just what Swift himself is

---

[31] Frank H. Ellis, 'Arthur Mainwaring as reader of Swift's *Examiner*', *Yearbook of English Studies*, xi (1981), 49-66, misses this point and so overestimates the effectiveness of the *Medley*'s response to the *Examiner*.

doing. This part of the pamphlet (*PW* iii.187-9) could have furnished material for a good *Examiner* paper; it may possibly be a reworking of material originally intended for one. From the moment that Swift turns to a detailed examination of Oldmixon's pamphlet, however, he loses force and direction. He makes some telling individual points, but the need to follow Oldmixon prevents their emerging as a coherent whole. The need to follow his opponent, instead of leading, blunted the effectiveness of Swift's rhetoric.

It became usual for a periodical essayist (who normally wrote under a pseudonym rather than strictly anonymously) to endow his assumed character or identity with as much verisimilitude as possible, especially through the use of invented biographical details. The model for this procedure was Steele's *Tatler*, which began publication as the work of 'Isaac Bickerstaff', a ready-made character familiar to the reading public from Swift's anti-Partridge hoax and the various squibs and pamphlets it had spawned. Bickerstaff developed into quite an elaborate character. Gay observed, in *The Present State of Wit* (1711; a witty survey of current journalism), that the various writers who, after Steele dropped the paper, tried to revive and imitate the *Tatler*, were careful to reproduce this '*Garnish*', mistaking it for the paper's substance.[32] Another much-imitated device was that of the club, as used by Addison and Steele in the *Spectator*. In the *Guardian* Steele used yet a third device, combining the eccentric individual with the supporting group: the venerable 'Nestor Ironside' appears as the paper's author, and much attention is given to the family of the Lizards with whom he is intimate. Once introduced into the early numbers of a paper, these devices provided a ready-made resource suited to the exigencies of the brief format. They could be used to present different points of view, and they helped to develop a familiar relationship with their readers.

The purely political papers avoided developing fictional identities of this kind. Both the whig *Observator* (1704-12) and its tory rival the *Rehearsal* (1704-09) used the form of a dialogue, but with no characterisation beyond the minimum required to present differing viewpoints.[33] The advantages of this

---

[32] *Poetry and Prose*, ed. Vinton A. Dearing and Charles E. Beckwith (Oxford, 1974), ii.454.

[33] Defoe's *Review* was untypical in this respect. For a comparative discussion of the 'images' or *personae* of the *Review*, the *Observator*, and the *Examiner*, see

impersonality can be seen in the awkwardness that often resulted when the usually apolitical *Tatler, Spectator*, or *Guardian* ventured into politics. Serious political comment came strangely from the whimsical Bickerstaff; readers were not used to the combination of politics and the individual, embodied voice. In the *Spectator*, political themes are indirectly and effectively dramatised, for example through the characters of Sir Roger de Coverley and Sir Andrew Freeport. But the great majority of its regular readers must have been disappointed and even outraged by No. 384 (21 May 1712), which is mainly a reprint of William Fleetwood's militantly whiggish preface to his new volume of *Four Sermons*. An exceptionally large number of this issue was printed and distributed, not of course because it was genuinely popular but as a whig propaganda measure.[34] It still strikes one, as it must have struck contemporaries, as a grave abuse of the readers who trusted Mr Spectator to provide them with his usual entertainment or edification. In the *Guardian* Steele (as editor) printed political letters from himself, at first under another pseudonym and then under his own name, a vacillation between subterfuge and honesty with which Swift made merry sport in *The Importance of the Guardian Considered* (1713; *PW* viii.8). It may have been accidental, the result of collective authorship, that when the *Examiner* was set up in August 1710 its *persona* was impersonal. But it is more likely that it was a conscious reaction against the very personal censorship of Bickerstaff in the *Tatler*, an attempt to create a more authoritative voice with which to affect impartiality. The precedent was followed by the *Whig-Examiner* and the *Medley*; by Steele himself when he dropped the *Guardian* in favour of the mainly political *Englishman* (1713-14; revived in 1715); and by Addison in the *Freeholder* (1715-16). None of these used the *persona* of disembodied authority more effectively than Swift in his series of *Examiner* papers. One of the respects in which the later papers written by Mrs Manley and William Oldisworth fall far short of Swift's is their inability to command this authoritative tone. Swift was greatly aided by the fact that he was writing a semi-official paper. Although he protests his independence of the government, it was sufficiently known that,

---

L.S. Horsley, 'Rogues or honest gentlemen: the public characters of Queen Anne journalists', *Texas Studies in Literature and Language*, xviii (1976), 198-228.

[34] The very large figure of 14,000 is mentioned by Fleetwood himself in his letter of 17 June 1712 to bishop Burnet; printed in the *Compleat Collection of the Sermons* and other works of Fleetwood (1737), p. vi.

as Gay put it in *The Present State of Wit*, the *Examiner* 'carries much the more Sail, as 'tis supposed to be writ by the Direction, and under the Eye of some Great Persons who sit at the Helm of Affairs'.[35] Swift often writes as an insider, as when he is confident of being able to reveal 'about eight or nine Thousand of the most scandalous Abuses' of the past twenty years of whig-dominated governments (No. 18, 7 December 1710; *PW* iii.32). Throughout the series he often speaks as though he has secret sources of information, though without ever making any very startling revelations. He likes to give the impression that he could tell much more than he chooses to. At the same time, Swift often emphasises his volunteer status, maintaining the fiction and image of a gentlemanly amateur motivated solely by his concern for the public interest. This protestation of independence is marked in his first paper (No. 13, 2 November) and is repeated from time to time. Thus Swift contrives to present himself as both above the conflict yet within the circle of authority, a well-informed but disinterested judge. If he gives his support to the tories (and it happens that he always does) it is entirely because of the merits of their case. Swift uses the same kind of pretence to identify the government with the nation at large, and the whig opposition with a mere faction.

Some writers found the discipline of the essay form, with its strictly limited length, the requirement of consistency of tone through a whole series of papers, and the frequent deadlines, positively liberating. Both Addison and Steele, though for different reasons, produced much of their best writing for the genre. Addison, who had a plentiful supply of material in his notebooks, needed the deadline to force him to work it up for publication and the protection of the essayist's mask (and the partnership with Steele to take care of the main editorial responsibilities) to overcome his natural diffidence. Steele had no great stock of material, but he seems to have had the knack of writing effectively under pressure, at least up to the usual length of the periodical essay; but he was often forced to construct a *Spectator* out of lightly edited contributions from his readers.[36] Swift was able to supply hints for such papers, but the form itself did not suit him. Although on friendly terms with Steele for most of the time, he contributed practically nothing to the *Tatler*,

---

[35] *Poetry and Prose*, ed. Dearing and Beckwith, ii.451.

[36] The introduction to Donald F. Bond's edition of the *Spectator* (5 vols, Oxford, 1965) contains much information about the methods of composition of the two chief authors.

only one proper essay (No. 230) and two short poems. For Swift, the cultivation of the disembodied voice required by the political paper was irksome, for he loved to impersonate with the richness of observed and imagined particularity that characterises *A Tale of a Tub* and *Gulliver's Travels*. After the long series of *Examiner* papers it must have given him great pleasure to write *A New Journey to Paris* (September 1711; *PW* iii.209-18), in which he created the fully developed fictional character of the Sieur du Baudrier, a pretentious and self-important Frenchman supposed to have acted as a servant to Matthew Prior on the French sections of his diplomatic journey to Versailles. This was an unofficial pamphlet, a labour of love written without the knowledge of the ministers or of Prior himself; it is full of the verisimilitude of *Gulliver's Travels*. Swift's skill in comic impersonations of this kind, and his enjoyment of them, can also be seen in *Toland's Invitation to Dismal* (1712; *Poems*, i.161-6), in which he sought to embarrass the high-church Earl of Nottingham (whose nickname was Dismal) after his defection to the whigs by associating him with freethinkers like John Toland. Another example is the *Letter of Thanks* supposedly addressed to bishop William Fleetwood by the rakish atheist Lord Wharton (1712; *PW* vi. 151-5). There is further evidence that Swift may have longed to break out from the lofty dignity needed for the *Examiner* in the only pamphlet that he found time to write while he had to meet the weekly deadline. The *Short Character of Wharton* (1710; *PW* iii.177-84) has an exuberant good humour and a virtuoso deployment of flashy rhetorical devices that suggest how constrained he may have felt in the writing of the *Examiner*. To compare the full-blooded attack on Wharton in the *Short Character* with the attacks on him in the *Examiner* (principally in the discussion of the 'Art of Political Lying' in No. 14, and in the adaptation of Cicero against Verres in No. 17), or with the character Swift gives of him in his *History of the Four Last Years of the Queen* (*PW* vii.9-10), is to realise how much energy Swift had to repress in order to achieve the lofty impartiality that he adopted as his pose both in the *Examiner* and the *History*. There is no sense of effort (in the *Examiner* at least; the *History* is altogether more laboured), but effort there must have been.

Some of Swift's *Examiner* papers are quite straightforwardly argued, for example those on the army and on the clergy (No. 20, 21 December, and No. 21, 28 December). But it was more characteristic of Swift to use fictional devices, as he does in most of the more memorable papers: for example, the attacks on the Duke of Marlborough in the paper on ingratitude (No. 16, 23 November) and in the 'Letter to Crassus' (No. 27, 8 February). Swift's use of classical material is infrequent but always striking. Only the attack on Wharton as Verres in No. 17 (30 November) is actually based on a classical original; the 'classical' attacks on Marlborough are largely imaginative. The parallel between Roman gratitude and British ingratitude in No. 16 depends for its effect on a very Swiftian combination of realistic detail and unsupported general assertion, while the 'Letter to Crassus' is Roman only in its form. The classical guise gave an appearance of universality and impartiality, and Swift sometimes gives a classical appearance to his fables, as with the genealogy of merit (No. 30, 1 March) and the fable of faction (No. 31, 8 March), which he dignifies through the invocation of Plato. Swift was fond of devices which create an appearance of impartiality, as do the parallel letters from a whig and a tory (No. 28, 15 February), which give the impression (an entirely misleading one) that the *Examiner* has been following a strictly non-partisan course which has exposed him to censure from both sides. So too with the parallel accounts of what whigs and tories mean by passive obedience in No. 33 (22 March); in order to refute the moderate statement of the doctrine that he there attributes to the tories, it is only necessary to turn back to the original *Examiner* No. 13, a paper that Swift suppressed in the reprints. Such balancing devices have their counterpart in some of Swift's characteristic syntactic effects: the balanced sentence whose equipoise conceals false opposites or excludes a vital middle term; the juxtaposition that hints at guilt-by-association without offering any evidence; the apparently fair-minded qualification that makes a more damning point; the ironic acquittal that condemns. There is no need to illustrate these points, for examples will come to hand on any reading of the *Examiner*. If Swift's arguments are designed to beg all the important questions, so too is his syntax.[37]

The aloof, dignified impartiality of the *Examiner* allowed Swift to treat his opponents with an affected indifference. They are consistently presented as little and contemptible; at one point Swift is so disappointed by the poor quality of whig propaganda that he threatens to write replies to himself, in order to see it better done (*PW* iii.36). In No. 22 (4 January) he

---

[37] For a mainly rhetorical analysis of the tory writings, see Richard I. Cook, *Jonathan Swift as a Tory Pamphleteer* (Seattle, 1967), especially pp. 31-77.

actually writes a parody of a feeble whig 'answer' to an *Examiner*, and towards the end of his series (No. 45, 14 June) he prints a petition for relief from the now starving whig scribblers. All this was never, of course, intended to be more than a rhetorical pose. In his first paper (No. 13) Swift moved quickly from his protest of impartiality to a thoroughly approving account of the tory interpretation of recent British history. As the series progresses, he comes out more and more openly as a tory partisan, speaking of 'we' meaning the tories and of 'the tories' as his party. This is not (as is sometimes suggested) because, in the course of time, he came more under the influence of the tory extremist St John instead of the instinctively moderate Harley.[38] It was the natural result of his rhetorical strategy, for he becomes more outspoken as he gets his audience more firmly under his control. In November 1710 he was addressing the timid and the uncertain, unsure how their recent victory at the polls would be translated into action in parliament; by the end of the parliamentary session, he was addressing victorious troops. In his *Letter to the Examiner*, St John had outlined the new tory strategy as he saw it, particularly the need for an early peace. But this theme is not taken up either in the pre-Swift series or in the first numbers that Swift wrote. It would have been premature. St John's *Letter to the Examiner* was a typically rash and impetuous piece; it gave too much of the tory game away. In the queen's speech from the throne at the opening of parliament, reference was made to the ministry's intention to prosecute the war vigorously, especially in Spain. This seems to have been intended and taken as a covert way of saying that the war effort in Flanders would be scaled down, but it also served to quieten accusations that the new government intended to negotiate a rapid peace at almost any price. In one of his first papers (No. 18, 7 December), Swift quotes part of the queen's speech, including the reference to Spain. It is not until No. 38 (26 April) that he feels able to come out openly against any attempt to recover Spain. By then he has succeeded in making the old ministry and their management of the war look corrupt and self-seeking. In this respect, the *Examiner* quietly prepared the way for the full-scale attack on the whigs and the Dutch that he launched in the *Conduct of the Allies*. It was not

[38] W. Speck, 'The *Examiner* examined: Swift's tory pamphleteering', *Focus: Swift*, ed. C.J. Rawson (1971), pp. 138-54; Downie, *Robert Harley and the Press*, p. 135.

that Swift's opinions changed, or that the policy aims of the
government altered; but it would have been impolitic to have
moved in advance of public opinion, which needed to be
educated to see the whigs not as patriots but as selfish
warmongers.

Swift, like most Englishmen, had initially supported the aims
of the allies in the War of the Spanish Succession, and he
continued to do so (if with no great enthusiasm) until about
1709. Between 1708 and 1709 the war became an increasingly
partisan issue, and Swift would only have been following the
current of public opinion in becoming more sceptical about its
continued necessity. As late as 1709, however, we find him
publishing two pieces that could be interpreted as expressing
continued support for the war. *A Famous Prediction of Merlin*
(*Poems*, i.101-5; early 1709) is a mock-prophecy in verse with an
accompanying prose explanation; it contains both a compliment
to Marlborough and a prediction of a successful campaign. In
June 1709 Swift published the third part of Sir William Temple's
Memoirs; the timing (when popular support for the war was
flagging) and Swift's own preface (reprinted in *PW* i.268-71)
amount to an endorsement of whig war policy. The *Memoirs*
themselves (as we should expect from Temple) are consistently
pro-Dutch and anti-French in their point of view; they end with
a lengthy account of France's expansionist aims and the need for
concerted opposition to frustrate them. Swift's preface contains
compliments to two leading ministers, Lords Godolphin and
Sunderland. Yet Swift never expressed the positive enthusiasm
for the war that we find in the writings of Addison and Steele, for
in principle he was opposed to war in a way that the whigs were
not. So it was quite consistent with his convictions to take on the
task of justifying the new ministry's peace policy. Swift's view of
the proper relations between Britain and the world was typically
tory. In the *Spectator* No. 69 (19 May 1711) Addison expressed
the characteristically whig ideal of a Britain at the hub of the
trading world, the capital of a great economic empire that would
diffuse enlightenment and all the benefits of whig civilisation
(such as the *Spectator*). In the *Freeholder* No. 22 (5 March 1716)
Addison satirises the typical xenophobia of the tory squirearchy
by pointing out how many of the ingredients of the tory fox-
hunter's favourite punch come from abroad. Addison, of course,
approves of this economic interdependence. Swift's ideal was
economic self-sufficiency. This is expressed imaginatively in the
societies of Parts II and IV of *Gulliver's Travels*, and in the

surprise expressed by Gulliver's Houyhnhnm master that England should be so barren as to need to import drink (*PW* xi.252). Swift's various proposals for the economic advancement of Ireland all include a greater degree of self-sufficiency through the increased consumption of its own manufactured goods. Swift distrusted the social disruption and the growth of luxury that inevitably followed economic expansion (as had happened in Sparta, Rome, and Venice). Far from being an agent of civilisation, trade (like war) was a selfish activity. In *A Tale of a Tub* Swift presents war as a disease or madness of kings (*PW* i.103), and in *Gulliver's Travels* he satirises wars that kill and enslave people in order to 'civilize and reduce them from their barbarous Way of Living' (*PW* xi.246).

As early as August 1710 informal, unofficial contacts had begun between the new English government and the French. The first official proposals were made in April 1711. In August Matthew Prior was sent on the secret mission that became the subject of Swift's *New Journey to Paris*, and on his return he brought with him the French agent who gave his name to the 'Mesnager Preliminaries' signed in London on 28 September. Their unofficial publication in the press provoked a storm of hostile whig criticism, and one of the tasks of Swift's *Conduct of the Allies* would be to counter this opposition. It is characteristic of Swift that his idea of defence was a sustained attack on the long-standing war policies of the whigs and the Dutch; he refocused the debate away from the new preliminaries onto past misconduct. Swift had, of course, been working on his substantial pamphlet long before September, and its aim was much wider than defending the recent preliminaries. He had been given help and access to official information by Harley (now Earl of Oxford) and St John, both of whom read the pamphlet and made suggestions. With the opening of the 1711-12 parliamentary session in sight, publication of the *Examiner* (dropped since the summer) was resumed, but it was now written by William Oldisworth.[39] Swift contributed a very few papers over the next two years, and he may have given Oldisworth hints and possibly exercised some kind of supervisory control. Certainly contemporaries continued to charge Swift with being the author of the *Examiner*, and much of the responsibility for the rather unsavoury reputation as a controversialist that

[39] For an account of Oldisworth and his political writings, see Robert J. Allen, 'William Oldisworth: "the author of the *Examiner*" ', *PQ* xxvi (1947), 159-80.

Swift acquired derived from this mistaken belief that he was largely responsible for the often scurrilous propaganda of Oldisworth's *Examiner*. In fact, Swift had moved on to more ambitious writings, of which the first was the *Conduct of the Allies*.

The Conduct of the Allies (*PW* vi.5-65) was published on 27 November 1711, timed to influence opinion for the forthcoming session of parliament. It was a great and immediate success, and Swift would proudly claim that resolutions of the House of Commons were 'almost quotations' from it (*JS* ii.482). There can be little doubt that it was Swift's most important single contribution to the tory cause. Several answers were written, some long but none very effective.[40] The task of the would-be answerer was indeed exceptionally difficult. He had, in the first place, to counter Swift's facts and arguments with alternative interpretations of those most seriously damaging (whether through truth or misrepresentation on Swift's part) to the whig case. This was relatively easy. More difficult was the problem of how to try to refute Swift's sly and subtly expressed innuendoes and insinuations. But nothing made the answerer's job more difficult than the eagerness of Swift's audience to believe what he told them. The majority of the tory squires in the House of Commons, and the majority of country gentlemen who had elected them were glad to see the blame for the unhappy state of the nation and the national finances placed squarely where they thought it belonged, on the whigs and the hated Dutch. They were not disposed to pay much heed to any facts, figures, or arguments that suggested otherwise and threatened to rob them of their comfortable convictions. The overwhelming success of *The Conduct of the Allies* owed much to its audience as well as to its author. This is not to suggest that any other pamphleteer would have enjoyed a similar success. Other pamphlets in fact made much the same points as Swift without his cogency. The particularly effective qualities of the *Conduct of the Allies* can be clearly seen if it is compared with a series of three pamphlets on the same theme that Defoe published shortly before the *Conduct*

---

[40] The various replies are listed in Teerink, *Bibliography of Swift*, pp. 287-8. Five are reprinted in *Swiftiana III: On Swift's 'Remarks on the Barrier Treaty' and his 'Conduct of the Allies'* (New York, 1974); this collection unfortunately includes only the first of the four parts of the most important reply, Francis Hare's *The Allies and the Late Ministry Defended* (1711-12). An interesting recent discussion of the pamphlet is J.A. Downie 'Polemical strategy and Swift's *Conduct of the Allies*', *Prose Studies*, 4 (1981), 134-45.

appeared. These pamphlets, like Swift's, were written on behalf of the Oxford government (it is a measure of the minister's deviousness, and of the imperfect confidence with which Swift was treated, that he seems not to have known that Defoe was also writing for Oxford). Defoe put the general case for an immediate peace in *Reasons Why This Nation Ought to Put a Speedy End to This Expensive War* (published 6 October). Defoe attacks the opponents of such a peace in a second pamphlet published a little later in October, *Reasons Why a Party among Us, and also among the Confederates, Are Obstinately Bent against a Treaty of Peace with the French at This Time.* In a third pamphlet, *The Ballance of Europe* (published 1 November), he argues at greater length against the particular issue of 'No Peace without Spain'.[41] Defoe was a rapid and voluminous writer; Swift lavished great care on the small number of pamphlets that he wrote. It is therefore reasonable enough to set these three pamphlets of Defoe's against the *Conduct of the Allies*; together they are about the same length and go over much the same ground. The contrasts between the pamphlets of the two men reflect personal differences of style, thought, and temperament. More generally, they illustrate the different kinds of pamphlet that were written, quite consciously, for different audiences within the politically-aware public as a whole.

What chiefly distinguishes Swift's *Conduct* from Defoe's pamphlets, and indeed from the general run of contemporary political writing, is something that had already characterised the *Examiner*, an authoritative tone. Impatient of contradiction, Swift brushes off opposition as either self-interested or ignorant. He is very much an insider who knows all the 'secret history' of the last several years; yet he speaks as though these supposed 'secrets' are no more than what everyone knows. Thus he contrives to unite the seemingly opposite methods of revealing secrets while appealing to common assent, a procedure that requires (what Swift had) a willing audience. Swift's arguments and rhetoric are usually of impressive generality, yet he can be detailed and specific when he needs to clinch a point. He often drops a fact or a figure with an air of contempt, as though daring contradiction. By contrast, Defoe's manner is workaday, practical, matter of fact. He assumes no great superiority over

---

[41] These dates of publication are taken from John Robert Moore, *A Checklist of the Writings of Daniel Defoe* (2nd ed., Hamden, Conn., 1971), pp. 88-90, in which these pamphlets are Nos 216, 217, and 219.

his readers; those who may disagree with him are treated as thoughtless or misinformed rather than self-interested or culpable. His use of detail is often illustrative or realistic, intended to bring a general or abstract argument within terms of common experience. He is sure that the reader will agree with him, when properly informed; but he does not ladle out truths with the bald, take-it-or-leave-it manner of Swift. Defoe's deferential rhetoric is much the commoner strategy in contemporary pamphleteering; a reader would not be many minutes into the *Conduct of the Allies* before being aware of an unusual kind of voice, speaking with an exceptional degree of assured authority.

Both pamphleteers, in arguing for an immediate peace, had somehow to come to terms with some awkward facts: that the government intended to negotiate a separate peace with France if the allies would not accept the British proposals, and had actually been negotiating secretly with France for over a year; that it had determined to repudiate the Barrier Treaty negotiated with the Dutch in 1709; that it did not propose to share trading concessions equally with the Dutch, as stipulated in the second Grand Alliance; and that it was willing to leave the Bourbon king, Philip V, in possession of Spain and Spanish America. Such facts could not be openly admitted. Defoe, indeed, ignores them altogether. His strategy is to take a pragmatic, forward-looking approach, stressing the advantages that will flow from a peace and the miseries that will multiply if the war is not concluded. He appeals for an end to old animosities and for a new national unanimity to take advantage of the prospects of the future, especially the increased opportunities for the expansion of trade. Swift's approach is quite different. He takes the offensive and meets the awkward facts straight on. He begins, it is true, with an apparently abstract and impartial account of the causes and motives that lead to wars. Here he begs all the important questions, for the possibilities that he pretends only to suppose turn out to be the very ones that the *Conduct of the Allies* happens to be about. In pretending to lay down a few self-evident truths that will be accepted as axiomatic by all sides, Swift conceals the controversial points under an account of the wars in which the English have been engaged between 1066 and 1688, an account which is so slanted as to make the post-revolutionary wars appear the most iniquitous in British history. Even civil wars are better, Swift suggests, because they take no money out of the country. The ability to generalise, to raise the argument above the particular issue or instance, is an important element in his success as a political writer. He pretends to detach himself from petty political squabbles; drawing on the greater prestige of general over particular truth, he makes his own values seem but reflections of the general laws of the universe. His opponents are relegated to the microscopic world of particularity, myopic denizens of a world of corruption and self-interested motives. In the *Conduct of the Allies*, Swift anticipates the charge that England is betraying the allies by himself taking the offensive against them. This results in a significant shift in the grounds of the debate, putting the onus on the whigs and the allies to defend their own past conduct. Swift develops a plausible 'conspiracy thesis' in which the former whig government is shown to have been involved in private agreements with the Dutch (and to a lesser extent with the other allies) for their mutual financial advantage. The British people, especially the tax-paying landed gentry, have been paying vast sums not (as they have been told) to reduce the exorbitant power of France but to enrich Marlborough and the whig financial interest and to conquer new provinces for the Dutch. Swift simplifies all issues to moral questions, which he presents as simple contrasts between virtues and vices. This kind of simplification perfectly suits his authoritative style. Defoe, consciously writing so as to appear more nearly on a level with his readers, chooses instead to complicate the issues. In *The Ballance of Europe*, for example, his way of recommending his own solution (which is the same as Swift's, that is, leaving Philip V in possession) is to make the question seem problematic and complicated. He therefore pretends to consider a number of options before coming out (on pragmatic grounds) in favour of Philip. This is Defoe's typical way of deflecting attention from the allies' moral commitment to the Austrian candidate, 'Charles III', by making it seem not such a simple matter as his readers may have thought.

Defoe's pamphlets, though they in effect recommend the same basic policies as the *Conduct of the Allies*, lack Swift's distinctively tory themes. Swift puts the onus of blame on the whig ministers for having started the war and for having conducted it in the wrong way in order to further their own interests. Worst of all, they rejected the advantageous offers of peace made by the French in 1709 because they preferred their own continuance in power to the real national interest. Swift minimises the value and importance of the military successes gained during the war, and he makes the favourite tory suggestion that the war should have been conducted primarily by sea rather than by land. Defoe does not complain at all of the allies, nor of the conduct of the war by the late ministry, although in *Reasons Why a Party* he does condemn the whigs' attempts to sink public credit after their dismissal. Defoe is generally much more concerned with financial matters than Swift is, and he looks at issues from the point of view of the trading interest. Thus he says nothing about the transfer of wealth, as a result of the war taxation, from the landed men to the monied interest; but he does deplore the effect that the war has had on trade, and he emphasises the advantages to trade that peace will bring. The financial bogeys that he raises are not a perpetually high land-tax (which is what Swift's readers were most afraid of) but a stop of the exchequer (which Swift comes close to recommending) and a general excise. It is clear that Swift's moral crusade is aimed at the landed class, tory in their prejudices and isolationist in their instincts, who will be glad to hear that the whigs have been lining their pockets at the nation's expense, that the allies have cheated and therefore deserve to be left in the lurch. Swift is addressing a thoroughly committed audience. Defoe's audience is obviously to be influenced by mainly economic arguments. His appeal is primarily to the trading classes, particularly those living in the larger urban centres that can expect to benefit from increased economic activity. They do not share the tory prejudices that Swift exploits in his readers, but neither are they so strongly committed to the whigs as to let ideology outweigh economic advantage. They want to enjoy the obvious benefits that peace will bring for traders; moral issues are not very important to them, and they are prepared to forget about the past and look to the future. In this contrast between the two different audiences that Defoe and Swift were addressing, we can perhaps see the distinction between the party faithful, whose general support can be assumed but who need to be inspired and mobilised (it is this kind of audience that Swift is writing for), and the less certain middle ground of the 'floating' or uncommitted voter open to conviction from the side (and on this occasion Defoe implies that it is the tory side) that promises success and self-advantage.

Defoe was very well-informed on all the subjects likely to be relevant to political arguments. Much more can be learned about contemporary society from his pamphlets and from the *Review* than from Swift's political writings. It is striking how much more Defoe uses factual material than Swift does. The success of Swift's pamphlets owes more to rhetoric: to their authoritative tone, to their fictional and generalising devices, to their reductive illustrations and metaphors. When, exceptionally, Swift does rely mainly on his material the result is disappointingly dull. Perhaps the least interesting of his pamphlets is *Some Remarks on the Barrier Treaty* (February 1712; *PW* vi.85-117). This consists mainly of the text of the 1709 Barrier Treaty (to which Swift alludes in the *Conduct of the Allies*; it was not then in print) with some introductory remarks by way of commentary. Swift was happier when he had to make a little evidence go a long way. Dr Johnson paid him an unintended compliment when he claimed that the *Conduct of the Allies* 'operates by the mere weight of facts, with very little assistance from the hand that produced them'. The criticism is a tribute to Swift's success in what Quintilian regarded as the most difficult of all rhetorical tasks, to say 'that which, once heard, all think they would have said, – a delusion due to the fact that they regard what has been said as having no merit save that of truth'.[42]

iii

By the summer of 1712, the tasks that Swift had begun in 1710 had been largely accomplished. The old ministry had been discredited; the power and influence of Marlborough curtailed; the war had been made unpopular; the public had been prepared for a peace that would leave Spain in the hands of a Bourbon. A note of self-satisfaction is evident in *Some Reasons to Prove, that No Person Is Obliged by his Principles, as a Whig, to Oppose her Majesty or her Present Ministry. In a Letter to a Whig Lord* (June 1712; *PW* vi.123-36). This pamphlet is unusual in that it is addressed (nominally at least) to the whigs. Its theme is that the opposition leaders are motivated purely by selfish considerations, their desire to get back into office and resume their plunder of the nation. Moderate and disinterested whigs should therefore support the government, since the two

---

[42] Johnson, 'Swift', *Lives of the Poets*, ed. George Birkbeck Hill (Oxford, 1905), iii.19; Johnson does recognise the part played in the pamphlet's success by its willing audience. Quintilian, *Institutio Oratoria* 4.ii.38; trans. H.E. Butler (1921), ii.71.

sides are no longer kept apart by principles but by men and profits. How far this pamphlet was really addressed to the whigs may be doubted; it may have been intended as a bid for the support of the more independent back-benchers by trying to divide them from their leaders. As an expression of confidence that everything is going right for the ministry, the pamphlet marks a high-point in the 'four last years'; soon things would begin going badly for Swift and for the government. Meanwhile, however, Swift's confidence and high spirits also found expression in two brief squibs. In *A Letter from the Pretender to a Whig Lord* (July 1712; *PW* vi.145-6) he deftly transfers the charge of Jacobitism onto the whigs themselves. The *Letter* purports to discuss the Pretender's agreement with the whigs about the division of the spoils of office, once their intrigue for his restoration has succeeded. Swift borrowed the character of his old enemy Lord Wharton, whom he had earlier lampooned for his corrupt government of Ireland, for *A Letter of Thanks from My Lord Wharton to the Lord Bishop of St Asaph* (July 1712; *PW* vi.151-5). The bishop, William Fleetwood, had published a volume of old sermons with a new and aggressively whiggish preface. The new preface had been given wide currency (14,000 copies are said to have been printed) through being reprinted in the popular *Spectator* and in the *Flying Post*. By having an irreligious old scoundrel like Wharton thank the bishop for his services to the whig cause, Swift wanted to make whig churchmen feel uncomfortable about their political company. The damaging association between the whigs and atheism and irreligion was of great value for tory propagandists, and Swift was always willing to exploit it.

In the eighteen months of its existence the Oxford ministry had achieved much. It had established itself as stable and creditworthy. It had begun negotiations for a peace while appearing to continue the vigorous prosecution of the war. A political alliance between the landed interest and the church had been forged through measures acceptable to both. The 1711 Qualification Act was an attempt to keep the 'moneyed' men out of the Commons by requiring members to have minimum landed estates. Swift regarded it as an important constitutional safeguard (*PW* iii.169-70), but it proved too easily evaded to have any other effect than to provide work for the lawyers. An act was passed to finance the building of fifty new churches in the newly built-up areas of London, and for the first time the lower house of Convocation had a government sympathetic to its aspirations. For Scotland, acts were passed to assist the episcopalian minority and to restore lay patronage. For England, an Occasional Conformity Act (which had been the subject of so much heat and discord in 1702-4) was easily passed, the whigs having withdrawn their opposition as the price for Lord Nottingham's support in December 1711 of the motion for 'No Peace without Spain'. Swift cherished hopes that, once a satisfactory peace had been negotiated, the government would be able to do much more in the way of constructive, tory legislation of this kind. A project that he had particularly at heart was the foundation of an English academy. In May 1712 he published his proposal for such an academy in his *Proposal for Correcting the English Tongue* (*PW* iv.5-21), dedicated in the most extravagant and fulsome terms to Lord Treasurer Oxford. Most unusually, Swift signed his name to this dedication, surely a mark of how far he desired to be publicly identified with the scheme. Obviously drawing its inspiration from the French Academy, Swift's idea was attacked in the press, predictably enough, on party grounds as showing typically tory francophilia.[43] The nominal purpose of the academy was to act as a guardian of the English language; critics then and since have often pointed out the impracticability of trying to fix a language, and the futility of trying to control language through an official body. But Swift probably attached greater importance to the academy as an instrument of patronage, both through appointments to the academy itself and to the role it would have played (somewhat like the modern Arts Council) in distributing government financial support for writers. Had such an academy been in existence in 1704, it would surely not have been necessary for the Chancellor of the Exchequer to have visited Addison in his garret to ask him to write a poem celebrating the great victory of Blenheim.[44] The task would have been assigned to an academician, or through the recommendation by the academy of a promising young poet.

To set against these positive achievements and projects, there were many delays, disappointments, and divisions. The negotiations for a peace went on very slowly. After Marlborough's dismissal at the end of 1711, the Duke of

[43] John Oldmixon, *Reflections on Dr Swift's Letter to Harley* (1712); and Arthur Maynwaring, *The British Academy* (1712); reprinted with an introduction by Louis A. Landa (Los Angeles, 1948; Augustan Reprint Society, No. 15).

[44] Peter Smithers, *The Life of Joseph Addison* (2nd ed., Oxford, 1968), p. 94.

Ormonde in 1712 conducted a futile but expensive campaign in Flanders, prevented by his 'restraining orders' from engaging in any substantial action. These orders led to a discreditable break-up with the allies, including (most unfortunately) the Elector of Hanover. The peace began to take on an increasingly partisan character, and the whigs began to exploit the elector's opposition to the tory government's foreign policy to lend credibility to their charge that the ministry was plotting to bring over the Pretender. There were increasingly apparent divisions, over personalities and policies, within the ministry itself: between Oxford and Bolingbroke (as St John had now become on his elevation to the House of Lords), and between moderation and tory 'high-flying'. When the Dean of Wells died in February 1712, Swift wrote a short letter to Oxford asking for this piece of desirable preferment (*Corr*.i.288); after torturing delays, he failed to get it, or any other of the deaneries that became available. Swift was also vexed and disappointed by the ministry's failure to get a bill to regulate the press through parliament. This was a cause that he had almost as much at heart as his academy. The stamp tax, which was introduced in August 1712 as in some measure a substitute for censorship, proved ineffective in suppressing whig propaganda although it had a temporary effect in depressing the circulation of newspapers. These various frustrations do not find much direct expression in Swift's writings, since the summer of 1712 marked the beginning of a barren period in his publications.[45] They can be sensed in a small way in a second attack he wrote on bishop Fleetwood, published in the *Examiner*, Vol. II, No. 34 (24 July 1712; *PW* vi.159-61). Although written within a few weeks of the high-spirited *Letter of Thanks from My Lord Wharton*, the second piece breathes frustration and exasperation. Swift's paper is built around a reprint of an earlier preface of Fleetwood's, to one of the old sermons when first published (in 1700), in which the future bishop had deplored whiggery and fanaticism as likely to lead to the establishment of a republic. This *Examiner* paper, unremarkable enough in itself, marks something of a turning-point in Swift's political writings. It is the first piece, as his *History of the Four Last Years of the Queen* would be the longest, in which he is on the defensive. Hitherto he had enjoyed almost unlimited scope in attacking the misdeeds

---

[45] They can, however, be followed in numerous passages in the *Journal to Stella* (e.g. ii.535, 540, 552, 556, 580).

and maladministration of the whigs; from the summer of 1712 his primary task (to which his rhetorical gifts were much less well suited) would be the defence of the record of the tory ministry.

Initially at least there was something of a lull in the war of propaganda, while the negotiations were in progress; for the peace could not easily be attacked until the terms were known. Nor did parliament meet, as it usually did, before Christmas; its first business session was postponed from time to time until April 1713 when the peace terms were finally announced. Swift used his freedom from routine pamphleteering for what he hoped would be a major historical work, intended as a defence of Queen Anne's change of ministers in 1710 and of the new ministry's negotiation of a good peace. Swift had long had ambitions of being an historian, and here he seemed to have an ideal subject.[46] In the tradition of Thucydides and Polybius, he had lived through, and to a degree had taken part in, important and complex events of European significance; and he had many opportunities of talking with men who had played major roles and of obtaining 'inside' information. He took his research very seriously, and the composition of the *History* can be followed in some detail through the *Journal to Stella*. On 7 August 1712 he spoke of 'an Affair I am upon' (*JS* ii.552); by 15 September it is 'a long work' (p. 556), yet on 28 October be still expected to finish it about Christmas (pp.566-7). 'I toil like a horse,' he writes, 'and have hundreds of letters still to read; and squeeze a line perhaps out of each, or at least the seeds of a line' (p. 569). By the end of December Swift had something ready to print, which he was holding back until his preferment was fixed (p. 590). Yet on 23 April 1713, just after his appointment as dean of St Patrick's had been confirmed, he wrote that he would not come to Ireland until his book was finished (p. 664). On 16 May he could finally report that 'I have finisht my Treatise & must be ten days correcting it' (p. 669). Some of the later delays were caused by the dilatoriness of the ministers to whom Swift showed his manuscript for advice, and who (for reasons that we shall see) were less enthusiastic than he had hoped and expected. The book had been written as a defence of the making of the peace, to be published when the treaties were submitted to parliament for approval. The procrastination of the ministers had made this

[46] On Swift's historical ideas and ambitions, see Irvin Ehrenpreis, *The Personality of Jonathan Swift* (1958), pp. 58-82; and F.P. Lock, *The Politics of 'Gulliver's Travels'* (Oxford, 1980), especially pp. 33-65.

impossible. Swift left for Ireland to be installed as dean. Parliament approved the treaties but rejected a bill to make the commercial clauses relating to free trade with France effective. When Swift returned to London in September 1713 the polemical occasion for his *History* had passed. He himself never lost his faith in the value of the work, and at least twice in his later life he made serious efforts to have it published. On each occasion discouragement from his friends combined with accidents of circumstance to prevent its appearance. It was eventually published, as *The History of the Four Last Years of the Queen*, in 1758.[47]

The title, though it has Swift's own sanction, is misleading, since the *History* is taken no further than the signing of the peace treaties and gives only a very selective account of the years with which it deals. It is divided into four books, of which Books I and III are occupied with affairs at home and II and IV with negotiations abroad. Despite Swift's protestations of impartiality, we are not many lines into the first page before a reference to the 'Heads of a discontented Party Faction' (*PW* vii.1) reveals the essentially partisan nature of the following narrative. The *History* is in fact a mixture of panegyric and satire, disguised as an historical account. Its theme is that of a moral fable, the triumph of virtue over selfishness and duplicity, and the presentation of character and events is slanted to illustrate the theme of the fable. Swiftian themes from the *Examiner* and the *Conduct of the Allies* are repeated and developed: the iniquities of the outgoing whig ministers, and the selfish perfidy of the allies, especially the Dutch.

It is not difficult to see why the ministers delayed and tried to discourage the publication of the *History*. It was far too obviously partisan to be accepted in the way Swift seemed to offer it, as impartial history, and yet it would be irrelevant to the real issues (especially the arguments about trade with France) that would be debated in parliament. Both Oxford and Bolingbroke probably felt that little would be gained by an attempt to defend the methods used to negotiate the peace, and that it would be better to focus on the undoubted advantages to Britain that the treaties themselves brought. In particular, what

---

[47] The fortunes of the *History of the Four Last Years of the Queen* can be followed in the introduction by Harold Williams, *PW* vii.x-xxvii. A slight glimpse of Swift at work on the *History* is afforded by a small sheet of rough notes, printed and discussed by George P. Mayhew, *Rage or Raillery: The Swift Manuscripts at the Huntington Library* (San Marino, 1967), pp. 26-36.

was needed was forward-looking pamphlets defending the commercial advantages of the peace, for it was on the proposed terms of trade that the whig opposition would focus. In this new situation, with the ministry on the defensive, it was the typical Defoe strategy that was appropriate. In *An Essay on the Treaty of Commerce with France* (1713), Defoe argued strictly in terms of the economic advantages to be gained by the treaty, as he did at greater length in his periodical *Mercator*.[48] Swift's *History* was irrelevant to this debate, and its appearance would only have provoked damaging and unnecessary counter-propaganda. Whether we regard it as a history or as a pamphlet, the *History* can only be considered a failure. Swift's rhetorical gifts were unsuited to the writing of history. His prejudices make him unwilling to draw a mixed character, or to accept mixed motives on both sides. His characters are the (historically unconvincing) vices and virtues of a morality play. He describes the peace negotiations in terms of moral contrasts between the participants, not as a human drama in which the actors on both sides are trying to outwit each other. Nor is Swift able to breathe life into the long and complex narrative. His accounts of the diplomatic moves in Books II and IV are particularly tedious, for the detail is not made meaningful. In the *Conduct of the Allies*, Swift was sparing of detail. Because his main attention was devoted to the rhetorical effect of the pamphlet, he never used more than was needed. In the *History* he seems to have regarded the detail as necessary, although he clearly feels no interest in it. There is the dry recital, without the impartiality, of the chronicler. Considered simply as a pamphlet, stripped of its historical pretensions, the *History* is diffuse and poorly proportioned. It fails to address the really topical issues, no polemical purpose is served by its raking over the past, and it is very dull. For the most part Swift sacrificed his usual repertory of rhetorical devices in favour of what he imagined to be the requirements of the dignity of history.

Despite its rhetorical failure, and its severe limitations as a primary historical source, the *History* contains many passages of considerable interest as specimens of Swift's style or for what they reveal about his opinions. The only passages which show real brilliance of style are the characters of the whig lords near

---

[48] For a modern study of the treaties, see D.C. Coleman, 'Politics and economics in the age of Anne: the case of the Anglo-French trade treaty of 1713', *Trade, Government, and Economy in Pre-Industrial England*, ed. D.C. Coleman and A.H. John (1976), pp. 187-211.

the beginning of Book I. These are masterpieces of character-assassination, and would have been in place in a political pamphlet. Swift's method is to seize on anything openly discreditable in the characters of the old ministers, and having exhausted that he twists their apparent virtues into disguised vices. The most vicious is the attack on Lord Nottingham, who earned his place among the whigs by his apostasy from the tories on the question of the peace terms. 'His *outward* Regularity of Life, his *Appearance* of Religion, and *seeming* Zeal for the Church' (*PW* vii.11; emphasis added); Swift will not allow any of Nottingham's virtues to be real. He could have forgiven Nottingham for being a narrow-minded bigot, if he had not deserted to the whigs. Yet the characters in the *History*, clever as they are, are inferior to the *Short Character of Wharton*, where the same use of innuendo and insinuation is allowed free play. In the *Short Character* there is a genial good-humour that wins the reader's sympathy. The fictive author never drops the mask that he is describing a character notable for its rarity, as one might an unusual specimen of animal life. The reader is left to supply the moral indignation. In the *History* the moral revulsion is already present, but there is no humour; and the too obvious unfairness of the portraits jars with the preceeding protestations of impartiality.

It seems curious that Swift did not balance the portraits of the whig villains by a corresponding set describing the important tory leaders.[49] The only one drawn at length is Oxford (*PW* vii.73-5). It is illuminating to compare this character, in which the minister's chronic procrastination is excused and even praised as a deep reach of policy, with what Swift really thought a year or so later, as he expressed it in his attack on Oxford's methods in *Some Free Thoughts on the Present State of Affairs* (*PW* viii.77-98). Even in the *History* the character of Oxford is surprisingly unfavourable for a professed panegyric. One of Swift's limitations as a political writer was his inability to praise with any degree of conviction. His preferred method of praising someone, by ironic or inverted criticism, is sometimes successful, as it is in *A Vindication of his Excellency the Lord Carteret* (1730; *PW* xii.153-69). More often, however, as in the group portrait of the new tory ministers in the *Examiner* No. 26 (1 February 1711), the infusion of ironic negatives fails to come off

---

[49] Swift does provide characters of Oxford, Bolingbroke, and Ormonde in the *Enquiry into the Behaviour of the Queen's Last Ministry* (*PW* viii.132-8).

and the reader is left with a rather unsatisfactory sense that Swift has nothing much to say in favour of men that he forbears to criticise rather than praises. In the *History* Swift seems afraid to draw an unreservedly favourable portrait of Oxford. Instead, in an absurd attempt (after the flagrantly biased portraits of the whigs) to maintain his avowed historical impartiality, he writes what is supposed to be a candid or 'mixed' character. The result is most unfortunate. For the list of Oxford's major achievements (which Swift really believed in) is misplaced as a defence against the petty accusation of cunning; and the overall impression left by the character is curiously negative. Swift was perhaps too convinced a pessimist to be happy in the role of panegyrist, unlike the facile author whom he ridicules in *A Tale of a Tub* for being 'so entirely satisfied with the present Procedure of human Things' that he proposes to write '*A Panegyrick upon the World*' (*PW* i.32). In the dedication of *A Tale of a Tub* to Lord Somers, only about ten lines of the three pages are spent on a bare list of the good qualities attributed to Somers. The rest of the dedication is spent where Swift's interest obviously really lay, in parodying and satirising dedications and their conventions. For a convincing celebration of Somers (who was by no means the most difficult of the whig lords to praise sensibly) we have to turn to Addison, whose eulogy published in the *Freeholder* shortly after Somers's death (No. 39, 4 May 1716) has a measured dignity of tone that prevents it sounding fulsome. Elsewhere, as in *The Campaign* and in the *Dialogues on Medals*, Addison celebrates the heroes of a Britain that he sees as worthy, in its cultural and military achievements, of comparison with the Rome of Virgil and Horace.[50] It is just this ability to communicate a sense of positive achievement that Swift needed to make his *History* come alive.

Apart from the character-sketches of the whig leaders, the most interesting passages in the *History* are those which reveal Swift's own opinions on various subjects. Thus his remarks on the bill to repeal the Naturalisation Act promoted by the previous whig government reveal his views on immigration policy, which are typically tory and xenophobic. He dislikes Holland, which had an 'open door' attitude to immigrants, and

[50] In the *Guardian* No. 96 (4 July 1713) Addison proposed that contemporary events should be commemorated on the current coinage. He had previously praised the Roman practice of doing this in his *Dialogues upon Medals* (written about 1702, posthumously published in 1721); *Miscellaneous Works*, ed. A.C. Guthkelch (1914), ii. 380-1.

which had long been a haven for political and religious refugees from the more repressive regimes in other parts of Europe. He fears that encouraging the immigration of protestant refugees from France will strengthen the dissenting interest; he would have liked conformity to the national church to have been a precondition of immigration (*PW* vii.94). More generally, Swift is opposed to the expansion of economic activity, particularly in the manufacturing trades, that immigrant craftsmen will bring; his ideal for both population and economic activity was a 'steady state' (p. 95). Swift was never in favour of any unlimited freedom of the press, and in the *History* he gives a lengthy account of his views on the subject in the context of the abortive Licensing Bill of 1712 (pp. 103-6; his giving so much space to a bill that failed to become law shows that he did not subscribe to the belief that the proper subject-matter of history is success stories). Most of this passage is an excuse for an attack on the malpractices of whig scribblers, but of independent interest in his objection to the clause in the proposed legislation which would have required authors to set their names and addresses to their books. In a spirited defence of authorial modesty and anonymity, he charges that only the 'Dull or Superficial, void of all Taste and Judgement' would be willing to print their names on their first publications (p. 105). This passage gives a clue to how he felt about someone like Steele, who (later in 1713) would sign his name to his political writings as a kind of guarantee of sincerity. Swift always felt that modesty and self-distrust made anonymity imperative, and only the 'Dull or Superficial' could think otherwise.

iv

In April 1713, soon after the announcement of the signing of the peace treaties and shortly before the completion of his *History of the Four Last Years of the Queen*, Swift's suspense about his own future ended with his appointment as dean of St Patrick's, Dublin. This bitter disappointment, after his hopes for an English deanery, made a fitting end to a year of frustrations and delays. In June he returned to Ireland for the first time since 1710, to be installed as dean, protesting and perhaps half-believing that he had finished with English politics. He spent the summer in quiet seclusion at his country parish of Laracor, but by August he was ready to listen to the blandishments of

Erasmus Lewis, who urged his return to London (*Corr*. i.383). On his return to the English capital he found the political situation there altered in every way for the worse. In June the government had suffered its first serious parliamentary defeat, on the commercial clauses of the treaty of Utrecht. This setback had to some extent been retrieved by the substantial tory majority returned in the general election held in August and September. But the conclusion of the peace settlement now allowed both Oxford and Bolingbroke more time and energy to fight each other. Swift had been one of the last to perceive the irreconcilable feud between the two ministers, and he would be one of the last to try to repair it. In the autumn of 1713 he could no longer ignore it, and over the next year he would waste much effort in futile attempts at peacemaking. Oxford, so far as his plans can be fathomed, wished to pursue a course of moderation and to win support, if possible, from the less intransigent whigs; he certainly wanted to retain as much power as possible in his own hands. To bid for moderate whig support without alienating the tories meant avoiding any divisive or controversial issues (which in 1713 meant practically all issues), and Oxford's policies led inevitably to the government beginning to drift without any clear lead from the top. Bolingbroke wished to capture power for himself by gaining the support of the tory majority through the pursuit of a distinctly tory programme of reaction. He was happy and even eager to alienate the whigs in the process. Swift's loyalties were awkwardly divided between the two men. He had a greater personal respect for Oxford, but he was fully aware of the bad effects of the minister's dilatoriness and procrastination and he had little temperamental sympathy for trimming or moderation. Instead his natural temperamental extremism, and his strong desire to see the implementation of a full tory programme to strengthen the church and the landed interest, and to break the power of the whigs and the moneyed interest, drew him towards Bolingbroke, despite his uneasiness about the secretary's defects of character and lax personal morality.[51]

Internally divided as it was, the ministry also faced a more

[51] One can agree with Ehrenpreis that 'it was Oxford's character but Bolingbroke's programme that held Swift' (*Swift*, ii.674), without supposing that Swift was looking for the father that he had lost in Harley (ii.393, 755) and for the son he never had in Bolingbroke (ii.455). For a detailed study of the relationship and quarrel between the two ministers (with many references to Swift), see Sheila Biddle, *Bolingbroke and Harley* (1975).

serious external threat than it had since the 'No Peace without Spain' crisis of December 1711. The whigs, though weak in the House of Commons, were making an improved propaganda effort, for which they had an ideal issue, capable of uniting their own side while dividing the tories and even the cabinet: the question of the succession to the throne. Nominally and in public at least, everyone on both sides was agreed in support of the Act of Settlement. Swift was really loyal to it, although very unenthusiastic about the prospect of the Hanoverian succession, which was expected to lead to a revival of the power of the whigs. Oxford and Bolingbroke, however, both toyed with the idea of a Jacobite restoration. Their motives for doing so are clear enough: to preserve their own power after the death of the queen. But with what degree of seriousness they regarded the negotiations is hard to say. In the event they got the worst of both worlds. During the negotiations for the peace, they had offended the future George I, so that they had little to hope for from his accession. Yet they made no serious attempt to effect a reconciliation with him. Nor did they take any serious steps to make a Jacobite restoration at all practicable. Admittedly the Pretender's refusal to change his religion was unhelpful; but it was hardly unexpected. By fighting each other rather than making active preparations for the inevitable next reign (Queen Anne, though not old, was in very poor and declining health), they increasingly paralysed the government and inflicted lasting damage on the party's prospects for the next reign. There is no doubt that the popular fears of popery and the Pretender were real enough. The whig writers thus had an easy task to exploit such feelings for their own ends, by branding the ministry (and the charge was credible enough) as crypto-Jacobites. For Swift, these fears of popery and the Pretender were less real than they were for most Englishmen, and this made it difficult for him to understand them and try to neutralise them. In his writings for the government in 1713-14 he had a much harder task than he had faced in 1710-11. Instead of articulating popular fears and prejudices that he felt himself, he had to try to combat fears and jealousies that he regarded as unreal and absurd; and he was writing against the tide of popular opinion.

When Swift reached London from Ireland on 9 September, the political world was full of a new writer and a new topic; his ex-friend Steele was the writer, new in his political importance at least, and the issue was Dunkirk.[52] Steele was not a completely

[52] The quarrel between Swift and Steele is treated in Bertrand A. Goldgar, *The*

inexperienced political journalist, for he had edited the government's *London Gazette*, and his periodical essays, though for commercial reasons they had been kept largely politically neutral, had included the occasional partisan paper. But he had not previously tried his hand at the longer form of the pamphlet. An impetuous man impatient of restraints of any kind, he had been out of sympathy with the new tory government from the very start. Economic motives, reinforced by the advice of his more responsible friends, had probably served to keep him reasonably quiet. He enjoyed a sinecure in the Stamp Office, as well as a pension as a former servant to the queen's late husband, Prince George of Denmark. He was perpetually short of money, and he seems to have come to a private arrangement with Harley (of which Swift certainly knew nothing) to refrain from attacking the government in return for keeping his incomes. In the summer of 1713, however, he became so dissatisfied with the government's policies, which he took to be leading to the restoration of the Pretender, that he decided to come out into open opposition. He resigned his place and pension, published some very outspoken criticism of the ministry in the *Guardian*, and decided to stand for parliament at the forthcoming general election. Private motives played their part in this decision, as hostile pamphleteers would soon charge him: the pressure of his creditors made the M.P.'s immunity from arrest for debt convenient. The issue that Steele (or rather, presumably, his party leaders) chose was Dunkirk. This port had long been a haven for French pirates in their operations against British merchant ships, and as part of the Utrecht settlement Louis XIV had agreed to demolish its fortifications and fill in its harbour. As an earnest of his good intentions, a small British force had been allowed to garrison the town in 1712, when the town had briefly been a political issue. Swift had written an amusing little squib on the subject, *A Hue and Cry after Dismal* (*PW* vi.139-41; the original broadside printing is reproduced as the frontispiece to *PW* vi). This has really less to do with Dunkirk than with Lord Nottingham, who had become one of Swift's favourite targets since his desertion to the whigs on the peace terms in 1711. Swift also wrote a dull ballad celebrating the British occupation of the

Curse of Party: Swift's Relations with Addison and Steele (Lincoln, Nebraska, 1961). The story is told from Steele's point of view in Calhoun Winton, *Captain Steele: The Early Career of Richard Steele* (Baltimore, 1964). On Dunkirk as a political issue, see John Robert Moore, 'Defoe, Steele, and the demolition of Dunkirk', *Huntington Library Quarterly*, xiii (1950), 279-302.

town (*Poems*, i.167-9). In 1713 the issue was that the time stipulated by the treaty for the demolition of the fortifications and harbour had expired without the work being done, and the British government was taking no steps to ensure that it would be carried out. Less directly, the whigs further insinuated that the reason that the government was not insisting on the demolition was that they were colluding with the French to leave it intact as a port of embarkation for the Pretender.

In the *Guardian* No. 128 (7 August 1713) Steele printed a letter signed 'English Tory'. The motto of this issue was the elder Cato's 'Delenda est Carthago'; its theme was a phrase several times repeated in the letter, 'The British Nation expect the immediate Demolition of Dunkirk.' In a later issue defending the letter, Steele's authorship of it was admitted. On 22 September a pamphlet on the subject, *The Importance of Dunkirk Considered*, was published with (most exceptionally) Steele's name on the title page. In the *Guardian* No. 168 (23 September) appeared a letter from Steele, signed, puffing his pamphlet and triumphantly crowing about his margin of victory in his recent election to parliament.[53] It became inevitable that the character and conduct of Steele himself would become an issue. The episode well illustrates the advantages of anonymity in political pamphleteering, for the substantive questions about Dunkirk were beclouded by irrelevant personal abuse of Steele. Technical anonymity, however well-known Steele's authorship became, would have confined such abuse to passing allusions (of the kind that one finds made about Swift, for example).

Steele himself, however, revelled in his notoriety and positively courted martyrdom. His writings were complained of in parliament, where he admitted and even gloried in their authorship. In March 1714 he was duly expelled from the House of Commons, for his various anti-government writings, after a debate that became a full-scale party conflict, with Steele supported by the best whig debating talent. The outcome, decided on party lines, was never in doubt. Even the whig leaders must have been a little embarrassed by Steele's antics, though they were no doubt glad to be able to make use of someone prepared to make an exhibition of himself. Steele's was a character out of its proper time, the type of the 'amiable

---

[53] *The Importance of Dunkirk Considered* is reprinted in Steele's *Tracts and Pamphlets*, ed. Rae Blanchard (Baltimore, 1944), pp. 83-124; an edition of the *Guardian* by John C. Stephens is forthcoming.

humourist' that by mid-century readers would begin to find endearing.[54] Swift and most contemporaries found Steele incomprehensible and infuriating. Steele was good-natured in his way, optimistic, sentimental; but he tended to confuse intention with action, and was erratic, unreliable, and irresponsible.[55] He was irked by restraints of any kind. In his literary enterprises this made him often an innovator, as in his journalism and in his plays and his writings about the theatre. He had an unusual perception of the importance and even the heroism of ordinary people and everyday life. But his deplorable lack of decorum in his own conduct was offensive to contemporaries. He was prepared to put his loyalty to principle above gratitude to a patron; and this the age found shocking. He was the temperamental opposite of his friend Addison, with whom he was nevertheless able to engage in a most fruitful literary partnership, at least while there were no political differences between them. It was politics that destroyed their friendship of thirty years standing in 1719. Swift and Steele were also temperamental opposites; but Swift was more abrasive and less tolerant than Addison, and politics soon took them into active opposition to each other. Swift's relations with Steele had been cool since the establishment of the tory government in 1710, and they reached breaking point early in 1713 on the occasion of an angry exchange between the *Examiner* (for which Oldisworth, not Swift was responsible, although Steele refused to believe this) and the *Guardian*. The broken friendship left Swift with a residue of bitterness against what he saw as Steele's ingratitude for his literary and political assistance; for this reason personal animosity has a greater share in *The Importance of the Guardian Considered* than it has in most of Swift's political pamphlets.

As a political propagandist, Steele was better in the short form of the periodical essay than as a pamphleteer. His most effective statement about Dunkirk is contained in the letter printed in the *Guardian* No. 128. The slogan 'Delenda est Carthago' expresses pretty much all he has to say. Writing without research, revision, or much thought, he is nevertheless able to communicate his simple slogan effectively enough. His rhetoric is clumsy: it

[54] For the type, see Stuart Tave, *The Amiable Humorist: A Study in the Comic Theory and Criticism of the Eighteenth and Early Nineteenth Centuries* (Chicago, 1960).

[55] For a contemporary description of Steele's vagaries, see the vicious caricature in Mrs Manley's *Secret Memoirs and Manners ... from the New Atalantis* (1709), pp. 187-93.

consists only of affirmation and repetition. Yet everyone could take his simple point, and it proved surprisingly hard to answer. Why had Dunkirk *not* been demolished? Steele's weaknesses become only too apparent in the pamphlet, *The Importance of Dunkirk Considered*. He is unable to construct an argument, indeed he has little to add to what he had already said in the *Guardian*, to which the pamphlet adds nothing of any substance.

Swift was by no means the first to take issue with Steele on the question of Dunkirk. As early as 13 August, only a week after the appearance of the *Guardian* No. 128, Defoe published *The Honour and Prerogative of the Queen's Majesty Vindicated and Defended*. Defoe here poses as an 'Old Whig' and praises the *Guardian*'s general record of cultural service before attacking the particular paper on Dunkirk. Defoe has little to say on the substantive question, and instead he concentrates on the insult to the queen implied by the word 'EXPECT', to which he gives a typographical prominence that it had not had in the *Guardian* (where, however, it was often enough repeated to make it stick in the reader's mind). There is little *ad hominem* material in Defoe's pamphlet until the end, where he has a fling at Steele's financial debts and at his supposedly borrowed wit. About a month later Defoe published a second, longer pamphlet on the same subject, *Reasons concerning the Immediate Demolition of Dunkirk*.[56] Here Defoe deploys whatever arguments his ingenuity and imagination can suggest, but his real tactic is to make the question seem much more difficult and complicated than Steele had pretended. He uses the same kind of deferential *persona* as he had in *Reasons why this Nation Ought to Put a Speedy End to this Expensive War* (1711), where his strategy had also been to make the question seem more difficult than it really was. A quite different tactic was adopted by William Wagstaffe in *The Character of Richard St—le, Esq.* (1713). This is a vicious personal attack, which Steele himself seems to have attributed to Swift.[57] Within a few pages Steele is exposed as a venal and parvenu plagiarist, who to escape the debts that his extravagance has contracted, has hired his pen (and his service in parliament) to the whigs.

---

[56] The two pamphlets are Nos 261 and 264 in Moore's *Checklist of Defoe*, from which the dates of publication are taken.

[57] That Steele himself thought that Swift was the author of the *Character* is apparent from the *Englishman*, No. 57 (15 February 1714); ed. Rae Blanchard (Oxford, 1955), p. 233. The pamphlet was commonly thought to be Swift's; Goldgar, *The Curse of Party*, p. 133.

Swift's contribution, *The Importance of the Guardian Considered* (*PW* viii.4-25), did not appear until the very end of October or the first days of November, by which time the issue was a little stale and Steele himself ripe for ridicule rather than invective. Swift makes no attempt to argue in the manner of Defoe's *Reasons why this Nation*, and his pose is anything but deferential. He takes up and develops the theme of Steele's monstrous impertinence that Defoe had used in *The Honour and Prerogative of the Queen's Majesty*, and he combines it with his own usual lofty tone to make Steele seem microscopic in his unimportance. Swift is just as abusive of Steele personally as Wagstaffe had been, but he is more adroit about it. Steele had cast his pamphlet in the form of a letter to the bailiff (mayor) of Stockbridge, the borough which had recently elected him to parliament. Swift jokingly employs the same form, pretending that Steele's letter needs a second letter of commentary or explanation for the provincial reader (who was not, of course, Steele's primary audience). Swift adopts a tone suitable for the relating of ordinary, matter-of-fact circumstances. The pose of writing for the information of the bailiff and his fellow-townsmen makes Swift's character assassination of Steele read like a weary headmaster's end-of-term report on an exasperatingly wayward pupil. Steele's self-importance is deflated, his gross ignorance is exposed, his lapses in grammar and sense corrected. Awkward biographical details are deployed to reveal Steele's really ignoble motives for his supposedly public-spirited posturings. Several of the devices that Swift had used in the *Examiner* are brought back into service. By the end of the pamphlet Steele has become the real issue; a question of politics has been transformed into one of taste and morality. Steele's high-minded patriotism has been exposed as no more than the indecorous antics of a self-interested, incompetent clown. The reader is left feeling that it would be bad manners to question the queen on the matter of Dunkirk. Loyal subjects should trust her to manage the problem as she (not Richard Steele) knows best. *The Importance of the Guardian Considered* is the most amusing of Swift's political pamphlets, but hardly the most effective. He shows that Steele is unimportant, and implies that Dunkirk is so too, but he has nothing to say to those whigs (and perhaps some tories) who were really worried by the question.

Dunkirk was a particular instance of a wider political issue. Presented both as a threat to English commerce and as a probable port of embarkation for the Pretender, Dunkirk symbolised the collusion between the British and French governments that the whig writers denounced. Deep and almost universal hatred of popery had forged the short-lived national alliance against James II in 1688, and fear of popery and (after James II's death) of the possible return of the Pretender had ever since been a potent factor in the making of public opinion on political matters. In 1708 the Jacobite invasion scare had won the election for the whigs. In 1713-14 the uncertainty of the government's policy on the succession allowed the whigs again to exploit this powerful issue, not only consolidating their own supporters but causing the most serious split in the ranks of the tories since the controversial plan to 'tack' the Occasional Conformity Bill to a supply measure in 1704.

Anti-popery propaganda took many forms. William Fleetwood, bishop of St Asaph, prepared an elaborate treatise on *The Life and Miracles of St Wenefrede* (1713). The waters at Holywell in his diocese were supposed to owe their curative powers to St Wenefrede, being the site of her martyrdom. The well had been popularly associated with popish frauds since James II had visited it in 1687 to pray for a son. Fleetwood's book is an elaborate exposure of the well's supposed powers and of the part played by 'pious frauds' in the popish system. He ends his preface with an insinuation that the government is plotting to introduce popery and the Pretender together, a theme that he developed in another preface, to his *Four Sermons* (1713). This preface achieved a much wider circulation by being reprinted as No. 384 of the popular (and usually non-political) *Spectator* (21 May 1712). Swift wrote both an *Examiner* paper (Vol. II, No. 34, 24 July 1712; *PW* vi.159-61) and a separate little pamphlet, the *Letter of Thanks from My Lord Wharton* (*PW* vi.151-5), attacking this preface.

The chief anti-catholic writers at this juncture, however, were Steele and Gilbert Burnet, bishop of Salisbury. Steele's hostility to popery was based on his belief in liberty. In particular, he thought that English liberty was the product of the variety of national 'humours', a variety which required the toleration of religious pluralism if it was to be maintained.[58] Thus for Steele anti-popery was essentially a political and patriotic attitude.

[58] Unlike Swift, Steele always regarded the personal liberty of the individual as the proper basis of political liberty; see, for example, *The Crisis*, in *Tracts and Pamphlets*, p. 137. For his belief that religious pluralism helped safeguard national liberty, see his *Letter on the Schism Bill* (1714), in *Tracts and Pamphlets*, pp. 237-54.

Burnet's hatred of popery was more genuinely religious, and it had an intellectual and personal basis that Steele's lacked. As the historian of the English Reformation, Burnet was closer than most of his contemporaries to a knowledge of what England in its catholic days (and especially under the Marian persecution) had really been like. He had travelled in catholic Europe (as neither Swift nor Steele had), shortly after the Revocation of the Edict of Nantes. He had published an account of his travels, *Some Letters containing an Account of what Seemed Most Remarkable in Switzerland, Italy etc*, mainly as a warning against catholicism, in 1686; it was a widely read book that went through many editions.[59] Burnet had seen both the more sophisticated Gallicanism of the court of Louis XIV and the degraded superstition of Italy. In 1713 he published three new pieces of anti-catholic polemic, increasingly hysterical in their tone: a preface to a new collection of his sermons; a preface to a new edition of his *Pastoral Care*; and an *Introduction* to the long-awaited third volume of his *History of the Reformation of the Church of England* (the first two volumes had been published in 1679 and 1681). Burnet was intimately acquainted with the iniquities of the reign of Bloody Mary; he himself had lived through the scare of the Popish Plot; and his message was that, in 1713, such times were again arrived.[60] To Swift all this seemed nothing but hypocritical party-inspired malicious nonsense; but it provided a popular rallying-cry for the whigs and it even managed to alarm many sincere tories.

Swift admired France and could not take either popery or the Pretender very seriously as a threat. As we have seen, he wanted to set up an English equivalent of the French Academy, and in general he was sympathetic to a greater degree of political authoritarianism than most contemporary Englishmen. The logic of his ideal of a national church of which membership should be compulsory made him admire the institutions of the Gallican church. While it would be wrong to suggest that Swift would have approved of the violent methods used to persecute the Huguenots after the Revocation of the Edict of Nantes, he was certainly hostile to religious dissent or pluralism and this made him less sympathetic than most contemporaries to the Huguenot exiles. For Swift, popery was the superstition of the

[59] Addison's *Remarks on Several Parts of Italy* (1705) was another whig travel book, in which the anti-catholic theme is more muted than it is in Burnet.

[60] Oldisworth's *Examiner*, Vol. v, No. 1 (30 November 1713), attacked Burnet's *Introduction* for drawing parallels between the reigns of Mary I and Queen Anne.

savage Irish; a much more potent threat to the national church was posed by the protestant dissenters. In his *Introduction*, Burnet branded the proposal for a union between the Anglican and Gallican churches as popish and Jacobite; in his *Preface to the B—p of S–r–m's Introduction*, Swift is sympathetic to the idea. Nor was it altogether absurd or impossibly impractical. While he was archbishop of Canterbury, William Wake would devote much effort over many years to exploring the possibilities of such a union.[61] Yet Wake was a good whig, having been Atterbury's principal learned antagonist during the convocation controversy.

The polemical brilliance of *The Importance of the Guardian Considered* was somewhat dimmed by Swift's inability to say much on the substantive issue. His two following pamphlets, while no less witty, both have much more cogent arguments to give them controversial backbone. The reply to Burnet, the *Preface to the B—p of S–r–m's Introduction* (*PW* iv.55-84) was published on 7 December 1713. *The Public Spirit of the Whigs* (*PW* viii.31-68) came out in February 1714 as a reply to Steele's *The Crisis* (a much-heralded pamphlet that finally appeared in January). These two pamphlets can be discussed together, for Swift used the same polemical techniques in both. He neither takes his opponents entirely seriously, nor is he contemptuously dismissive. His tone throughout both is predominantly serious; in the *Preface*, for example, there is a quite straightforward exposition of his views on how the financial problems of the church can best be solved (*PW* iv.65). But variety is provided through passages of humour and irony, as when Swift pretends to think that Burnet is coyly asking for a subscription (*PW* iv.59). In the *Public Spirit* there is a mock-serious discussion of the comparative literary merits of Ridpath, Dunton, and Steele (by no means company in which Steele would be proud to find himself), concluding with a bathetic enumeration of Steele's only literary defects as his lack of style, grammar, and information (*PW* viii.32). In both pamphlets Swift's basic strategy is to expose the whig writers as the self-interested tools of their factious party chiefs, who cannot possibly really believe their own lies. Sometimes this is done by association, as at the beginning of the *Public Spirit*, where a description of the methods used by the whigs in disseminating their poisonous pamphlets is likened to a fraudulent popish crying-up of a

[61] Sykes, *William Wake*, i.252-314.

miracle (*PW* viii.34) and culminates in a striking image of the whigs as bees kept together by the sound of brass. More often, Swift exposes genuine inconsistencies in the whig case and links them with the writers' stylistic defects. Burnet and Steele are made to appear muddled thinkers and incompetent hacks. Swift does not so much argue with them as show why no argument is needed. He avoids having to defend the ministry from the charge of Jacobitism by showing that the whigs do not really believe it themselves; they only use it, he suggests, for their own factious ends. For example, in the *Public Spirit* Swift makes the point that Steele is inconsistent in claiming both that the danger of popery and the Pretender is near and real and that no attempt to restore them could succeed because practically everyone is violently opposed to them. He dissects Steele's image of the origin of government as analogous to an angry crowd cooling under the influence of some respected individual,[62] convicting Steele of having stolen the image from Virgil (*Aeneid* I.148-53) and of having made nonsense of what he has stolen (*PW* viii.43-4). With Burnet, Swift accuses the bishop of being anti-clerical, and hints that his hostility to popery may possibly be because it would prevent his taking a fourth wife (*PW* iv.63-4).[63] With both writers, Swift links their exaggerations and their sensationalism (typified by Steele's cheap emotionalism in his invocation of the Catalans, and in Burnet's image of the fires again burning in Smithfield) with their concern for remote dangers at the expense of near ones. The bishop is afraid of popery, but not of the more immediate (as Swift sees it) threat from the dissenters; Steele is worried about the succession to the throne, but not about his loyalty to the present queen. In both cases, it is because whipping up public hysteria about popery and the Pretender serves their purposes and those of their party.

The *Public Spirit* was Swift's last great success on behalf of the ministry; it went through several editions and was translated

[62] An interesting sample of Steele at work can be seen in a corrected draft of this passage (the first paragraph of the preface to *The Crisis; Tracts and Pamphlets*, p. 134) among the Steele papers formerly at Blenheim and now British Library, Add. MS. 61688, ff.85-6.

[63] Burnet claimed in his *History* that 'The pleasures of sense I did soon nauseate'; the true reading of Swift's note on this passage, which Davis prints as 'Not so soon with the wine of some elections; (*PW* v.294) is 'Not so soon, with three Wives and some Etcetera's', a far more scurrilous remark that confirms the depth of Swift's antagonism to Burnet after politics had driven them apart. I am grateful to the Earl of Shelburne for kindly allowing me to examine Swift's copy of Burnet's *History*, now at Bowood.

into French. But it proved a hollow victory. Public opinion continued to be worried by popery and the Pretender; Oxford and Bolingbroke continued their destructive in-fighting; and the progressive deterioration in the queen's health meant that time was on the side of the whigs. Though Steele had been expelled from the House of Commons for the *Crisis* and other provocative writings, the whigs were able to use their strength in the Lords against Swift. An indiscreet passage in the *Public Spirit of the Whigs* (*PW* viii.50) had reflected on the numerous but poor Scottish nobility; it seems to have been aimed chiefly at the Duke of Argyle, who after supporting the tory government had recently returned to his earlier association with the whigs. The passage was complained of in the House of Lords, where two of Swift's old enemies, Lords Wharton and Nottingham, were prominent in the attack. The government was able to stifle the enquiry by taking it *sub judice*, but it was forced to offer a reward of £300 for information about the author of the *Public Spirit* (the proclamation is reproduced in *PW* viii, facing p. xxii).[64] Instead of receiving an English deanery for his efforts on behalf of church and state, Swift found himself with a price put on his head. The episode must have seemed typical of the fate of the man of integrity and principle caught up in the corrupt world of contemporary politics; though he did not pay the supreme penalty, Swift was sharing in a smaller way the rewards of Socrates and Sir Thomas More.

In May 1714, at last despairing of being able to reconcile Oxford and Bolingbroke, Swift retired to the country, to the parsonage of his acquaintance John Geree at Letcombe Basset in Berkshire. Not that his situation there was so very remote from affairs. He sent and received many letters, keeping in close touch with political developments through Erasmus Lewis and Charles Ford. Pope, who visited Swift at Letcombe, wrote an amusing description of the frustrated politician in a letter to their common friend and Scriblerian, Dr Arbuthnot.[65] Why did not Swift return to Ireland? He must have wanted to remain within easy reach, either to follow Oxford into a dignified retreat (Oxford's resignation or dismissal was constantly expected) or to rejoin in an official or unofficial capacity a regrouped tory

[64] The fullest study of the episode is Maurice J. Quinlan, 'The prosecution of Swift's *Public Spirit of the Whigs*', *Texas Studies in Literature and Language*, ix (1967), 167-84.

[65] Letter of 11 July 1714; *Correspondence*, ed. George Sherburn (Oxford, 1956), i. 233-5.

administration under Bolingbroke. Some insight into his intentions is provided by a pamphlet which he wrote while at Letcombe, *Some Free Thoughts upon the Present State of Affairs* (*PW* viii.77-98). Written for immediate publication, its appearance was delayed by various circumstances until the death of the queen on 1 August made it irrelevant; it was not published until 1741. It seems clear that, when he wrote the pamphlet, Swift did not expect the queen to die so soon as she did, but that he envisaged a tory ministry staying in office long enough to hold another session of parliament and consolidating their power sufficiently to be able to negotiate with the successor from a position of strength. The pamphlet presents Swift's advice about how the tories can best reunite to fight both the whigs at home and the presumed hostility of Hanover abroad.

Swift seems to have been unusually anxious to conceal his authorship of *Some Free Thoughts*, even from Bolingbroke and his friend the printer John Barber. He disguised his style, to the extent of eschewing humour, irony, and other typical Swiftian devices. Perhaps his mood was so sombre that this came naturally. But the tone and character of the fictive author are deliberately pitched at a lower level than Swift usually adopted. The pamphlet is therefore rather slight in obvious literary interest, but it makes up for this by containing an unusual proportion of Swift's own thoughts and opinions, for here he was writing more on his own account than on behalf of the government. He begins, in the manner of the *Conduct of the Allies*, with a question-begging statement of general principle, one that he had learned from Sir William Temple: the superiority of the politics of commonsense to the politics of mystery and refinement.[66] It is in keeping with this theme that Swift adopts, so far as he can, a plain, matter-of-fact approach and style. The principle is illustrated both with historical examples (though these are, somewhat disappointingly, merely listed; one would have liked to have had Swift's comments on Louis XI and the Borgias) and from personal experience. Here it becomes apparent that the real object of attack in the pamphlet is the unsearchable depths of policy of Lord Treasurer Oxford, suspected by the whigs of plotting to introduce the Pretender and by the tories of planning a coalition with the whigs. Such are the results of mystery and refinement; they lead to mistrust on both sides. It is again Oxford who is aimed at (though never, of

[66] Lock, *The Politics of 'Gulliver's Travels'*, pp. 25-31.

course, named; there are similarities here with Swift's *Some Advice to the October Club*) in the second part of the pamphlet, which poses the question why, with all the advantages that it started out with, the tory government after less than four years is falling to pieces. Swift attributes the failure squarely to the Lord Treasurer's reserve and secrecy, and to his unwillingness to pursue thoroughly Tory measures and to employ only staunch tories in all official positions (in other words, Swift is recommending the policies of the October Club and Bolingbroke). All this is preliminary to Swift's advice as to what should be done, at this late stage, to retrieve the situation. He stops just short of a thoroughgoing endorsement of Bolingbroke, whom he follows, however, in recommending a purge of whigs from office and influence. His hostile remarks on the dissenters are presumably to be taken as supporting Bolingbroke's Schism Bill, the purpose of which was to make it much more difficult for the dissenters to operate their own system of alternative education. This bill (which Oxford opposed) was before parliament when Swift was writing. In another recommendation, however, Swift aligns himself with Oxford against Bolingbroke in proposing a scheme of reconciliation with Hanover through the elector's grandson (the future Frederick, Prince of Wales; at this time he was seven years old). In April the elector's envoy in London, Baron Schütz, had (with whig encouragement) demanded a writ to summon the elector's son (the future George II) to the House of Lords as Duke of Cambridge, a title that had been conferred on the prince. When the demand was discussed in cabinet, Bolingbroke had argued for a refusal of the writ, Oxford in its favour. This stand may have been an important cause of his declining favour with the queen, who hated the idea of a successor, however remote, coming to England.[67] Swift's idea was something of a compromise, since although the son would have been old enough to be a focus for whig opposition, the grandson was not. These proposals, taken together, illustrate the kind of policy that Swift favoured at this point. He wanted, so far as possible, to reverse the effects of the Revolution of 1688 by excluding the whigs and the dissenters from public office; but he was not prepared, or he thought that it would be too unpopular and therefore impracticable, to restore the Pretender. What was important to him was the preservation of the tory alliance between church and state. In this alliance, the church was all-

[67] Gregg, *Queen Anne*, p. 381.

important; it did not so much matter whether the state was represented in the person of a Stuart or a Hanoverian.

If Swift had wanted to bring these ideas to the attention of Oxford or Bolingbroke, he had enjoyed ample opportunities to do so, indeed he had probably done so, without going through the elaborate charade of addressing them through a pamphlet. The real audience for which *Some Free Thoughts* was written was the unhappily divided rank and file of the party, most especially those who were suspicious of the ministry's intentions on the succession question. Swift tried to conceal his authorship so that the pamphlet would not appear as a pro-government apologetic, as it inevitably would if his identity as author had been guessed. There are suggestive parallels in tone and technique with an earlier pamphlet addressed specifically to the back-benchers, *Some Advice Humbly Offered to the Members of the October Club* (published January 1712; *PW* vi.71-80).[68] The purpose of *Some Advice* was just the opposite of *Some Free Thoughts*. Its aim was to defend Harley (as he then was) and his policies of trimming and compromise. The reader is given a sense (remarkably enough in a printed pamphlet) of being an insider, and is flattered into feeling that he is being let into the secrets of Harley's deep game. In particular, hints and innuendoes (many picked out by being printed in italic, so that the dullest reader could not miss them) are plentifully scattered, all tending to the exculpation of '*one great Person*' who has worked hard against certain '*unknown Impediments*' (*PW* vi.75). In *Some Free Thoughts* Swift uses the same technique of appearing to reveal secrets while actually giving nothing away. A good example of this is the discussion of 'the late Dissensions at Court', where he speaks of 'the most plausible Topicks' (without naming any of them) that have been suggested, before confiding that they were really 'partly owing to very different Causes' (which are not, however, specified) and 'partly to the Scituation of Affairs' (not further detailed). His conclusion is that things 'could not easily terminate otherwise than they did' (*PW* viii.79). The reader is privileged to receive an inside view, but he is kept blindfolded. As in the *Advice to the October Club*, in *Some Free Thoughts* Swift tried to allay the fears of the government's supporters. In particular, he seems to have had in mind the 'Hanoverian tories'

---

[68] On the membership and political importance of the club, see H.T. Dickinson, 'The October Club', *Huntington Library Quarterly*, xxxii (1970), 155-73.

who, led by the independent Sir Thomas Hanmer, had deserted the government on the crucial vote in the House of Commons on whether the succession was in danger. This important vote of confidence, on 15 April 1714, saw the government's large paper majority dwindle to less than fifty. Swift devotes a paragraph of *Some Free Thoughts* to a defence of the Revolution of 1688 from the point of view of 'the highest Tories', taking the line that whatever guilt was involved (and he seems to accept that some guilt was involved), the episode is now ancient history: passive obedience, non-resistance, and hereditary right are ideas that must now be applied to the present settlement of things (*PW* viii.91-2). The paragraph seems intended to assure the 'Hanover' tories that no real threat to the protestant succession will be posed in supporting Bolingbroke's policies of excluding the whigs and pursuing partisan measures such as the Schism Act, while at the same time Swift offers a rationale to those sentimentally attracted to Jacobitism for transfering their authoritarian doctrines to a more attractive object than the Pretender. Both wings of the party are urged to unite, so as to establish tory control of the country so firmly that it will not be in the power of the successor to introduce the opposite party. It has been suggested that Swift would have felt obliged to join Oxford in political retirement in the event of a Bolingbroke ministry being established.[69] But the programme advocated in *Some Free Thoughts* is so close to Bolingbroke's that this seems unlikely. To be sure, Swift might have felt that in respect and sympathy for Oxford, a decent interval should elapse before he returned to active political involvement. But the attraction of Bolingbroke's tory-reactionary policies would have been a very powerful one. It was the great tragedy of Swift's political life that the dismissal of Oxford on 27 July 1714 was followed by the death of the exhausted queen on 1 August, before Bolingbroke had any chance to consolidate and extend tory power, so badly shaken and weakened by the bickerings between the two leaders. The death of the queen broke the alliance between church and state to which Swift felt his deepest political attachment. The 'four last years' of Queen Anne always retained a special place in Swift's personal mythology as a kind of golden age before the flood-tide of whiggism swept away the last remnants of the old political order that had been fatally weakened by the Revolution of 1688. Arbuthnot, writing to Swift in November 1714

[69] Ehrenpreis, *Swift*, ii.754-5.

(*Corr*.ii.144), borrowed Panthus's lament for Troy from the *Aeneid* to express his sense of the passing away of the age of Queen Anne:

> *fuimus Troes, fuit Ilium et ingens*
> *gloria Teucrorum; ferus omnia Iuppiter Argos*
> *transtulit; incensa Danai dominantur in urbe.* (2.325-7)

CHAPTER TWO

Swift and the Revolution

MORRELL 640
STANTA
II

In *Part of the Seventh Epistle of the First Book of Horace Imitated* (published October 1713; *Poems*, i.169-73) Swift described his involvement in English politics as a propagandist for the tory government as he wanted it to be seen. He describes himself in the poem as a disinterested patriot and wit, sought out by a great statesman (Harley) who enlisted his aid in support of a ministry dedicated to the good of church, queen, and country. Less cheerful, more realistic retrospects are found in two poems that Swift wrote during his retirement at Letcombe in 1714, neither of which was published until many years later. These, unlike the 1713 imitation of Horace, which is a public statement, are more private, introspective poems. 'The Author upon Himself' (published 1735; *Poems*, i.191-6) is a particularly bitter little piece about the ingratitude with which he has been treated in return for his services to the nation, and about the ill-will of his enemies in high places. In another imitation of Horace (this time of 'Hoc erat in votis', *Satires* II,vi) Swift looks back in a more good-humoured mood, developing a theme that recurs in the *Journal to Stella* the contrast between the worries and frustrations of the London politician and the carefree pleasures that he can enjoy at his rural retreat of Laracor (*Poems*, i.197-202; first published in 1727). Nor do these poems, even taken together, tell the whole truth, for Swift's mixed motives certainly included ambition and a desire to raise his station in the church through the patronage available to the ministry. Yet Swift genuinely believed that the tory government was acting in the national interest, and that his writing for it was therefore an act of public service.

Swift's enemies and political opponents naturally placed very different interpretations on his motives and conduct. They saw an unbelieving priest, who had already ridiculed religion in *A Tale of a Tub*, and who had failed to find preferment from the whigs, become a venal political turncoat who prostituted his literary talents as the willing tool of a corrupt ministry bent on introducing popery, arbitrary power, and the Pretender. Swift was subjected to partisan attacks in these and similar terms both while he was actually engaged in writing for the tory ministry and afterwards. The most amusing of these attacks are *An Hue and Cry after Dr S—t* (1714) and *Dr S——'s Real Diary* (1715), which present the charges of irreligion, venality, and Jacobitism through shrewd parodies in the manner of Swift's own account books and journal-letters.[1] Such accusations were commonly levelled at all those who served in, or who were associated with, Queen Anne's last ministry, and they found ready belief not only among the whigs but also from those tories who were most afraid of the threat from Jacobitism. These charges were made much easier to sustain after Bolingbroke and Ormonde, in 1715, fled to France to join the Pretender.[2] Their actions lent credibility to the association of the tories in general with Jacobitism. Oxford was impeached, and although as a result of the 'whig split' and a dispute between the two houses of parliament he was eventually acquitted, the evidence (not available to the whigs in 1715) of the correspondence preserved in the French archives shows that he too at least dabbled in Jacobite intrigue during his ministry.[3] Swift always vehemently denied the charges, both in relation to the ministry and as they related to himself. But if it is known that they were guilty, doubt is raised about Swift's testimony about himself.

In Swift's own case, there are good reasons for believing that he was telling the truth when he denied the charges of Jacobitism. But his contemporaries were not unreasonable in suspecting him, for his expressed hostility to the Revolution settlement and later to the Hanoverian regime looked very like Jacobitism. 'I always professed to be against the Pretender,' he

---

[1] Both pamphlets (*An Hue and Cry* from the third edition) are reprinted in *Swiftiana II: Bickerstaffiana and Other Early Materials on Swift, 1708-1715* (New York, 1975).

[2] Oldisworth, Swift's successor as editor of the *Examiner*, also joined the 1715 rebellion; Robert J. Allen, 'William Oldisworth: "the author of the *Examiner*" ', *PQ*, xxvi (1947), 175.

[3] J.H. Plumb, *Sir Robert Walpole: The Making of a Statesman* (1956), pp. 254-6; Walpole had been one of Oxford's most bitter enemies, yet he now (for his own factious reasons) stage-managed the earl's acquittal. L.G. Wickham Legg, 'Extracts from Jacobite correspondence, 1712-1714', *English Historical Review*, xxx (1915), 501-18, prints letters that implicate Oxford (with whatever seriousness on his part) in the Jacobite intrigues.

wrote to archbishop King in 1716, but the reason he gave was a strangely negative one: 'because I look upon the coming of the Pretender as a greater Evil than any we are like to suffer under the worst Whig Ministry that can be found' (*Corr*.ii.238-9). That, for Swift, was to say a great deal. A full understanding of his attitude to the Revolution, the Pretender, and the Hanoverian government is an essential element for the interpretation of the parts he played in English politics. Such an understanding in turn needs to take account of several relatively less-read works which, while not central to Swift's literary achievement, are crucial to his politics. The first of these is the 'Ode to Sancroft', written in 1692 but not published until many years after Swift's death, which shows how early his political attitudes were determined by his concern for the church. Swift was drawn to the tories as the 'Church Party'. Because of his awareness of the damage the Revolution had done to the church, he tended to put more emphasis on what he called its 'very bad effects', to dwell on these rather than its positive achievements. His attitude to the Revolution (a very guarded, grudging, balance-sheet approval) would also be his attitude to the Hanoverian succession, as we have seen in the quotation from his letter to archbishop King. Swift's hostility to the new regime is strongly, though obliquely, expressed in two pamphlets that combine a repudiation of Jacobitism with a severe indictment of the corrupt and arbitrary proceedings of the new whig government. *An Enquiry into the Behaviour of the Queen's Last Ministry* was written between 1715 and 1719, but not published until 1765. The 'Letter to Mr Pope' was written in 1721 but not published until 1741. Neither is among Swift's more commonly read pamphlets. None of the major texts discussed in this chapter (major, that is, as political statements) were published at the time of writing. Taken in conjunction with Swift's comments in his other works, they provide a more balanced and complete view of his political thought in general, and of his attitude to the Revolution in particular, than was available to contemporaries outside his own immediate circle. By helping to explain the precise nature of Swift's hostility to the Revolution, they tend to support his denial of Jacobitism. Contemporaries tended to think in simple categories: to be against the Revolution was to be a Jacobite. Swift's dilemma was that he was theoretically unable to come to terms with the Revolution, but in practice equally unable to support the restoration of the Pretender.

i

Very little biographical evidence is available for Swift's life and opinions in the 1690s. There are only a very few surviving letters for the whole decade, and not much else to supplement them. Such biographical inferences as can be drawn from the literary works of the period must be used to fill the gap. There are always problems in trying to look for biographical information in literary works. Swift's love of indirection and his skill in the use of a fictive speaker in his works make the search doubly difficult in his case. Certainly his presentation of himself in his later poetry has been the subject of much disagreement and controversy.[4] Fortunately, however, the most important sources for our knowledge of Swift's immediate reactions to the Revolution of 1688, and of his mood and opinions in the early 1690s, are the poems written between 1690 and 1693, and especially the four 'pindaric' odes.[5] These poems are among the most directly expressive pieces that Swift ever wrote. They patently express the young poet's thoughts and feelings at the time of writing. When they are obscure, it is through their difficult manner not because of any ambiguity of content. These poems have been little read or studied, even though Swift's poetry as a whole has recently enjoyed a remarkable revival of interest. They have often been dismissed as unsuccessful exercises in a poetic style unsuited to Swift's 'natural' bent. Particular passages in the poems have been used to support various arguments, and the ways in which they anticipate many characteristic Swiftian themes have been recognised.[6] But the

---

[4] Most notably in the controversy about the interpretation of *Verses on the Death of Dr Swift* (1731); see Arthur H. Scouten and Robert D. Hume, 'Pope and Swift: text and interpretation of Swift's *Verses on his Death*', *PQ*, lii (1973), 205-31.

[5] 'Ode to the King, on his Irish expedition' (1691; *Poems*, i.4-10); 'Ode to the Athenian Society' (1691; *Poems*, i.13-25); 'Ode to Sir William Temple' (1691?; *Poems*, i.26-33); 'Ode to Dr William Sancroft, Late Lord Archbishop of Canterbury' (1692; *Poems*, i.33-42). Only the 'Ode to the Athenian Society' was published at the time of writing; the others were not printed until after Swift's death.

[6] W.B. Carnochan, *Lemuel Gulliver's Mirror for Man* (Berkeley, 1968), sees uncharacteristic ultra-Platonism in the 'Ode' (pp. 169-70); Max Byrd, *Visits to Bedlam* (Columbia, S.C., 1974), sees in it anticipations of the world of the *Dunciad* (pp. 59-64); Emile Pons, *Swift: Les Années de Jeunesse et le 'Conte du Tonneau'* (Strasbourg, 1925), sees its themes as the *Tale of a Tub* and *Gulliver's Travels* in embryo (pp. 165-6).

poems have been little studied in their own right. While they are certainly not in any of Swift's later (and what we therefore regard as his more natural) manners, they deserve attention if only because Swift himself devoted so much care and effort to them that he clearly regarded them, at the time, as important statements. And although he no doubt came to regard their manner as fustian, he carefully preserved them. We can see how seriously Swift took himself as a poet from the most important extant letter of the period, that written to his cousin Thomas Swift on 3 May 1692 (*Corr*.i.6-11). He banters himself about his over-fondness for his own writings, but at the same time he speaks seriously enough about his difficulties of composition to imply a belief in his own inspiration. The odes are public poems, intended for publication. The 'Ode to the Athenian Society' was actually published in 1692, and the 'Ode to Sancroft' was certainly begun with publication in mind. But their complexity and density, and the evidently quite deliberate obscurity of metaphor and meaning suggest that the audience for which they were written was a much smaller, more highly educated and elite readership than Swift would usually write for later. Unlike his later 'public' poems, these pindaric odes were written not to persuade but to express his own views and feelings, which he expected to find unpopular. In these early poems Swift is most truly 'not heard, but overheard'. In these poems, which Swift regarded as in some sense inspired, he needed to make no concessions to his audience. We know that the 'Ode to the Athenian Society' was taken seriously by his contemporaries, and in the prevailing vogue for these 'pindarics' there is every reason to suppose that the others, if published, would have found small but appreciative audiences.[7]

The pindaric odes are nominally poems of celebration. What they celebrate, however, are the few exceptions that Swift recognises to the general degeneration, corruption, and pollution of the times. They are negative in tone and mood. It was not unusual for such odes to contain satire and criticism as well as panegyric. Thomas D'Urfey's *Pindaric Poem on the Royal Navy* (1691), for example, balances its stanzas of praise and

[7] The 'Ode to the Athenian Society' was quoted approvingly (and in the same paragraph with a quotation from Cowley) by Charles Gildon in his *History of the Athenian Society* (1691), p. 15. This praise (though hardly from an independent source) was gratifying to Swift (*Corr*.i.8). When the 'Ode' was published in the *Athenian Mercury*, it was given exceptionally lavish typographical treatment; I take this to be an implied compliment to the seriousness and dignity of the poem.

celebration with two complaints. Neptune laments how Britain has grown 'Degenerate and Vile', while Oceanus offers a more comprehensive indictment of factions in politics, schism in religion, and the growth of materialism. D'Urfey, like Swift in the 'Ode to Sancroft', complains of the fickleness of the British who can 'as the Weather instantly' change 'from hot to cold, from moist to dry' in their political loyalties.[8] D'Urfey, of course, had in mind William's loss of his initial popularity; Swift, how quickly the people had forgotten Sancroft's services to the nation. Yet Swift's odes are unusually bleak, and remarkable for the intensity with which his disgust at the corruption of the times is expressed. This is all the more notable since we might have expected the poems of a young Irish refugee to have been fuller of joy at the recently achieved liberation from slavery and popery. Thus where the 'Ode to the Athenian Society' might have celebrated the new enlightenment, instead the society is praised for the negative virtue of not joining in the age's propagation of atheism and irreligion. A theme that recurs in each of the odes is that the poet has found (in William III, in the Athenian Society, in Sancroft, in Sir William Temple) qualities that he did not expect to meet with outside romance, certainly not in contemporary reality. The poems employ the typical satiric strategy of contrasting hard-pressed virtues with numerically superior vices, and in foreseeing the likely extinction of the virtues altogether in the all-too-near future. Even the virtues that Swift chooses to celebrate are usually negative ones: self-denial, renunciation, modest anonymity. Although only two of the odes are primarily political in their content, all four reflect Swift's basic political and ethical values. His main object of attack is the pride of individualism, whether it finds expression in the megalomania of Louis XIV or in the uppish conceit of the modern half-educated female. His political ideal is an ordered and stable hierarchy.

The 'Ode to Sancroft' is the most interesting of the group of odes from the political point of view, and it is also (with the 'Ode to the Athenian Society') one of the most difficult.[9] It is the best guide we have to Swift's immediate reaction to the Revolution,

[8] *A Pindaric Poem on the Royal Navy* (1691), pp. 6, 11-14; the quotation is from p. 13.

[9] Earlier criticism of the 'Ode' is summarised in Edward W. Rosenheim, Jr., 'Swift's "Ode to Sancroft": another look', *Modern Philology*, lxxiii (1976), Supplement, pp. 24-39. Rosenheim's remains the fullest discussion of the 'Ode'; none of the recent books on Swift's poetry give it more than passing attention.

and is worth close examination. Several problems of interpretation present themselves. There is the apparent incongruity between the praise of William III in the 'Ode to the King' and the celebration of Sancroft in this ode for refusing to recognise the authority of the new king and the new settlement.[10] There is some uncertainty about the date of the poem. In the manuscript from which the poem was first printed (and which is unfortunately not now extant) it is dated 1689. But in his letter to his cousin of 3 May 1692, Swift speaks of the ode as begun within the last few months (*Corr*.i.8). Such a discrepancy might seem unimportant, if those three years in question had not been a time of rapid political developments. Praise of Sancroft in 1692 had altogether different implications from such praise in 1689. Then there is the question of the poem's incompleteness. Swift told his cousin that he was finding it a difficult poem to write. Yet we know that he added three more stanzas to the poem as it stood on 3 May 1692, and if he never completed the poem, he did not destroy it. If its abandonment could be linked to a change of attitude towards Sancroft, this would help with the interpretation of the poem. To understand the genesis of the 'Ode', and to see why Swift, though never a non-juror himself, could describe the most eminent of the non-jurors as 'a gentleman I admire at a degree more than I can express' (*Corr*.i.8), we need to go back before the Revolution to the period of tory reaction in the closing years of the reign of Charles II.[11]

Sancroft was promoted to the see of Canterbury following the death of Sheldon in 1677. Like his great predecessor, whom we know Swift admired (*PW* v.272), Sancroft was an anglican 'reactionary' in the sense that his ideal was a truly 'national' church to which all Englishmen should belong. This was what the English reformation had tried to create, and this was what the restoration settlement had tried to re-establish. But in practice the religious pluralism of the interregnum proved impossible to eradicate, and the church was really (though not legally) a voluntary society to which men might belong or from

[10] Irvin Ehrenpreis, *Swift: The Man, his Works, and the Age* (1962-7), i.130, is troubled by this point.

[11] I have found the following modern accounts and interpretations of the Revolution of 1688, its background, and its aftermath, particularly useful: Stephen B. Baxter, *William III* (1966); John Carswell, *The Descent on England* (1969); J.R. Jones, *The Revolution of 1688 in England* (1969); J.R. Western, *Monarchy and Revolution: The English State in the 1680s* (1972); and J.P. Kenyon, *Revolution Principles: The Politics of Party, 1689-1720* (Cambridge, 1977).

which they might dissent in favour of one of the numerous religious alternatives available. Swift shared the ideal of Sheldon and Sancroft; his intolerance of religious dissent was deep and lifelong. In 1681, when the Exclusion Crisis ended with the decline of the whigs after the dissolution of the Oxford parliament, Charles II sponsored a conscious programme of tory reaction, aimed at excluding whigs and dissenters from political power in both national and local life. Sancroft was at the centre of a nationwide movement to suppress dissent by a systematic attempt to enforce the laws on ecclesiastical uniformity. Prosecutions for non-attendance at church were greatly increased, and serious attempts were made to suppress conventicles. Sancroft vigorously opposed the alternative policy, espoused by such prominent 'liberal' churchmen as Stillingfleet and Tillotson and by such leading anglican laymen as Daniel Finch, later second Earl of Nottingham, of conciliating the more moderate dissenters by some 'comprehension' proposal. This would have meant offering concessions on some sensitive points, such as making the wearing of the surplice and the use of the sign of the cross during baptism optional. An Ecclesiastical Commission was set up in 1681, to advise the king on important church appointments. It sought out for promotion reactionary divines, of whom the most notable was Francis Turner, who rose rapidly through the hierarchy to become dean of Windsor, bishop of Rochester, and bishop of Ely. It was at Turner's suggestion (as he tells us in the crucial letter to his cousin) that Swift wrote his 'Ode to Sancroft'. Swift would have been entirely in sympathy with this programme of anglican reaction.[12]

The accession of James II in February 1685 did not, at first, make any difference to the prosecution of these firmly anglican policies. Throughout the Exclusion Crisis, the anglican party (or the tories as they came to be called) had been strong supporters of the hereditary principle and therefore of James's right to succeed. James was, in a sense, the tory candidate for king, so that his accession was greeted with loud protestations of loyalty from the church party. These often overemphatic expressions of devotion proved hostages to fortune; after the Revolution, choice specimens were from time to time reprinted by whig

---

[12] For the 'tory reaction', see Robert Beddard, 'The Commission for Ecclesiastical Promotions, 1681-84; an instrument of tory reaction', *Historical Journal*, x (1967), 11-40; and G.V. Bennett, 'The Seven Bishops: a reconsideration', *Studies in Church History*, ed. Derek Baker, xv (Oxford, 1978), 267-87.

propagandists to expose the inconsistency between high-church principles and practice. In 1685, however, the failure of the attempted rebellions by Monmouth in England and by Argyle in Scotland produced a further revulsion of opinion against whiggish ideas and memories, and this benefited James. Few anglicans in 1685 can have foreseen how soon their doctrines of passive obedience and non-resistance would prove an embarrassment. It was not until James began to seek the repeal of the penal laws against catholics and (much more importantly) of the test acts that gave anglicans a monopoly of national political power that his support from the tories in general and the anglican hierarchy in particular started to fall off. In a notable debate in the House of Lords on 19 November 1685, bishop Compton of London attacked the employment of catholic officers in the army. Many preachers attacked popery in their sermons, including bishop Turner of Ely, one of the bishops most closely identified with James and the policies of anglican reaction.[13] In March 1686 James issued a general pardon that halted all proceeedings against dissenters both in the civil and in the church courts. The church was not, however, cowed by this royal interposition in favour of their enemies, and the enforcement of the acts against conventicles was continued and even reached a peak of activity and prosecutions. Later in 1686, despairing of assistance from even those anglicans whom he had helped promote, James began instead to seek allies from his old enemies the whigs and the dissenters. This about-turn culminated in the issue (on 4 April 1687) of a Declaration of Indulgence, suspending the laws that guaranteed the anglican ascendency. By this time prosecutions in the church courts had ceased. Swift would always regard the test acts as the great security of the anglican church, and he wrote consistently in their favour from as early as 1709, when he may have spoiled his chances of obtaining preferment through the whigs by publishing his *Letter concerning the Sacramental Test* (*PW* ii.111-25). He would never forget that under James II, while the church had stood nobly against the king (in defence of its own privileges, to be sure, but this was not exactly how Swift saw it), the dissenters had basely prostituted themselves to obtain royal favour by servilely supporting the king's catholicising policies (disguised as religious toleration).

---

[13] Sir John Bramston, *Autobiography*, ed. T.W. Bramston (1845; Camden Society, No. 32), pp. 216-17; Bennett, 'The Seven Bishops', p. 275.

In May 1688 James re-issued his declaration, and ordered it to be read in churches. Bishop Turner took the lead in organising anglican resistance to the reading of the declaration, a campaign in which he was largely successful. In order to maximise support for this policy, it was necessary to attract both moderate anglican opinion and, so far as possible, to detach the more moderate dissenters from any support of the royal policies. Thus when the bishops petitioned the king against the order to read the declaration, they emphasised that it was not from 'any want of due tenderness to Dissenters' with whom they were willing to come to 'such a temper' as would be agreed in 'Parliament and Convocation'.[14] In the light of the way Convocation in 1689 treated the proposals for comprehension, it is easy to treat this miniscule concession on the part of the bishops as a mere subterfuge. Yet it is not certain that, if the Revolution had not awakened its most conservative and reactionary instincts, a convocation held under James II and the threat of encroaching popery would not have been less ferociously hostile to any compromise on comprehension. In 1688, certainly, the bishops had sufficient credibility to secure the support of the moderate dissenters. When the decision to prosecute the bishops for their petition to the king made them martyrs, and when their refusal to enter into recognisances forced the court to remand them to the Tower, they were visited there by a deputation of prominent dissenting ministers as well as by the principal anglican nobility. When Macaulay spoke of Sancroft's willingness to 'wear fetters and to lay his aged limbs on bare stones', his rhetorical evocation of primitive martyrdoms hardly reflected the conditions in which prisoners of Sancroft's rank were actually lodged in the Tower.[15] But it is the language in which Swift would have clothed the incident, and his celebration of the primate in his 'Ode' as 'primitive Sancroft' (1. 149) surely alluded to this willingness to undergo imprisonment for the sake of the true church. After a spectacular trial the bishops were acquitted to become popular heroes. Yet within two years Sancroft and his non-juring brethren (several of whom were among the seven bishops put on trial by James) had lost their popularity to an extent that suggested to Swift (as no doubt to many others) a parallel between the fickleness of the modern English and that of the

[14] 'The Petition of the Seven Bishops, 18 May 1688', reprinted in *The Stuart Constitution*, ed. J.P. Kenyon (Cambridge, 1966), pp. 441-2.
[15] Macaulay, *The History of England from the Accession of James II*, ed. C.H. Firth (1913-15), ii.1036.

jews who cried for the crucifixion of Christ so soon after his triumphal entry into Jerusalem ('Ode', ll.117-20).

The triumph of the bishops was only one of the mortifications that James had to endure during the course of 1688, culminating in the successful invasion mounted by William of Orange and James's ignominious flight from his capital in the early hours of 11 December. The trial of the bishops was symptomatic of James's alienation of his 'natural' supporters, and to this extent it made many people sympathetic to William's invasion who otherwise might well have lent James their active support. As it was, when James fled on 11 December he had no support of any substance outside the hard-core of catholic adventurers and extremists. The bishops had even refused to sign a declaration condemning the invasion by William. Such a mood of national unanimity could be sustained in opposition to James's attack on the established order, but it began to break up as soon as the question became what to do to provide for the government after James's flight. A meeting of peers was called and met at the Guildhall on 11 December. This meeting was apparently engineered by Sancroft and the Earl of Clarendon (the historian's son, and a prominent anglican layman), and their intention was to use it to mount a rearguard action against the incipient revolution and to prepare the way for James's eventual return. In the event, they were unable to get the meeting to adopt the kind of proposals they wanted, and it produced a declaration (which they signed only reluctantly) much more radical than they would have liked.[16] The split revealed at the Guildhall meeting between the loyalists and those they characterised as the 'violent party' would soon widen. For James's flight proved abortive when his disguise was penetrated and he was, with even greater ignominy than he had left, sent back to London. This very indignity, however, caused something of a popular reaction in James's favour, and on his return to London he was attended by many prominent people, including Sancroft. James's second flight, this time successful and permanent, was virtually ordered by William. Unlike the first, it was not obviously voluntary, and it made the idea that James had 'deserted' his throne (plausible enough after the events of 11 December) controversial. After James's second flight, Sancroft took no further part in public business. Clarendon, Turner, and

---

[16] Robert Beddard, 'The Guildhall Declaration of 11 December 1688 and the counter-revolution of the loyalists', *Historical Journal*, xi (1968), 403-20.

other loyalists, however, waged a vigorous and nearly successful rearguard action on James's behalf at the constitutional convention called by William for January to settle the government.

When this Convention, which assembled on 22 January 1689, met for substantive business (the Commons on 28 January, the Lords on the 29th), there were four main alternatives for consideration.[17] One was the establishment of a regency in James's name; another was to regard James as somehow legally demised and to crown Mary as the hereditary successor (ignoring James's son as of doubtful birth). A more serious break with the hereditary principle was represented by the radical proposal to crown William. The compromise finally adopted was to declare William and Mary joint sovereigns. The most conservative of the proposals, that for a regency, derived its main support from the bishops and the tory peers. In the Lords it was only narrowly defeated (51-48), but it attracted little support in the lower house. Its strong appeal to anglican loyalists was that it preserved intact at least the theory of passive obedience and indefeasible hereditary right, since (if only by a legal fiction) James would still be king. After the events of the Civil War and the trial and execution of Charles I, the church and the monarchy seemed to stand or fall together, and no anglican could be easy at the prospect of deposing a king, even one who had done as much harm to the anglican cause as James II had. Those who supported the proposal for a regency can be divided into two groups. For some, those who retained a personal loyalty to James, the regency proposal was essentially a device to gain time. It was intended to prevent any transfer of the crown (which would be extremely difficult to reverse) and to establish a compromise, temporary machinery of government until conditions should become more opportune for the return of James.[18] It was presumably to be hoped that James, restored by means of the anglican interest, would this time see more clearly

[17] The fullest account of the constitutional debates at the Convention is in Lois G. Schwoerer, *The Declaration of Rights* (Baltimore, 1981). This book has a wider focus than its title suggests, but its interpretation is decidedly whiggish. The story could profitably be told from the point of view of those who favoured the regency, as well as from that of the supporters of the Bill of Rights.

[18] On 17 February 1689 Turner wrote to an unidentified sympathiser that he regarded the regency proposal as 'onely to amuse & gaine time'; printed in Robert Beddard, 'The loyalist opposition in the interregnum: a letter of Dr Francis Turner, bishop of Ely, on the Revolution of 1688', *BIHR*, xl (1967), 101-9; the quotation is from p. 107.

who were his true friends. This group included Turner and Clarendon. The others were tories like Finch (now Earl of Nottingham), who had no desire to see James return but who scrupled to depose him. There is some evidence to suggest that, for this group, Mary's accession would have been an acceptable second best. Many of the crypto-Jacobite wing of the supporters of the regency proposal refused to recognise the new regime and became non-jurors; some, like Turner, became active Jacobites. Those who thought like Nottingham were able to reconcile themselves to the Revolution settlement on a pragmatic basis. The importance of this distinction between the two kinds of supporters of the regency is not that it affected the outcome (it was pressure from William that finally forced the Lords to agree to the Commons' motion that the throne was indeed 'vacant'), but that it is important in assessing Swift's position. For in the *Examiner* No. 43 (31 May 1711; *PW* iii.163) Swift refers approvingly to the regency proposal, and he specifically associates it with the church party. He expresses similar views elsewhere, for example in his marginalia on bishop Burnet's *History* (*PW* v.291) and in his 'Sermon upon the Martyrdom of King Charles I' (*PW* ix.229-30). The question was an academic one in 1711, but the constitutional point still seemed important to Swift at the time of the sermon (probably delivered in 1726). It would be very interesting to know the grounds on which he would have supported the regency in 1689, when it was a real question. It is certainly suggestive that about this time Swift was friendly with Turner, one of the leading crypto-Jacobites, whereas Lord Nottingham was one of the politicians whom he came most heartily to detest.[19] Unfortunately, there is no evidence for Swift's attitude to Nottingham in 1689. Certainly he would always describe the scruples of the conscientious non-juror with respect; yet he never became, nor so far as we know was he ever tempted to become, a non-juror himself. One of the very remarkable qualities of the 'Ode to Sancroft' is how deeply felt is Swift's respect for opinions that he does not himself share. This is so uncharacteristic of the later Swift as to deserve notice. For in this poem we can sense Swift agonising between his respect for

[19] In 1711-12, following Nottingham's apostasy from the tory camp on the peace terms, Swift consistently aspersed him as a venal turncoat (see above, p. 50). Henry Horwitz, *Revolution Politicks: The Career of Daniel Finch, Second Earl of Nottingham, 1647-1730* (Cambridge, 1968), shows that Nottingham was a man of principle, consistent (like Swift) to certain political values as he saw them.

Sancroft and his renunciation and his own acceptance of the new order, an acceptance with which he is obviously far from happy.

Central to the meaning of the 'Ode' itself is the analogy that Swift develops between Sancroft and Christ. He speaks scornfully of 'these forsaken wretches who to-day/ Revile His great ambassador', that is, Sancroft, and thereby show 'what they would have done/ ... To his undoubted Master, Heaven's Almighty Son' (ll. 130-4). Modern readers have found this analogy somewhat excessive and embarrassing, but it would not have seemed extravagant or even inappropriate to Swift's contemporaries, for whom a similar analogy between Christ and Charles I had become a homiletic commonplace. One of the earliest examples of this is found in a sermon preached before Charles II at Breda in 1649, only a few months after the martyr's death, by Henry Leslie, an Irish bishop for whom Swift would later express a particular admiration ('one of the most extraordinary Men of his Age'; *PW* v.79) and the father of Charles Leslie of the *Rehearsal*. In this sermon Leslie drew a very elaborate parallel between the crucifixion of Christ and the execution of Charles I, with this aggravating circumstance in Charles's case that his judges could not plead ignorance. Leslie concludes that the murder of Charles I was a crime so dreadful as to be paralleled only by the killing of Christ.[20] In 1662 an annual service on 30 January was added to the anglican liturgy to commemorate the martyrdom of Charles I, and the occasion was usually further marked by an appropriate sermon. The service itself developed both explicit and implicit analogies between Christ and Charles I. The second lesson at morning prayer was Christ's trial before Pilate (Matthew 27); the second collect made the point that, like Christ, Charles had prayed for his murderers. In the communion service, the epistle was a classic text on passive obedience (1 Peter 2.13-23), and the gospel lesson was the parable of the ungrateful husbandmen who kill the son of the owner (Matthew 21).[21] The typical sermon preached on the occasion used the same analogy to inculcate the favourite anglican doctrines of passive obedience and non-resistance. The extravagance of such sermons was by no means curtailed after the Revolution. Many preachers pretended to deprecate the

[20] *The Martyrdom of King Charles, or his Conformity with Christ in his Sufferings. In a Sermon on 1 Cor. 2.8* (The Hague, 1649); see especially pp. 11-12.
[21] 'A Form of Prayer with Fasting, to be Used Yearly upon the Thirtieth of January', in *The Book of Common Prayer*.

comparison between Charles and Christ, often as a prelude to using it. Even so good a whig as Thomas Tickell, Addison's cousin, friend, and assistant, could in 1713 publish a poem in which Charles is described as only just falling short of Christ's example. It is in the context of this anglican tradition that Swift's 'Ode to Sancroft' must be read.[22]

We have already seen that, after the trial of the seven bishops, Sancroft could reasonably be presented as an example of the primitive Christian ready to suffer for his faith. There are two ways in which Swift, in his 'Ode' develops the implications of the parallel with Christ. One is through the theme of the fickleness of popular opinion: Sancroft, not long since a popular hero, is now the object of popular obloquy. This theme illustrates Swift's point (ll.81-2) that while Sancroft may appear to have behaved inconsistently in first opposing James II but then refusing to acknowledge William and Mary, his principles have in reality remained firm. It is public opinion that has changed. Even more important politically is the precedent of Christ at his trial before Pilate remaining silent, refusing to exculpate himself or to recognise the legitimacy of Pilate's authority but passively submitting to it. In the same way, Sancroft had neither basely complied with the new regime nor actively resisted it. Instead he had accepted the penalties imposed for his refusal to take the oaths required and had suffered, if not martyrdom, at least deprivation and a kind of exile. Other analogies (though not made in the 'Ode') can be suggested with other Swiftian heroes such as Socrates, Cato, and Sir Thomas More, who could all be seen as examples of the same kind of loyalty to a higher power or principle, and passive acceptance of the penalties attached to it. Swift does indeed bring in the example of Cato at the end of the extant portion of the poem, to make the point that both heaven and Cato will be pleased with Sancroft's behaviour. This compliment (made by way of allusion to Lucan's famous line, 'Victrix causa deis placuit, sed victa Catoni') implies a favourite Swiftian belief, that defeat may be a greater kind of victory than earthly success. Here in the 'Ode to Sancroft' Swift uses the

---

[22] For the political importance of the 30 January sermons, see J.P. Kenyon, *Revolution Principles*, especially pp. 69-76. E.W. Rosenheim, Jr., 'Swift and the martyred monarch', *PQ*, lv (1975), 178-94, gives some attention to the genre as well as to Swift's sermon on Charles I. Tickell's poem, 'Thoughts Occasioned by the Sight of an Original Painting of King Charles I, Taken at the Time of his Trial', appeared in *Poetical Miscellanies*, ed. Richard Steele (1714, but actually published in November 1713), pp. 172-6.

allusion to suggest that while the success of the Revolution may imply providential approval of William's mission, Sancroft's self-sacrifice may also be pleasing to God.

In the letter to his cousin in which he describes his difficulties with the 'Ode', Swift says that if he could finish it to his own satisfaction he 'would send it to my Bookseller and make him print it with my name and all', partly as a gesture of 'respect and Gratitude' to Sancroft and also to 'perform half a Promise' made to Turner (*Corr*.i.9). The bravado with which Swift here speaks of printing his name, together with the fact that by 1692 Turner (who had been implicated in the 1690 Jacobite plot) was a fugitive from justice, have led to the suggestion that the publication of the 'Ode' would have been 'imprudent and illegal'.[23] To suppose this is to misunderstand both what the poem says and how it would probably have been received in 1692 if it had been printed. It was 'imprudent' in a worldly sense to be a non-juror, or to hold Jacobite opinions, for the first would certainly, and the second would for a person of conscience, preclude the acceptance of any position in the church or government. But it was not illegal to be a Jacobite. Swift's 'Ode' praises one particular non-juror, but as we shall see he was in some respects an untypical one; the 'Ode' itself is not a non-juring or non-juror's poem, still less a Jacobite one. There was widespread sympathy, especially among loyal anglicans, for the conscientious non-jurors, and especially for the deprived bishops, at least until the Assassination Plot of 1696 caused a natural revulsion of public opinion against anything associated with Jacobitism. William himself had been prepared to excuse the clergy from taking the new oaths, at least as part of a compromise involving the repeal of the test acts in favour of the protestant dissenters. This proposal proved unacceptable to the Commons. Burnet, a staunch whig, had worked for this compromise, and he later tried to secure some mitigation of the provisions of deprivation in favour of the bishops. William Wake, later a prominent whig churchman and archbishop of Canterbury, had no scruples about taking the oaths himself, but he respected the scruples of those churchmen who felt that they could not conscientiously take them.[24] There is very little in

---

[23] Rosenheim, 'Swift's "Ode to Sancroft" ', p. 30.

[24] Henry Horwitz, *Parliament, Policy, and Politics in the Reign of William III* (Manchester, 1977), p. 23; Burnet, *History of his Own Time* (Oxford, 1833), iv.16; Norman Sykes, *William Wake, Archbishop of Canterbury, 1657-1737* (Cambridge, 1957), i.44-5.

Swift's 'Ode' that would not have been acceptable to a churchman of moderate whig convictions, except (significantly) for the attack (ll.245-58) on the project of comprehension.

If Swift's poem had been printed in 1692, it would have been as likely to have offended the Jacobite wing of the non-jurors as the whigs. For Swift praises Sancroft for remaining neutral and unmoved at the centre of the revolutionary storm, a passivity for which he was censured not only by whigs like Burnet but by some of the non-jurors themselves. Burnet's hostility was partly motivated by personal rancour, for Sancroft had refused to consecrate him on his nomination to the see of Salisbury. Sancroft had commissioned three of his suffragans to perform the consecration, but had later removed this commission from the diocesan records, an act Burnet interpreted as an attempt to cast doubt on his episcopal orders. Burnet would later write that Sancroft had acted a 'very mean part' that led to his being despised on both sides, and it is certain that he displeased some people on his own side. Clarendon, for example, regretted that Sancroft would attend neither the important informal meeting of peers on 24 December nor the Convention itself in January. 'His declaring himself at this time would have been weight among us', he wrote in his diary after the 24 December meeting. On 15 January Clarendon dined with Sancroft at Lambeth, but failed to extract a promise to attend the forthcoming Convention. On 21 January Clarendon's language is much sharper: 'We pressed the Archbishop to be at the Convention; but he was obstinately resolved not to be there'. Bishop Turner, who took the lead in organising parliamentary (in so far as the Convention can be regarded as a parliament) opposition to a pro-William settlement through championing the regency proposal, was so little satisfied with Sancroft's part that he wrote to a friend on 17 February 1689 that 'Things could hardly haue come to this wofull pass, but for the Archbps strange Obstinate passiveness wch makes him both hated & despisd'. Here Turner confirms, from the opposite side in politics, Burnet's testimony that Sancroft's conduct was widely regarded as pusillanimous.[25] Thus Swift's 'Ode' was very far from expressing a point of view with which Turner, at whose suggestion it seems to have been written, would himself have approved. It may be that, in

---

[25] Burnet, *History*, iii.375; *The Correspondence of Henry Hyde, Earl of Clarendon*, ed. S.W. Singer (1828), ii.234, 248, 252; Beddard, 'The loyalist opposition in the interregnum', p. 109.

discussing Sancroft's case with Turner in 1689, Swift defended the archbishop against Turner's censure of his passive conduct. A major motivating force behind the composition of the 'Ode' may well have been a desire to defend a man of integrity who was, as Swift perceived the case, being unfairly attacked by both sides for remaining true to his conscience.[26] Without more information than we have, we can only speculate what Swift meant by the 'half a promise' that he gave Turner (did he promise two things, of which the poem was one, or did he only half-promise something, not necessarily the poem itself?). We would also like to know just what Swift thought Sancroft had done to earn his 'Gratitude' as well as his 'respect' (*Corr*.i.8).

A much more plausible reason can be suggested for Swift making such a point of his willingness to put his name to the 'Ode' than bravado in the face of likely political danger. After all, the poem was to be published quite openly by 'my Bookseller', evidently a respectable member of the trade. Swift was probably afraid of the charge of vanity. He would always prefer anonymous publication, and in his 'Ode to the Athenian Society' (published shortly before this letter to his cousin was written) he had particularly praised the members of the society for modestly concealing their real identities (ll.306-7). In 1712 he would object to a clause in the proposed licensing law that would have forced authors to print their names with their works. Also in 1712, when he (quite exceptionally) signed the dedication to Lord Oxford of his *Proposal for Correcting the English Tongue*, it is evident that he regarded this break with his usual practice of anonymity (and of eschewing dedications) as a special compliment that he was paying his much-admired Oxford.[27] In 1692 he had probably so regarded the signing of his name to his poem as a particular personal tribute to 'a gentleman I admire at a degree more than I can express' (*Corr*.i.8). He was willing to be seen in Sancroft's defence, confident perhaps that such an unfashionable posture as defending a man whom both sides had agreed to condemn, would be a sufficient defence against vanity as the world understood it.

It is important to remember that while the 'Ode' presents an exalted and idealised Sancroft, it does not endorse the non-juring position in general. Sancroft's transcendent virtue is an

---

[26] Swift's marginal comment on Burnet's criticism of Sancroft is 'others think very differently' (*PW* v.291).

[27] See above, p. 45.

example beyond imitation, remarkable for its uniqueness, something too good for and therefore unappreciated by his contemporaries (as in ll.149-53). It may be asked how Swift could praise Sancroft so extravagantly, and yet at the same time accept the Revolution, as he seems to do in the 'Ode' itself (ll. 98-106, where the 'Royal Rose' must be William III). Yet in terms of seventeenth-century political ideas, there need have been no inconsistency in admiring both the characters and conduct of Sancroft and William III. Even Sir Robert Filmer, the most extreme proponent of royal absolutism, thought that kings might justly be deposed: not by their subjects, of course, but by God. Filmer argues that God will use unrighteous instruments to depose offending kings, and that these wicked instruments would themselves be called to account by God. Other jurists took a view less favourable to absolutism. Hugo Grotius, for example, the century's most respected writer on the topic, thought that although subjects might not resist their sovereign, one sovereign prince might rightfully make war on another to rescue that prince's subjects from his tyranny.[28] It was thus perfectly possible to feel, in 1692, that both William and Sancroft were acting rightfully in taking their different courses. A bishop like William Lloyd of St Asaph, whom Sancroft at one time hoped would refuse to take the new oaths, felt able in a sermon in 1691 to justify the Revolution in terms of William's providential mission to rescue the nation from popery and tyranny.[29] So that Swift would not have been at all unusual in relieving William himself (though not by any means Englishmen in general; Swift continued to think that some national guilt was involved in the Revolution, as appears in *PW* viii.92) of any wrong-doing, or even in celebrating him as an agent of providence, while at the same time revering Sancroft as a martyr to his church principles. It is remarkable that in the 'Ode to the King' (*Poems*, i.6-10), where Swift's endorsement of William is naturally much more prominent than the oblique strokes he ventures in the 'Ode to Sancroft', he celebrates the King not for the successful revolution he engineered in England, but for the catholic-Jacobite revolution that he had defeated in Ireland. In the 'Ode to the King' attention is as much as possible deflected away from

[28] Filmer, *Patriarcha and Other Political Works*, ed. Peter Laslett (Oxford, 1949), p. 62; Grotius, *De Jure Belli ac Pacis*, II,xx,xxv; trans. Francis W. Kelsey (Oxford, 1925), iii.504, 584.

[29] Kenyon, *Revolution Principles*, pp. 29-30. On Lloyd, see further A. Tindall Hart, *William Lloyd* (1952).

the (to Swift) problematical conflict between William and James
to the much more straightforward (from the anglican point of
view) contrast between William III and Louis XIV (especially ll.
119-46). In the 'Ode to Sancroft' Swift celebrates William as the
'Royal Rose' (ll. 104-5) while reviling not James but the over-
ambitious politicians who are a prime cause of Britain's political
ills. 'Ev'ry stinking weed so lofty grows' (l. 103), and by these
noxious pests Swift means primarily the whig politicians, that
they feel able to challenge royal authority. This complaint would
apply just as well to the pre-revolutionary period as to the
difficulties William in turn had with his British ministers and
opponents from the moment of his taking power. Swift believed
in political order and hierarchy, and these values were more
important to him than the precise identity of the 'Royal Rose',
provided that it was universally respected as such and ambitious
weeds knew their proper place. He even manages to suggest a
link between William and Charles I (his grandfather, it should
be recalled) when he hints, through the image of the rose and the
weeds, that kings can be too mild for their own and their
country's good. Here Swift warns William not to allow himself to
become a prisoner of the whigs (the weeds), as Charles I had
through being too mild and conciliatory with his factious
opponents.[30] This is not, perhaps, how we see Charles I's
mistakes today, but in Swift's time it was a standard means of
excusing Charles's political mismanagements, particularly
useful to anglican apologists who wanted to draw as complete a
contrast as possible between the virtues of Charles I and the
enormities of James II, in order to distinguish the 'great
Rebellion' from the Revolution. By saying, at the end of the
poem, as we have it, that both heaven and Cato are
pleased, Swift implies that while God has blessed William with
success in order to preserve the Church (again a commonplace of
post-Revolution sermons), Cato would have approved Sancroft's
self-sacrificing renunciation and refusal to comply with the
change of the times. The attitude to the Revolution expressed by
the 'Ode to Sancroft' (an attitude that Swift takes elsewhere) is
that it was a regrettable necessity to preserve the church, which
James had been intent on subverting. Thus while the poem
evinces a great sympathy for the position of the conscientious
non-juror, it is not a Jacobite poem nor even a non-juror's poem.

[30] This is essentially Clarendon's interpretation of Charles I; *History of the
Rebellion*, xi.241; ed. W.D. Macray (Oxford, 1888), iv.490.

As we shall see, this position is very close to that of the much-maligned anglican pragmatist, William Sherlock.

It is characteristic of Swift's later pre-occupation with the threatened position of the anglican church that his greatest scorn in the 'Ode to Sancroft' is reserved for the physician-reformers who, under the pretence of trying to reform the church, are actually working to destroy it (ll. 245-58). After the Revolution, the promises made to the protestant dissenters that there would be moves towards compromise and comprehension had in some measure to be honoured, but in circumstances altogether less favourable to the church than had seemed likely at the time of the opposition to the reading of the declaration in 1688.[31] For after the defeat of the regency proposal in the Convention (which would have been much the most acceptable settlement to the anglican clergy at large), and the elevation of William and Mary to the throne, the church was seriously divided within itself about its proper attitude to the new regime. William himself was thought to be far too favourably disposed to the protestant dissenters, and as a Calvinist to have little sympathy for anglican doctrines and less for the church's temporal privileges. William certainly favoured the abolition of the test acts, so far as they affected protestant dissenters, and Swift and other anglicans saw these as the very bulwarks of the church. With Sancroft standing aloof from public business, the leadership of the church was also seriously weakened. Sancroft had himself been responsible for the drawing up of measures of comprehension in 1688. The details of his plans are not known, but it is quite possible that Swift knew (Turner would be an obvious source) more of these proposals than is now available to us. That they did not go very far is certain, for as early as 3 September 1688 Turner wrote to Sancroft that 'many of our divines ... intend upon any overture for Comprehension (which time shall serve) to offer all our ceremonies in sacrifice to the Dissenters'.[32] These divines can be readily identified with the 'wild reformers' of Swift's 'Ode' who wanted to 'tear Religion's lovely face;/ Strip her of ev'ry ornament and grace' (ll. 248-9). Many years later, at the trial of Sacheverell in 1710, William Wake, then bishop of Lincoln, who had acted as secretary to a committee that in 1688 had been engaged in considering possible

---

[31] Roger Thomas, 'Comprehension and indulgence', *From Uniformity to Unity, 1662-1962*, ed. Geoffrey F. Nuttall and Owen Chadwick (1962), pp. 191-253; on the difficult circumstances of 1689, see especially pp. 242-53.

[32] Quoted in Bennett, 'The Seven Bishops', p. 285.

revisions to the liturgy, gave an account of the proposals, in very general terms, to the House of Lords. Sacheverell, in the notorious sermon for which he was prosecuted, *The Perils of False Brethren* (1709), had vilified the schemes of toleration and comprehension proposed after the Revolution. Wake's strategy in replying was to father the idea of comprehension on Sancroft, who had become a kind of patron saint to the high-flying wing of the church. Wake's statement shows how little of a 'wild reformer' Sancroft was:

> The design was, in short, this: To improve, and if possible, to inforce our discipline; to review and enlarge our liturgy; by correcting of some things, by adding of others; and if it should be thought advisable by authority, when this thing should come to be legally considered, first in convocation, then in parliament, by leaving some few ceremonies, confessed to be indifferent in their natures, as indifferent in their usage, so as not to be necessarily observed by those who made a scruple of them; till they should be able to overcome either their weakness or prejudice, and be willing to comply with them.[33]

These 'concessions' are remarkably hedged with qualifications. It is possible that Swift had this passage of Wake's speech in mind when he set out his own policy for comprehension in 'The Sentiments of a Church-of-England Man':

> As to Rites and Ceremonies, and Forms of Prayer, he allows there might be some useful Alterations; and more, which in the Prospect of uniting Christians might be very supportable, as Things declared in their own Nature indifferent; to which he therefore would readily comply, if the *Clergy*, or, (although this be not so fair a Method) if the *Legislature* should direct: Yet, at the same Time, he cannot altogether blame the former for their Unwillingness to consent to any Alteration; which, beside the Trouble, and perhaps Disgrace, would certainly never produce the good Effects intended by it. (*PW* ii.5)

Here, as elsewhere, we see Swift offering a deceptively liberal-sounding statement and then qualifying it out of existence. In trying to claim Sancroft as a patron of comprehension in 1688,

[33] 'The bishop of Lincoln's speech to the House of Lords'; *The Trial of Dr Henry Sacheverell* (1710), reprinted in *A Complete Collection of State Trials*, ed. T.B. Howell, xv (1812), col. 505. Fuller details are found in Wake's diary, printed in Robert Beddard, 'Observations of a London clergyman on the Revolution of 1688-9: being an excerpt from the autobiography of Dr William Wake', *Guildhall Miscellany*, ii, 9 (1967), 406-17.

Wake was conveniently glossing over the fact that much more liberal schemes than any Sancroft (or Swift) would have approved were in the air, and of course it was to these that Sacheverell had been referring.

In 1689 the Earl of Nottingham sponsored two measures in the House of Lords, one for comprehension, the other for a very limited degree of toleration for those dissenters who remained outside the enlarged terms of communion. In the event, probably as a result of an arranged compromise, only the Toleration Act was passed, allowing dissenters freedom of worship but excluding them from political office. The measure for comprehension was referred to Convocation, where it was overwhelmed by high-church opposition (for which, in the above quotation, Swift 'cannot altogether blame' the clergy).[34] The compromise reached, limited toleration but no comprehension, was less liberal than Nottingham would have liked; but it was still much too favourable to the dissenters for Swift's taste. In 1710-14 he was a strong supporter of measures that tried, so far as was possible, to restrict the measure of toleration that had been granted in 1689.

Just as in the 'Sentiments of a Church-of-England Man' Swift asserts the primacy of church over state by describing the church as permanent while governments are temporary (*PW* ii.14), so too in the 'Ode to Sancroft' he uses the striking image of the 'weathercock of state/ Hung loosely on the Church's pinnacle' (ll. 73-4). The image is used to imply that, just because there has been a revolution in government, it is not necessary that there should be any corresponding revolution in the more stable fabric of the church. The image also justifies Sancroft's standing still (like the church steeple) while the giddy populace has been turning round and round (like the weather vane). This was the priority of a high tory like Sir Edward Seymour, who in 1680 had told the House of Commons, 'That the Protestant Religion may be preserved, I am for the preservation of the Crown.'[35] Because he saw the preservation of the church as more important than the particular monarch or royal family, Swift did not become a Jacobite or a non-juror.

It remains to ask why the poem was abandoned.[36] Several

[34] Horwitz, *Revolution Politicks*, pp. 87-95.

[35] Anchitell Grey, *Debates of the House of Commons from the Year 1667 to the Year 1694* (1769), viii.78.

[36] Rosenheim, 'Swift's "Ode to Sancroft" ', pp. 36-7, suggests that the poem may be complete, or at least that the ending we have is a satisfying one. But the

political reasons can be suggested. In June 1692, just a few weeks
after Swift's letter to his cousin about his difficulties in
completing the poem, news broke of the Jacobite plot scare in
which bishop Sprat of Rochester was arrested and in which a
crucial piece of evidence (though it was later discredited as a
forgery) was a Jacobite letter signed by (among others) Sancroft
and Turner. Swift must have known of this plot, and it may have
shaken his faith in Sancroft's integrity. We cannot be sure
whether Swift knew of another development that began in 1692-
3, the moves to perpetuate the non-juring schism by consecrating
new bishops. The actual consecrations (which did not take place
until 1694, after Sancroft's death) were kept a close secret.[37] But
it is possible that news of Sancroft's approval of the idea of
consecrating new bishops reached Swift. For all his serious
reservations about the Revolution and its aftermath, Swift could
never have looked favourably either on Jacobite plotting or on
the perpetuation of the schism. His ideal of a national church,
and his conviction that the church must remain though the
system of government change, would have prevented his support
of any schismatic movement. He retained his admiration for
Sancroft, as we know from his marginal comments on Burnet's
History (*PW* v.291), but developments in 1692 and later may
have sufficiently shaken his picture of the stable Sancroft to
have discouraged him, in conjunction with such other factors as
his literary difficulties with the poem, from finishing his 'Ode'.

ii

The 'Ode to Sancroft' shows that Swift's attitude to the
Revolution was primarily determined by his concern for the
church. In Ireland, in the 1690s, such an attitude was not
incompatible with being a whig in politics. In his *Letter
concerning the Sacramental Test* (1709), Swift reports that he
had told King William that 'the highest Tories' in Ireland would
make 'tolerable Whigs' in England (*PW* ii.283; the passage was

---

first part of the last stanza (ii. 245-7) seems to anticipate a general treatment of
the 'nation's crimes' which I believe the poem, if completed, would have
contained.
    [37] The consecration of George Hickes was not revealed to his friend and fellow
non-juror Robert Nelson, nor (as late as 1711) was the usually well-informed
Jacobite Thomas Hearne aware of it; J.H. Overton, *The Nonjurors: Their Lives,
Principles, and Writings* (1902), p. 90.

omitted in the 1735 edition of Swift's _Works_). In England itself, however, loyalty to the church naturally implied tory politics, for it was the tories' preferred designation to be known as 'the church party'. In 1694 Swift was ordained, and he served briefly in the parish of Kilroot near Belfast. He had few anglican parishioners there, and the experience confirmed (if it needed confirmation) his hatred of the presbyterians who formed the majority of local protestants. It may also have been his time at Kilroot that made him regard his mission in the church not primarily as a pastoral one, or as a missionary or outward-looking vocation, but rather in military terms as 'defending a post assigned me, and for gaining over as many enemies as I can' (_PW_ ix.262). Despite this reference to 'gaining over enemies', Swift came to see clergymen who tried to compromise with those outside the church less as evangelists than as betrayers; hence his later bitter hostility to whiggish churchmen like bishop Burnet. About 1702-3, on a visit to England following the publication of his first political pamphlet, the _Discourse_ of 1701, when his acknowledgement of its authorship had introduced him to several of the whig leaders, Swift told Lord Somers (whom he had defended as Aristides in the _Discourse_) that he was 'much inclined to be what they called a Whig in politics', partly as a result of the love of liberty that he had imbibed from his reading. of the classics, and partly because he found it impossible otherwise to accept the Revolution. But he qualified his being a whig by adding that in religion he was 'an High-churchman' and could not understand how a clergyman could be otherwise (_PW_ viii.120).

This formulation, his being a whig in politics and a tory in religion, remained a favourite one with Swift.[38] There were certainly good reasons why, in 1702-3, he should wish to disown the civil policies of the tories. Ever since the Revolution, the tories, and especially the high-church wing, had been suspected of crypto-Jacobitism. In 1702, with the accession of Queen Anne (herself a natural high tory, especially in church matters) Jacobitism became less of an immediate issue than the question

[38] On 27 May 1713 he wrote to his estranged friend Steele that 'I have in print professed myself in politics, to be what we formerly called a Whig' (_Corr_.i.359). In an age when party allegiances were often disguised by claims of impartiality, this kind of formulation was something of a commonplace, as is suggested by Steele's own use of it in the _Guardian_: 'I shall be impartial, though I cannot be neuter: I am, with relation to the government of the church, a Tory; with regard to the state, a Whig' (No. 1, 12 March 1713).

of occasional conformity, on which the tories were accused of wanting to inaugurate a persecution of the dissenters on the model of 1681-5. The whigs had captured the word 'moderation' as their password, and the tories were associated (not always incorrectly) with extremism in their civil and religious policies. In a kind of political testament, written just possibly as early as 1704 and by Swift's own account in 1708, 'The Sentiments of a Church-of-England Man' (*PW* ii.1-25), Swift tried to define the position of a churchman as somewhere much nearer the middle of the road than whig propaganda allowed, or than was really the case. The title would itself have identified the author as a tory, and behind the pamphlet's smokescreen of rhetorical moderation tory positions are easy to detect. Its real purpose was to show that a good churchman (that is, a tory) could not justly be suspected of Jacobitism or of wanting to sell the nation to France, popery, and slavery. In 1704, it would have been written at the time of the 'tack', the attempt of the tory extremists to force their Occasional Conformity Bill through the Lords by tacking it to a supply bill, a measure of dubious constitutionality that split the party. In 1708, it would have been written against the background of the Jacobite invasion scare and the attempt by the whigs to make election propaganda out of the tories' suspected leanings towards Jacobitism. Swift would later claim that he had published the 'Sentiments' during the 'highest dominion of that faction' (which must mean 1708-10; *PW* viii.122). This is wrong, for although the tract appears in a list of 'Subjects for a Volume' dated 1708, it was not published (although it was almost certainly written earlier) until it appeared in Swift's *Miscellanies in Prose and Verse* (1711).[39] By then Swift was publicly identified with the new tory government, and the text of the 'Sentiments' as we have it is likely to differ in important (but unfortunately unknowable) respects from whatever he had written in 1704 or 1708. The pamphlet must therefore be considered as expressing Swift's views in 1711, though probably incorporating earlier material.

For the purpose of illustrating the nature of Swift's toryism, the most important idea expressed in the 'Sentiments' is that of legislative supremacy. Official anglican doctrine (as expressed for example in the *Book of Homilies*) had always been politically conservative, and since the Restoration the doctrines of passive obedience and non-resistance had been the distinctive political

---

[39] The list is reprinted in Ehrenpreis, *Swift*, ii.768-9.

slogans of both the church and the tories.[40] It was even proposed at one point that these should be formally incorporated into a fortieth article of religion.[41] This idea was not taken up, but the church party did greet the accession of James II with extravagant professions of loyalty that, after the Revolution, proved a serious liability. In 1689-91 various makeshift expedients had to be found to reconcile acceptance of the Revolution with passive obedience. None proved so satisfactory as the idea which, though it is found earlier, did not really come into prominence until it was used by Sir Simon Harcourt in defence of Sacheverell at the great trial in 1710. Harcourt boldly transfered passive obedience from the king (to whom, in the traditional notion of the doctrine, it was certainly due) to the national legislative authority as a whole. This new interpretation could be combined with the idea, expressed by Lord Nottingham at the Convention in 1689, that a king who repudiated the legal framework of the constitution and set up to govern by his own will and pleasure, could be deemed to have abdicated.[42] Thus the events of 1688 need not have involved 'resistance' at all in the new sense, an interpretation attractive to tories for its reconciliation of passive obedience with the Revolution. It is this doctrine of legislative supremacy that Swift puts forward in the 'Sentiments' in answer to the question of whether resistance is ever lawful. He argues that it is not, but that obedience is due to the legislature and not to the person of the monarch (*PW* ii.16). Here Swift agrees with absolutist theorists like Charles Leslie in allowing no appeal from the final political authority, against more 'liberal' political thinkers like Locke and Hoadly. Swift, although he was willing to allow that the people were the ultimate source of political authority, and that the people as a whole might very occasionally rise as a body against the grossest

---

[40] 'An Homilie against Disobedience and Wilfull Rebellion', *Certaine Sermons or Homilies* (2 vols, 1623; rpt. in one vol., Gainesville, 1968), ii.275-319; R.A. Beddard, 'The Restoration church', *The Restored Monarchy, 1660-1688*, ed. J.R. Jones (1979), pp. 155-75, especially pp. 166-8.

[41] The idea was Peter du Moulin's, and he made the suggestion to (then dean) Sancroft about 1668; R.A. Beddard, 'Of the Duty of Subjects; a proposed Fortieth Article of Religion', *Bodleian Library Record*, x (1981), 229-36.

[42] For Harcourt's speech, see Howell's *State Trials*, xv, cols 196-213; Harcourt quoted the anglican homily (cols 204-5). On the trial generally and the political arguments involved, see Geoffrey Holmes, *The Trial of Doctor Sacheverell* (1973), especially pp. 181-6; and Kenyon, *Revolution Principles*, pp. 88-9, 136-8. For Nottingham's speech in 1689, see Cobbett's *Parliamentary History of England*, v (1809), col. 82.

misgovernment, refused to allow the individual the exercise of any judgment over the legislative power. This he thought could only lead to chaos. On the other hand, he stopped short of endorsing passive acceptance of tyranny, as seemed to be involved in the acceptance (as in Hobbes and Leslie) of the executive power as absolute. Swift found the distinction between legislative and executive very useful, for it allowed him to be an absolutist without being a Hobbesian; indeed, he complacently attributes 'all the political Mistakes' in Hobbes to a confusion between the two powers (*PW* ii.16).

In one of his marginal notes on bishop Burnet's *History*, Swift wrote that while (like Burnet) he believed that kings ruled by virtue of an original contract with their people, he would nevertheless (against Burnet) still have favoured a regency in 1689 (*PW* v.291). Yet in the *Examiner* No. 25 (25 January 1711), Swift ridicules the notion of government by contract, listing among extravagant whig resolutions, 'That by the Original Contract the Government of this Realm is by a Junta, and a King or Queen; but the Administration solely in the Junta' (*PW* iii.72). The quotation from the *Examiner* is more typically tory in its outlook, and it may seem strange that Swift should later (in his note on Burnet) affirm his belief in a contract, and stranger still that he should think such a belief consistent with supporting the regency proposal. The idea of a contract was not, of course, exclusively whiggish; it is found in the writings of the great anglican apologist Richard Hooker. In its more extreme forms, however, the idea was associated with the whigs, and especially with their theorist John Locke. What tories objected to was not so much the idea of the contract itself (at the Convention, the Earl of Clarendon objected in the strongest terms to the phrase 'Original Contract', but this was not one of the parts of the resolution of the House of Commons that the Lords as a whole took exception to) but the notion that seemed to be deduceable from it, that the people could, on maladministration (of which they were the judge) resume the power they had given the government. Making the people the judges seemed to make all government precarious. Thomas Long, for example, in a moderate tory reply to Abednego Sellar's Jacobite *History of Passive Obedience* (1689) called *The Historian Unmasked: or, Some Reflections on the Late History of Passive Obedience* (1689), sought (like Swift) to present anglican political attitudes as a middle way between the extremes of despotism and popular power. Long makes the point (with which Swift would have agreed) that even if one takes the people to be the origin of political power, public tranquillity would be very much impaired if the people were made its judges.[43]

The doctrine of legislative supremacy is calculated for a situation where the different branches are able to work in harmony with each other. It could hardly, by itself, justify two branches acting together to depose the third. Swift raises this problem in the 'Sentiments', where he attributes it to a well-meaning non-juror (*PW* ii.21-2). In framing his reply to this point, Swift stops well short of asserting a deposing power. Instead he uses historical examples to construct a *reductio ad absurdum*. This is, in effect, the argument from necessity, used often in 1689-91 and again at the trial of Sacheverell, that it is always understood that in cases of unforeseen extremity the ordinary rules no longer apply, but that it is wrong to weaken the authority of the rules by anticipating and discussing such cases while they are merely hypothetical.[44] Swift's refusal to attempt any justification of the Revolution on theoretical grounds was partly because (as we shall see) he had important reservations about all the various arguments available. But he also thought that, since the Revolution had involved guilt on the part of its active promoters, it was better to rely on the argument from necessity. In 1714, for example, he used the argument (attributing it to the 'highest tories' who were less than forty years old, that is who had come of age since the Revolution settlement) that the present establishment is the one to which passive obedience is due, and the crime of excluding James ('if it were any') rests with those who did it, and not with those who have inherited the present regime (*PW* viii.92) A similar argument would later be used by Swift's whig antagonist Steele in the *Englishman*, second series, No. 22 (23 September 1715).[45] Such an argument was not needed for the whigs, nor did Steele himself believe that any guilt had been incurred at the time of the Revolution. He simply uses it as an argument that the tories,

---

[43] Long particularly objects to the idea that 'the Original of all Power is from the People, and that they may resume it on Male-Administration'; *The Historian Unmasked* (1689), p. 7. This possibility of the people's resumption of power was far more frightening to the conservative mind than the theoretical issue of the origin of political power; hence Swift is willing to make the people the source of political power (*PW* i.195).

[44] Harcourt, in *State Trials*, xv, cols 201-2, citing St Paul.

[45] *The Englishman*, ed. Rae Blanchard (Oxford, 1955), pp. 339-40.

by their own principles, will find unanswerable, that they are obliged to support the establishment that they found in being at the time of their responsible entry to society.

There were three main kinds of argument that had been used to justify the Revolution of 1688.[46] A distinctively whig idea was that resistance to properly constituted authority was, in some circumstances, lawful and justifiable. The notion that the success of the Revolution implied providential approval was one that drew bipartisan support. Reluctant tories who could accept neither of these arguments might still feel that, whatever the guilt or otherwise of the Revolution, since the new regime had succeeded in establishing itself, obedience was due to it on a *de facto* basis. The first of these arguments, asserting the legality of resistance, was naturally completely unacceptable to Swift or to any tory. As we have seen, it seemed destructive of political order and authority to allow the governed to judge their governors. This could only lead to anarchy. Even the whigs, as they became the party of government rather than a party of opposition, began to back away from any defence of the idea of resistance. By 1716 the doctrine of passive obedience had more to offer the whigs, as the party in power, and consequently Addison in his *Freeholder* papers completely rejects resistance and the idea of the power of the people. Whenever he mentions the absurdities and excesses associated with passive obedience, Addison is careful to associate the doctrine with the tories; but he claims the substance of passive obedience (not under that name, of course) as due to the present whig government.[47]

The idea that the success of the Revolution had been providential was one that could appeal to both parties. Much could be made of the peculiar way in which the changes of the wind had assisted the movement of William's fleet while preventing James's from moving into action against it. Burnet, in a sermon preached on 31 January 1689, took this line, and he was still satisfied with it when he wrote his *History*, in which the Revolution plays a crucial role in one of the five great crises of the

---

[46] The best general discussions are in Kenyon, *Revolution Principles*; and Mark Goldie, 'The Revolution of 1689 and the structure of political argument: an essay and an annotated bibliography of pamphlets on the allegiance controversy', *Bulletin of Research in the Humanities*, lxxxiii (1980), 473-564.

[47] Addison ridicules tory passive obedience in No. 3 (30 December 1715), yet in No. 5 (6 January 1716) he demands it (not under that name, of course) on behalf of 'the Wisdom of our Legislature' (that is, the whig government); *The Freeholder*, ed. James Leheny (Oxford, 1979), pp. 51, 59.

European reformation.[48] Swift's view of history prevented his acceptance of this interpretation of Burnet's. While he believed, of course, in a general providential order, he did not believe in the particular providential approval of single events or people, or that providence would always support the winning side. Many of his heroes were precisely men who, in worldly terms, had failed: Socrates, Cato, Sir Thomas More, Clarendon, Sir William Temple. In the 'Ode to Sancroft', as we have seen, Swift supposes that God may well be pleased with the individual whose course of action leads to apparent failure. Swift saw chance, accident, and the individual as determining the events of history, rather than a minutely-guiding hand of providence.[49] Burnet's theory seemed to involve a facile acceptance of whatever happened as right. Whereas the course of history in Swift's own time showed, as in the triumph of the whigs in 1714-15, that evil might well flourish in the short term, and no one could tell how short that term might prove to be.

The main exponent of the *de facto* school was the Earl of Nottingham, a high tory churchman of sincerity and integrity. His political views on most subjects were so close to Swift's that there is a temptation to look for the source of Swift's inveterate hostility to the earl in some personal slight. Possibly Nottingham was one of the tory lords whose treatment of the clergy with 'insolence and haughtiness' Swift complained of (*PW* viii.120). On this particular issue, however, Swift disagreed with Nottingham. He objected to the *de facto* theory as a piece of legal quibbling designed as a hypocritical attempt to preserve both conscience and employment. It seemed as odious for Nottingham to accept employment in a government that he believed to be an usurpation as it did for the dissenters to accept occasional communion in the anglican church in order to qualify themselves for civil places. Swift's lampoons on Nottingham had an immediate and additional provocation (in 1711 Nottingham had joined the whigs in opposition to the tory peace) but their viciousness suggests a previous latent hostility.[50]

[48] Burnet, *A Sermon Preached ... on 31 January 1689* (1689); *History of his Own Time*, i.569-88; Kenyon, *Revolution Principles*, pp. 24, 169.

[49] For Swift's view of history, see above, p. 47, n.46.

[50] For the *de facto* argument, see Kenyon, *Revolution Principles*, pp. 21-34; and Goldie, 'The Revolution of 1689', pp. 487-8. On the importance of Nottingham's acceptance of the new government, see Horwitz, *Revolution Politicks*, pp. 82-5. Swift refers jestingly to the *de facto* theory and the worldly wisdom of its adherents in his letter to Pope of 30 August 1716 (*Corr*.ii.213).

If Swift found all the usual reasons unacceptable, and consequently did not find it easy to justify the Revolution to himself, this need not imply that he had much (at least before 1714) sympathy for Jacobitism. In the 'Sentiments', in fact, he claims that the opposition to James II came 'altogether from the Church of *England*, and chiefly from the *Clergy*, and one of the Universities' (*PW* ii.9). The dissenters, on the other hand, as Swift noted in a comment on Burnet's *History*, slavishly complied with James's proposals (*PW* v.285). Thus Swift contrives to appropriate to the tories whatever credit is to be had from the events of the Revolution, leaving the whigs and the dissenters with the much larger amount of opprobrium. There were probably few churchmen who genuinely wanted a Jacobite restoration, and Swift was certainly not one of them. Yet he would always be very sympathetic to the conscientious non-juror. The dissenters, who wanted to remain outside the national church and yet enjoy a share of the employments in the national government, earned only his hatred and contempt. But he could respect the scruples of conscience by which the individual was sure to be a material loser. This was an attitude also shared by sincere whig churchmen like William Wake.[51] In the 'Sentiments' Swift argues respectfully with the scruples of Robert Nelson, being careful to clear him from the imputation of Jacobitism (*PW* ii.21-2). In the *Memoirs* that he wrote or revised for Captain Creichton Swift presents the non-juring point of view with sympathy and understanding (*PW* v.168). Of greater political significance are his references to Charles Leslie, the prominent Jacobite journalist whom (unlike Nelson and Creichton) he seems not to have known personally. In the *Examiner* No. 15 (16 November 1710) he draws a contrast between the whig journalists Defoe and Tutchin ('two stupid illiterate Scribblers') with their opposite number Charles Leslie, 'whose Character and Person, as well as good learning and Sense, discovered upon other Subjects, do indeed deserve Respect and Esteem' (*PW* iii.13). Even the qualification that Swift goes on to make, that Leslie's political papers are 'more pernicious' than those of the whigs, carries the implied compliment that they are more dangerous because more able. Leslie's *Rehearsal* had in fact ceased publication by the time that Swift was writing, whereas Defoe's *Review* and Tutchin's *Observator* were still appearing. The *Examiner* was actually in its political point of

[51] Sykes, *William Wake*, i.44-5; see above, p. 85.

view something of a successor to the *Rehearsal*, a connection Swift was anxious to play down. Hence the allusion to Leslie, to give the appearance of his being a medium between two extremes. Yet it is suggestive that he speaks much more kindly of Leslie than he does of the whigs, and many of Swift's political ideas (usually less temperately expressed) can be found in the pages of *Rehearsal*.[52] Swift paid Leslie a more direct compliment in his *Preface to the B—p of S–r–m's Introduction*, where he contrasts Burnet's self-interested hysterical outbursts with Leslie's more solid and worthwhile efforts 'to the confounding of *Popery*' (*PW* v.79-80). Nor should the fact that Leslie wrote an attack on Swift's early *Discourse* be taken to imply that they were politically at odds, for Leslie recognised the really illiberal tendencies of the *Discourse* (with which he agreed), though it suited his own polemical purpose to point out their incompatibility with the surface classical republicanism of the author of the *Discourse*.[53]

While Swift was sympathetic to the non-juror who acted from what Swift regarded as a mistaken principle of conscience, his loyalty to the ideal of a national church prevented his approving any schism from that church on any point (however conscientiously felt) of government rather than doctrine. Only heresy could justify separation; otherwise the great body of the protestant dissenters could similarly justify themselves.[54] In the 'Sentiments' Swift is careful not to identify the church with any particular form of civil government (*PW* ii.14). He was willing to

[52] Leslie asserts (against Locke and Hoadly) the absolute and arbitrary nature of the power of last resort; the *Rehearsal*, No. 38 (21 April 1705), No. 49 (7 July), and No. 56 (25 August). Swift makes a nominal protest against 'arbitrary Power' (which had an unpopular sound), but gives 'an absolute *unlimited legislative* Power' to the supreme constitutional body (*PW* ii.15, 23), so that he only differs from Leslie in the placing of the power. Any reader of the *Rehearsal* will be struck by Swiftian themes, though expressed without Swift's characteristic rhetorical moderation. Thus the ingratitude of the people to their benefactors (the main theme of Swift's *Discourse*) is found in No. 70 (3 November 1705) and No. 111 (8 June 1706), and the irrational behaviour of people in groups (*PW* i.226-7) in No. 72 (10 November 1705). For an account of Leslie, see Bruce Frank, ' "The Excellent Rehearser": Charles Leslie and the tory party, 1688-1714', *Biography in the Eighteenth Century*, ed. J.D. Browning (New York, 1980), pp. 43-68.

[53] See below, p. 160.

[54] Edward Stillingfleet, *A Discourse concerning the Unreasonableness of a New Separation on Account of the Oaths* (1689); for the various views held by the non-jurors, see Mark Goldie, 'The non-jurors, episcopacy, and the origins of the Convocation controversy', *Ideology and Conspiracy*, ed. Eveline Cruickshanks (Edinburgh, 1982), pp. 15-35.

claim for the church the privileges that went with establishment. But he neither claimed for the church as a temporal institution the independence of civil government asserted by Dodwell and the non-jurors, nor did he believe that monarchy was necessary for episcopacy, though he thought it was best.[55] Swift rejected independency because he wished the church to retain the sanctions that could only be applied by the civil power; only in association with the civil power could the church retain its monopoly. At the same time, it might be equally unfortunate for the church to become too closely associated with a particular regime. Bishop Sprat, in his apology for serving on James II's Ecclesiastical Commission and for resigning from it just before the government collapsed, justified his apparent timeserving with the arguments that he served on the commission to exert a moderating influence and that he resigned when it seemed safe to do so because the commission was breaking up. Sprat makes the point that the cause of episcopacy in Scotland was ruined by the Scottish bishops becoming too closely identified with James II, and not deserting his cause in time (as Sprat had); hence William had no option but to establish presbyterianism, because the bishops were all obstinate Jacobites.[56] Whatever one thinks either of Sprat's personal conduct, or of the chances of survival of the Scottish episcopal church, the argument had some force when applied to the English church. If it was to remain the national, established church, it would in practice have to come to terms with whatever government achieved permanent effective control. It was more difficult to say just when the church should decide to, in Swift's phrase, 'fall in with' the new government (*PW* ii.14).

In 1689 the question had been an urgent one. In his 'Ode' Swift praises Sancroft for his firmness, that is, for not going over immediately to William. Others thought that it might have been better for the church if Sancroft had taken a more active role in public affairs at this crucial time.[57] Swift may even have come to

---

[55] For the doctrine of independency or the 'two societies', see John Kettlewell, *The Measures of Christian Obedience* (1681), pp. 135-6; and for its use by the non-jurors, see Goldie, 'The non-jurors'. In 'The Sentiments of a Church-of-England Man' (*PW* ii.5), Swift stops just short of the extreme claims for episcopacy advanced in Henry Sacheverell, *The Political Union* (Oxford, 1702), pp. 16-17.

[56] *A Letter from the Bishop of Rochester to ... the Earl of Dorset* (1688, but published 1689).

[57] Francis Lee, writing for a non-juring audience in the 'Life' prefixed to *A Compleat Collection of the Works of ... John Kettlewell* (2 vols, 1719), defends

regret that Sancroft did not feel able, eventually, to take the oaths to the new regime, for the non-juring schism undoubtedly damaged the church. William Sherlock, Master of the Temple, was (like Sancroft) a non-juror at first. He failed to take the oaths before the time appointed, and even wrote against them. But he came to accept the new regime when he thought it had become firmly settled, as many (including perhaps Swift) must have wished that Sancroft would have done. Sherlock took his main argument from bishop Overall's *Convocation Book*, a collection of canons prepared and approved by convocation in 1606 but never given royal approval by James I and therefore never having any legal validity though possessing some moral authority. They had remained in manuscript until 1689, when Sancroft arranged for their publication in order to strengthen the non-juring case. It was therefore ironic that the main controversial use to which (certainly unforeseen by Sancroft) they were put was by a non-juror converted from his previous conviction by this very book. For the *Convocation Book* asserted that passive obedience was due to a settled government. In 1606 the purpose of this canon had been to discourage the support of rebellions against existing regimes in Europe, but in 1690 it could be used to justify obedience to William's government, which (after his great victory at the Battle of the Boyne) seemed reasonably firmly settled. In taking this line, Sherlock was uncomfortably close to Hobbes, who had divorced authority from right, and indeed his attempt to defend himself from the charge of being a Hobbesian is not altogether convincing. But for Swift, who (as we have seen) regarded Hobbes's main error as a confusion between the executive and the legislative powers, Sherlock's argument was perfectly acceptable if it was applied to the legislature as a whole. Once a properly functioning government of king, lords, and commons was in effective operation, it was not for the private citizen to question the title of the king, any more than it was to question particular election results or claims to nobility, since these were properly cognisable

---

Sancroft and others against those non-jurors who 'blamed them exceedingly for their Reserves, and their not acting so Openly and Vigorously' as others, and who censured them as 'Unconcerned and Unactive with regard to the State it self' (i.103; this last phrase must mean a refusal to enter into Jacobite conspiracies). Lee later defends Sancroft for having given the commission to consecrate Burnet against those who thought he ought to have refused (i.135-6). For the dissatisfaction of Turner and Clarendon with Sancroft's neutrality, see above, p. 86.

only by the legislature itself. Such an argument was also all the more acceptable for allowing a clear distinction to be made between the Revolution of 1688 and the illegal regimes that had usurped power between 1649 and 1660, which were never properly constituted legislatures in the manner of the ancient constitution. Sherlock's arguments provoked a large debate, and he was naturally attacked as self-interested, a charge that was not made less credible by his promotion in 1691 to the deanery of St Paul's.[58] But whatever the intellectual validity of the arguments he used, they were powerfully attractive to churchmen who (like Swift) wanted the church to be able to 'fall in with' the established civil power. By the time Swift wrote his 'Sentiments' the post-Revolution government was too firmly established for the particular point at which it had become so to have much importance. The 'weathercock of state' had turned, but the church was still the same fixed point.

iii

The success of the Revolution of 1688, and the permanence of the settlement worked out in 1689, did more than determine the character of English politics and the course of events for the next thirty years or more. It also decisively changed the character of national life. Its repercussions extended well beyond the dynastic change, important as such a change was in the seventeenth century. There were far-reaching constitutional innovations, the result of a shift in the balance of power between the monarch and parliament. Political parties became a permanent fact of national and local political life. The struggle for control of parliament, rather than the pursuit of influence at court (important as that remained) became the primary objective in the business of politics. Hence the new importance of journalism and public opinion. Other changes affected more than the politically active minority. The religious settlement, with its (however limited) recognition of dissent, ended the ideal (not the less cherished for having been long divorced from reality) of a single national church. England's involvement in two long and expensive European wars led to a massive increase in taxation and in the bureaucratic machine needed to organise it and to supervise the expanded government activities that the

---

[58] On Sherlock, see Goldie, 'The Revolution of 1689'.

war began but which tended to become permanent. Both these developments resulted in a weakening of the traditional structures of power and authority. Political power was now increasingly wielded by 'new men' whose fortunes derived from government service or funded money rather than from inherited landed estates. In the familiar tory analysis of this movement, it was usually asserted and believed that the wars had been paid for by the landed interest while the profits accrued to the moneyed men. These political and economic changes can be traced back to well before the Revolution; but they were quickened and strengthened by the events of 1688-9, and it became something of a commonplace (for tories) to trace all the national ills back to 1688 and no further, a date that the whigs as naturally tended to treat as a kind of birth-date of liberty.[59]

There are a number of places in Swift's works where, sometimes in a serious and sometimes in a comic context, the Revolution is treated as a point from which to measure decay and degeneration. In *Mr Collins's Discourse Put into Plain English* (1713), Swift credits '*Free-thinking* and the *Revolution*' between them with banishing the devil and the fear of him from England (*PW* iv.30). In the introduction to *Polite Conversation* (published in 1738, but begun as early as 1704), Simon Wagstaff (the fictive author) dates the 'Refinement' of 'abbreviating, or reducing Words of many Syllables into one, by lopping off the rest' as 'having begun about the Time of the Revolution' (*PW* iv.106). We know that Swift seriously regarded this practice as a symptom of linguistic decay (*PW* ii.175-6). In 'A History of Poetry' (a Swift-Sheridan exercise in punning) the decline of poetry is dated from the Revolution (*PW* iv.274), while it is the neglect of philology from the same period that is complained of in 'A Discourse to Prove the Antiquity of the English Tongue' (*PW* iv.231). These references suggest a habit of mind cognate

[59] For a succinct statement of the tory case, which would later be elaborated by Swift, see Henry St John's letter of 9 July 1709 to the Earl of Orrery; 'The letters of Henry St John to the Earl of Orrery, 1709-1711', ed. H.T. Dickinson, *Camden Miscellany*, xxvi (1975), 146. For the standard modern study, see P.G.M. Dickson, *The Financial Revolution in England: A Study in the Development of Public Credit, 1688-1756* (1967). The *Medley* printed a letter in No. 32 (7 May 1711) which (ironically) traces all current evils back to the Revolution. This parody of a tory complaint is attributed by Oldmixon, *The Life and Posthumous Works of Arthur Maynwaring* (1715), p. 194, to Anthony Henley, a whig M.P. with whom Swift had been on friendly terms in 1708 (*Corr.* i.101-2). By December 1710 the views parodied were Swift's, so it is not surprising to find him seeking to avoid Henley's company (*JS* i.115).

with that of the Jacobite fox-hunter in the *Freeholder* No. 22 (5 March 1716), whom Addison ridiculed for his belief that 'there had been no good Weather since the Revolution'. Jacobite satires did not fail to load William with responsibility for the poor weather and harvests of these years.[60] In the light of these jests, the discontents that lie behind them, and of Swift's more serious comments, it is rather surprising that Swift's unequivocal support for the Revolution should usually have been taken, by modern scholars, as axiomatic.[61] For his contemporaries would have marked the author of such remarks as a probable crypto-Jacobite.

It is well known that Swift was hostile to all the developments characteristic of post-Revolution England. From *A Tale of a Tub* (1704) to *The Presbyterians' Plea of Merit* (1733), he fought a strong rearguard action in defence of his ideal of a national church. He attributed the general decline in religion and morality to the weakened position of the anglican church. He would have liked, so far as was possible, to circumscribe the legal toleration (or as he and the tories preferred to call it, 'indulgence') allowed to the dissenters. More generally, he was opposed to the various manifestations of the 'whig' view of the world, epitomised in the *Spectator* and so congenial to Macaulay: the world of individualism, secularism, commercialism, and imperialism.[62] Swift's attitude to the Revolution was an extremely guarded and qualified approval, arrived at through a balancing of accounts that showed the smallest of surpluses. Revolutions he regarded as being justified when 'those evils which usually attend and follow a violent change of government' are less than 'the grievances we suffer

---

[60] *The Freeholder*, ed. Leheny, p. 131. Bevil Higgons (?) attributes 'ten Years of War and dismal Weather' to William's baneful influence in 'The Mourners' (1702); *POAS*, vi.362.

[61] Among those who have mistaken Swift's politics for a kind of Lockean liberalism are some distinguished scholars: Louis A. Landa, 'Introduction to the Sermons', *PW* ix.224; Ricardo Quintana, *Two Augustans: John Locke, Jonathan Swift* (Madison, 1978), p. 76. Herbert Davis puts the common view when he says that 'Swift never wavered in accepting the Revolution settlement of 1688' (*PW* ii.xvii).

[62] For an account of a typical 'whig' view of the world see (apart from such primary sources as the *Spectator*) Chapter iii of Macaulay's *History of England*; and Peter Earle, *The World of Defoe* (1976). In *The Curse of Party: Swift's Relations with Addison and Steele* (Lincoln, Nebraska, 1961), Bertrand A. Goldgar discusses some of the reasons for Swift's hostility to the whig world-picture.

under a present power'. He allows this to have been the case in 1688, but adds the rider that the Revolution produced 'some very bad effects, which are likely to stick long enough by us' (*PW* ix.31). These 'very bad effects' are the subject of frequent comment and extended analysis in Swift's serious political and historical works.

The ideal monarch, in the tory scheme of things, is well represented by David in Dryden's *Absalom and Achitophel* (1681), particularly in David's long speech at the end of the poem where he composes factional strife and restores order. The divine sanction of the monarchy is suggested when God 'nodding, gave Consent'; the rule of 'Godlike *David* was Restor'd,/ And willing Nations knew their Lawfull Lord'. Swift draws such a 'godlike' monarch in the lofty king of Brodbingnag, whose contempt for the party strife of England expresses the ideal of a 'patriot king' in a way that anticipates Bolingbroke's *Idea of a Patriot King* (written about 1738, although not published until 1749). After the Revolution, it was less easy to treat the office of kingship so reverently as Dryden had been able to. The reality of the post-1688 monarchy was unglamorous, neither William nor Queen Anne (nor George I) having any taste for the theatrical pageantry that had contributed so much to the public image of the earlier Stuart courts.[63] Queen Anne resumed a practice disused by William, that of touching for the King's Evil (she touched Samuel Johnson in 1712), and this ceremony was perhaps the last vestige of the formerly magical and even divine nature that the kingship had once possessed. Of much greater practical significance than the essentially symbolic aspects of monarchy was the fact that both William and Anne were forced, though with great reluctance, to take sides in party strife. In his *Examiner* papers Swift makes much of the rudeness and insolence of the way the queen had been treated by her whig ministers (*PW* iii.37,80,117). This theme is extended in *The Importance of the Guardian Considered* (1713), where Swift condemns Steele's language in 'expecting' the demolition of Dunkirk, comparing it to Bradshaw's at the trial of Charles I (*PW* viii.4). It was always Swift's strategy to identify Queen

---

[63] For Charles I's interest in his 'image', and the role of the theatrical at his court, see Peter W. Thomas, 'Charles I of England: the tragedy of absolutism', *The Courts of Europe*, ed. A.G. Dickens (1977), pp. 191-211. The character of the post-1688 monarchy is best studied through biographies: Baxter, *William III*; Edward Gregg, *Queen Anne* (1980); and Ragnhild Hatton, *George I: Elector and King* (1978).

Anne with the nation as a whole, not just with the tories; in this way she is made to appear above party strife, and her support for the tories looks as disinterested a choice as Swift's own (it should be said that Queen Anne genuinely was a reluctant partisan). Swift's basic charge against George I was that he had allowed himself to become the king not of the nation but of the whigs.[64] This is a view that Swift expresses historically in several pamphlets, allegorically in the 'Account of the Court and Empire of Japan' (1728; *PW* v.99-107), and imaginatively in the character of the Emperor of Lilliput in *Gulliver's Travels.*[65]

One pernicious effect of the rise of party was the way each party sought to force itself on the monarch as a group. This was not especially a whig notion, although naturally it is on the insolence of the whigs that Swift focuses. In the *Examiner* No. 17 (14 December 1710) he attacks the way in which individual whig ministers placed conditions on their willingness to serve the queen. While it was still the theory, and to some extent still the case in practice, that ministers were the personal servants of the crown, it seemed a sinister development that ministers should try to make terms in this way.[66] While individual ministers remained responsible primarily to the crown, there seemed some check against the possibility of an over-mighty group of ministers (such as the whig Junto) seizing control of the government, as Swift thought had happened during the period of whig domination under Queen Anne. Swift was always distrustful of groups of men, especially of professions or corporations who banded together to practice some fraud on the public (*Corr.*iii.103). Political parties (by which in practice Swift meant the whigs) were formed to do just this. In the *Project for the Advancement of Religion* (1709) he argues that merit and even more morality should be the proper qualifications for public employment (as in the uncorrupted state of Lilliput), and attacks the way men of vicious lives and no obvious qualifications are given jobs because they are reliable party men (*PW* ii.62). Swift was here speaking from personal feeling and experience. The *Project* was published in April 1709. On 8 March

[64] Hatton, *George I*, pp. 119-28, palliates the extent to which George favoured the whigs on his accession.

[65] See below, p. 170.

[66] As late as the 1740s the friction between the theory that ministers were royal servants and the practical importance of their securing parliamentary support could lead to serious political instability; John B. Owen, *The Rise of the Pelhams* (1957).

1709 Swift had written to his friend Ford of his disappointed hopes of preferment, attributing his failure to his being 'thought to want the Art of being thourow paced in my Party, as all discreet Persons ought to be' (*Corr*.i.125). The systematic use of patronage for political ends was not, of course, a post-Revolution phenomenon. It had been used against the whigs in the tory reaction of 1681-5. But to Swift it seemed one thing to reward the friends of the constitution in church and state (the tories), and quite another to reward a faction that intended the overthrow of both (the whigs). It is true, of course, that in his days of influence under the tory ministry of 1710-14, Swift often tried to help whig friends obtain or retain public employment. To this extent he practiced what he preached about rewarding merit.[67] But the kind of scheme of promotion by piety that he advocates in the *Project for the Advancement of Religion* would have been more partisan than he pretends. It would have ended the use of patronage for party advantage only in the sense of giving it almost exclusively to the tories. When Swift sought to turn the clock back to before the Revolution, it was naturally to the period of tory reaction of 1681-5 that he turned.

The Revolution had inaugurated a period of nearly twenty years of almost continuous war, Britain's part in which had been financed largely by borrowing on the public credit. The result was the creation of a new 'moneyed interest' which rivalled and threatened to dominate the traditional power of the landed men. This sinister new factor in politics was the subject of the first *Examiner* paper that Swift wrote (No. 13, 2 November 1710; *PW* iii.5). There were several reasons for regarding the new development as alarming. Landed wealth was thought to be the safest base for political power because it was the most stable form of property and most closely identified its owners' interests with those of the nation at large. A landowner could not take his wealth with him, and would therefore be the less tempted to act or to approve action that was against the national interest. Even the capital of a trading merchant was not so dangerous as money in the stocks, because most of the merchant's time and energy would be taken up with the management of his trade, leaving him little leisure for political activity. Men whose money was in

---

[67] Swift reported to Stella his efforts on behalf of Steele and Philips (*JS* i.128-9) and of Congreve (*JS* i.295). In the 'Letter to Mr Pope' he claims that he tried to help Addison, Congreve, Rowe, and Steele; this is where he records the ministers teasing him that 'I never came to them without a Whig in my sleeve' (*PW* ix.28-30; quotation on p. 29).

government securities and other funds, however, were not only free to engage full-time in political activity but had the ready cash with which to buy their way into parliament through bribery and corruption. Money in the funds was also untaxed. Worst of all, from the point of view of political stability, apart from being less 'real' than land, the value of money in stocks and funds could be manipulated by the owners themselves. It was in the power of the largest stockholders, or of a group of them, to raise or depress the market by large-scale buying or selling. The same people could make it easier, or more difficult, for the government to borrow money. From the conservative viewpoint of Swift and his like, the creation and growth of this 'moneyed interest' was probably the single most pernicious result of the Revolution.[68] In 1701-2 Charles Davenant, the tory economist, argued that the recent war (the Nine Years War) could have been financed from taxes raised within each year, without the need for public borrowing and the creation of a vast national debt. He argued that the policy of deficit financing and public indebtedness had been adopted in order to settle the new government more firmly, since all those who invested any money in the funds would certainly support the Revolution settlement against the threat of a Jacobite restoration, which would inevitably be accompanied by a repudiation of public debts. Further, the debt had grown to such monstrous proportions as a result of corruption on the part of those charged with its management, who had raised vast estates for themselves by robbing the public purse. Davenant made these charges more vivid and effective by dramatising them in a dialogue between 'Tom Double' and a subordinate 'Mr Whiglove'. In Tom Double Davenant drew what he claimed was the type of the modern or 'new' whig, a man who had been destitute at the time of the Revolution, but who had subsequently raised himself a fortune of £150,000 through various corrupt dealings with government money. Davenant describes all the government's main expedients for raising funds in terms of how advantageous they proved for men like Tom Double.[69] The result of the war was thus

---

[68] There was a bipartisan dislike of the stock-jobber and financial manipulator, and praise from both sides for the genuine merchant; see John Loftis, *Comedy and Society from Congreve to Fielding* (Stanford, 1959), especially pp. 77-100. Hostility to the 'moneyed men' was, nevertheless, a distinctively tory theme; see Isaac Kramnick, *Bolingbroke and his Circle* (Cambridge, Mass., 1968), especially pp. 59-60.

[69] *The True Picture of a Modern Whig* (1701), especially pp. 32, 34, 51; *Tom*

the transfer of vast amounts of wealth away from the rightful, hereditary proprietors to a set of rascally whig upstarts like Tom Double; and with this wealth naturally went political influence. In 1710-11, towards the end of another and even more expensive war, Swift offers exactly the same analysis as Davenant had done ten years earlier. In the *Examiner* and in the *Conduct of the Allies* Swift develops a conspiracy thesis similar to Davenant's yet with even wider ramifications, involving the allies as well as the whigs. Swift adopts Davenant's account of the finances of the 1690s (that the debt was deliberately created to keep people loyal to the government and the Revolution), and extends it to the War of the Spanish Succession. This war, he suggests, has been fought less for the official pretexts given (such as to protect the protestant interest in Europe, to reduce the excessive power of France, to improve the prospects for British trade) than for the private advantage of Marlborough, the Dutch allies, and the rapacious whig financial interest at home. It has been paid for, however, by the now impoverished tory squires.

One of the most pernicious ways, as Swift saw it, in which the 'financial revolution' had direct political consequences was in the development of public credit. In particular, with the development of a stock-market trading in government securities as well as in the stocks of private companies, the price of such securities came to be regarded as an index of national well-being. The stocks would naturally rise with 'good' news (that is, with news that was welcome to the body of the proprietors of the stocks) and fall with bad. This was a most sinister development. It introduced a new 'popular' element into political life, for the rise or fall of share prices involved simple figures easily taken up and spread around, like the simple political slogans ('No Peace without Spain') that proved so effective as political rallying cries. This meant that the unpopularity (with the fund-holders) of government decisions or policies could be readily and instantly publicised in an extra-parliamentary way. Swift was especially annoyed at the way stocks rose and fell with reports of the queen's health in 1713-14. The worse her health, the closer

---

Double Returned out of the Country (1702), especially pp. 32-43. The same characters reappear in *Sir Thomas Double at Court* (1710) and repeat many of Davenant's earlier points. The account of Davenant's ideas in J.G.A. Pocock, *The Machiavellian Moment* (Princeton, 1975), pp. 436-46 suffers (in my view) from purposely disregarding the immediate political context in which Davenant lived and wrote, for which see D. Waddell, 'Charles Davenant (1656-1714): a biographical sketch', *Economic History Review*, xi (1958), 279-88.

seemed the inevitable Hanoverian accession and the return to power of the whigs. Nothing better symbolised the factiousness and selfishness of the whigs than their rejoicing at the queen's near-fatal illness in December 1713. The deliberate manipulation of the stocks was, of course, practised by the professional stock-jobbers (who in the Queen Anne period were almost universally regarded, by whigs as well as tories, as iniquitous parasites) for purely financial reasons. In the *Examiner* No. 24 (18 January 1711) Swift describes their spreading reports that are calculated to lower prices and therefore allow their friends (who will know that the reports are untrue) to buy at advantageous prices (*PW* iii.67). But the same thing could be done for political purposes. In 1710 the whigs were accused of deliberately trying to lower the public credit in order to increase the difficulties faced by the incoming tory government.[70] In *Gulliver's Travels*, one of the devices of the 'profound Politicians' described in the Academy of Lagado, who invent plots in order to exploit them, is to 'raise or sink the Opinion of publick Credit, as either shall best answer their private Advantage' (*PW* xi.191). So long as the government needed to borrow money (which in practice it constantly did), it was at the mercy of those who in could command large sums of cash; whereas in Swift's view it was the proprietors of the land who should exercise political influence.

Swift thought it a pernicious innovation that 'the Wealth of the Nation, that used to be reckoned by the Value of Land, is now computed by the Rise and Fall of Stocks' (*PW* iii.6). This was a typically tory view. A forward-looking whig like Addison had no such reservations about the value and importance of credit. In the *Spectator* No. 3 (3 March 1711) he drew an allegorical representation of 'Public Credit' as a main bulwark of the constitution. In this allegory Addison places Magna Carta between the Act of Uniformity on one side and the Toleration Act on the other, giving formal recognition of the dissenters' claim (which Swift could never accept) that the 'toleration' was legally and morally the equivalent of the establishment of the church. The main threat to credit (and therefore to national well-being) comes of course from the threat of the Pretender, although Addison makes a show of coupling anarchy with

[70] For the problems of credit and finance faced by Harley on taking office, see B.W. Hill, 'The change of government and the loss of the city, 1710-11', *Economic History Review*, xxiv (1971), 395-413.

tyranny and bigotry with atheism as equal threats. Credit has a fainting-fit at the threatened approach of the Pretender, to be revived by monarchy in the guise of the Hanoverian successor and by religion in the form of 'moderation'; in other words, credit is restored by whig foreign and domestic policies. Swift may have intended a paragraph in the *Examiner* No. 37 (19 April 1711) as a response to Addison's vision, for he picks up a phrase which Addison had attributed to 'none of her well-wishers', that Credit seemed 'troubled with vapours'. Swift writes that to hear 'some of these worthy Reasoners' talk about credit 'you would think they were describing a Lady troubled with Vapours or the Cholick' (*PW* iii.134).[71] He goes on to make a distinction between true national credit and the irrelevant phantom that is the creature of the opinions of a few self-interested stock-jobbers. In the *Conduct of the Allies* he makes a similar distinction when he says that he took it as a 'good Omen' when the stocks fell as a result of the ministerial changes in 1710, as though 'the young extravagant Heir had got a new Steward ... which made the Usurers forbear feeding him with Mony, as they used to do' (*PW* vi.56). This analogy between a private and the public estate was a favourite one with Swift. It expresses his commonsensical opposition to the idea that it was a good thing for the public to be in debt. Later he would make the King of Brobdingnag fail to understand 'how a Kingdom could run out of its Estate like a private Person. He asked me, who were our Creditors? and, where we found Money to pay them?' (*PW* xi.131). It gives a significant indication of the audience for whom Swift was writing in the *Conduct of the Allies* that he could rather casually propose the expedient of suspending payment on the debts contracted in the previous war as a sensible way of helping to finance the present one (*PW* vi.18). This would have been a most irresponsible financial decision, but one likely to appeal to the heavily taxed tory squires.

In his first *Examiner* paper Swift directed his readers to examine the newest and smartest equipages about town; most would be found to belong to the newly rich military and financial adventurers, many of them men who would formerly have belonged on the outside of such coaches (*PW* iii.5). His objections to such redistribution of wealth are not just financial but social and political: too rapid shifts in wealth cause

---

[71] For the iconography of credit, see Paula R. Backscheider, 'Defoe's Lady Credit', *Huntington Library Quarterly*, xliv (1981), 89-100.

dislocation and disturb the social hierarchy on which political stability depends. Once it became possible and even easy for a shameless go-getter to rise '*from the dregs of the People*' (*PW* iii.78) to become Lord Chancellor and Lord President of the Council, as Somers had done; or to raise, in Marlborough's case, the largest private fortune in Europe from royal favour and a happy knack of winning battles; more people would become discontented with their appointed places in society and would try to improve their fortunes. This inevitably led to the worst kind of economic and political adventurism, typified by the case of William Wood and his corruptly-obtained patent for coining copper money for Ireland. From the beginning of the first of the *Drapier's Letters*, Swift refers again and again to Wood's humble social origins (*PW* x.4). Swift expressed his belief in the need for a stable and hierarchical social system through the ideal educational institutions of Lilliput, which perpetuate the existing class-system (*PW* xi.61-3), and more generally still through the caste-divided society of the Houyhnhnms. The Lilliputian politicians who gain advancement by their dexterity in leaping, creeping, and rope dancing perfectly symbolise the new breed of post-Revolution politicians whose special skills (like electoral and financial management) made them necessary in the corrupt world of contemporary politics.[72] Only if politics could be cleaned up would it be possible to dispense with such men and to employ only the men of birth, virtue, and integrity who were the natural leaders of society.

Swift's views on all these post-Revolution developments can be related to the 'neo-Harringtonian' political ideas that had been advanced much earlier, by the Earl of Shaftesbury and his followers about 1675, in opposition to the corrupt government of Charles II.[73] These ideas, which derived from the classical-republican tradition of political thought, emphasised the part played by 'corruption' in subverting traditional institutions. In 1675 the twin threats of a 'standing' parliament (there had been no general election since 1661) and a 'standing' army seemed to

---

[73] The important texts are 'A Letter from a Person of Quality, to his Friend in the Country'; 'The Earl of Shaftesbury's Speech in the House of Lords' on 20 October 1675; and 'Two Seasonable Discourses concerning the Present Parliament'; all printed in *State Tracts: Being a Collection of Several Treatises Relating to the Government* (1689), pp. 41-71. Their interpretation is discussed in J.G.A. Pocock, 'Machiavelli, Harrington, and English political ideologies in the eighteenth century', *Politics, Language, and Time* (1972), pp. 104-47.

provide the court with the means to control parliament, with the consequent loss of parliament's ability to act as a check on the executive. In 1675-7 this was 'opposition whig' doctrine. After 1688, as the whigs themselves became more closely identified with government rather than opposition, such ideas gradually became the property of the 'country tory' backbenchers (although many 'old whigs' continued to share them). To such tories, the 'Financial Revolution' seemed to have completed the long decline of the ancient and stable 'gothic' constitution. The king was now dependent on parliamentary supplies even for the normal business of government. High taxation to pay for the wars meant that the nobility was increasingly attracted to the pursuit of employments in the court and the army in order to supplement their incomes and retain their participation and influence in political life. The independent country gentlemen in the House of Commons were similarly liable to corruption through the distributions of civil and military places and pensions. Thus in both houses of parliament, independence was replaced by subservience, either to the king and the court party (as seemed to be the case in 1675), or (as most commonly after the Revolution) to whatever minister, group, or party was able to control the flow of royal patronage. Further, the membership of both houses was increasingly being filled by men whose qualifications were personal (as proven administrators, financial 'experts', useful 'managers', or whatever) rather than representative of the traditional hereditary and territorial ruling classes. That this critique of contemporary political developments became, after the Revolution, essentially a tory one, a way of explaining the increasing whig domination of politics despite the fact that the tories regarded themselves as (and almost certainly were) a majority party, is why Swift's highly conservative and authoritarian political thought happens to contain so much that is, in one sense, 'whig' and even republican. The attraction of these 'republican' ideas and institutions for Swift was that they could provide a strong authoritarian structure within which to contain individualism, as in Lycurgus's Sparta or the Rome of the early republic.

The most important difference between Swift's analysis of the post-1688 political corruptions and Shaftesbury's 1675 critique of the corrupt court of Charles II is in respect of the church. It is this difference that reveals Swift's essential toryism. In 1675 the bishops had been widely regarded as royal stooges, self-interested men who played up to claims of royal absolutism and preached the divine right of monarchy, passive obedience, and such doctrines in exchange for the crown's support of their own extravagant claims for the church's wealth and power.[74] Swift, of course, could never have subscribed to such ideas. In 1675 he would certainly have been a supporter of Danby's government, which was trying to reforge the old cavalier-Clarendonian alliance between church and state. After the Revolution, when the church was very much on the defensive and began to play a somewhat reduced role in national political life (a trend that became much more pronounced after 1714), Swift continued to think of it as a central organisation in the state.

Swift thus regarded every post-Revolution change and development in politics, religion, and society with distrust and hostility. Yet for all his serious reservations, he always accepted the Revolution, if only from greater fear of the more destructive effects of any counter-revolution. To this extent he became a conservative rather than a reactionary. Many of the particular policies that he would have liked to have seen adopted were reactionary ones, but he accepted the broad outlines of the Revolution settlement. He even came to see himself as a moderate, mediating between slavish Jacobitism on the one hand and atheistic whig republicanism on the other. This is his strategy in *A Tale of a Tub* (at least in the religious satire) and in the 'Sentiments of a Church-of-England Man'. In fact, of course, this grudging, 'balance-sheet' approval of the Revolution put Swift firmly on the tory side. Most people, even most tories, accepted the Revolution with less uneasiness than Swift did. He was exceptional in the importance that he attached to the ideal of a truly national church; in his scepticism about the value of Marlborough's victories, and of military conquests and glory generally; and in his indifference to the material prosperity, economic growth, and national prestige that the new order was supposed to bring. In all these respects his backward-looking attitudes contrast with the cultural optimism of whig contemporaries like Addison, Steele, and Defoe. It would have been an easy transition from these views to the kind of backwoods Jacobitism represented after 1714 by William Shippen and Sir William Wyndham. Swift did not follow them because (despite his temperamental bias towards the authoritarian) his dislike of popery and political absolutism was

---

[74] This is a prominent theme in the 'Letter from a Person of Quality', and recurs in 'The Earl of Shaftesbury's Speech'.

as real as his hatred of whiggism. He could never be a Jacobite any more than he could ever be a whig. He distrusted the individual, whether (to take examples from *A Tale of a Tub*) Louis XIV or Descartes, the Pope or Jack of Leiden. Papal (or royal, or intellectual) infallibility was as obnoxious to him as the pretence of individual inspiration.

iv

In the early morning of 1 August 1714, Queen Anne died in her palace at Kensington. One of the first to be informed of the fact was Lord Bolingbroke, Secretary of State, and effective head of the government since the dismissal of Lord Treasurer Oxford on 27 July. He sent an express with the news to his brother-in-law's house near Faringdon in Berkshire. About noon the courier passed through Wantage, only a few miles from Letcombe Basset, the village where Swift had been staying in 'retirement' since he left London in disgust in May. He received the news about 1.30 (*Corr*.ii.98), just six hours after the queen's death. It was unwelcome but expected, and he knew what it would mean, for himself and for the tory cause. The new king, George I, was certain to favour the whigs, and the new government would initiate an almost complete reversal of the domestic and foreign policies of the old. Swift did not at first think that his exclusion from English politics would be permanent. On 16 August he left for Ireland to take the necessary oaths to the new king, thinking it probable that he would return to London for the winter and politics (*Corr*.ii.112). Just two days after the queen's death, Bolingbroke wrote to Swift with at least an affectation of cheerfulness, either not foreseeing the troubles ahead or else with a euphoria engendered by despair, suggesting that he should come to London to resume his political writing: 'the Whigs are a pack of Jacobites. that shall be the cry in a month if you please' (*Corr*. ii.102). Swift's reply to this letter was altogether more sober in mood and tone. He offers some free criticisms of the past conduct of the tory ministers, but he still sees some hopes of a possible tory revival. Tacitly assuming that Oxford is now discredited and unacceptable to either party, he invites Bolingbroke to assume the position that will most naturally attract Swift's own loyalty: 'To be the head of the Church-interest is no mean station, and that, as I take it, is now in your Lordship's power' (*Corr*.ii.112). Swift offers his services as a writer to the new tory opposition. It would have been very much to the advantage of the tory cause if Bolingbroke had followed Swift's advice. Instead he lost his nerve under the threat of impeachment, fled to France, and briefly (and unsuccessfully) served as Secretary of State to the Pretender. It was Oxford who justified Swift's admiration for his superior steadiness of personal character by staying to face accusation, imprisonment, and eventual acquittal; but he never managed to make a political come-back. Bolingbroke joined the Pretender because he hated the whigs, he was afraid of their revenge, and he saw (temporarily at least) a Jacobite restoration as the best hope of overturning the new whig establishment.[75] For Swift, in 1714 as in 1688, the preservation of the church and its interest was the primary consideration, as he tried to persuade Bolingbroke in his letter. The church could hope for little from George I, but it had much more to fear from the Pretender. Swift himself returned to Ireland, where at first he tried to live quietly, privately, and uninvolved in politics. He would not revisit England until 1726. In 1715 his mail was opened and he was suspected of involvement with the Jacobites; it was even rumoured that he had been arrested.[76] There can be no doubt that the whig government would have liked to have been able to incriminate him, in order to further discredit the queen's last ministry by associating another of its prominent friends with Jacobite intrigue. For several years Swift published nothing, yet in 1715 he began once more to write about politics. His twin themes were the defence of the queen's last ministry, and the abuse of the present whig one; and in treating these themes he would take up Bolingbroke's hint, raising the cry that 'the Whigs are a pack of Jacobites'.

Was Swift a Jacobite? His association with the tory ministry was enough to brand him as one in the opinion of many contemporaries. In 1716 archbishop King, reporting to Swift a rumour that Bolingbroke (recently dismissed from the service of the Pretender) would shortly be pardoned and would return to England, added the gratuitously needling speculation that 'certainly it must not be for nothing, I hope he can tell no ill story of you' (*Corr*.ii.228). Swift's dignified rebuttal of the implied accusation, expressed towards the end of his reply in a tone of

---

[75] For his own account, see his 'Letter to Sir William Wyndham' (written in 1717, though not published until 1753), *Works* (1844), i.111-79, especially pp. 127-35. For a modern biography, see H.T. Dickinson, *Bolingbroke* (1970).

[76] The Duke of Ormonde, writing to Swift from England on 3 May 1715, had heard that his 'papers were seized' and 'Messengers were sent to fetch you over' (*Corr*.ii.166). Swift himself reports the opening of his mail in a letter to Knightley Chetwode (*Corr*.ii.172).

injured innocence that carries conviction, is a most important statement. He assures King that 'had there been ever the least Overture or Intent of bringing in the Pretender during my Acquaintance with the Ministry, I think I must have been very stupid not to have pickt out some discoveryes or Suspicions' (*Corr.* ii.238). It is now known that both Oxford and Bolingbroke were, with whatever intentions, actively carrying on Jacobite negotiations during a great part of Swift's residence in London. It is hard to escape from the alternatives that he was indeed 'stupid' (or perhaps a better word would be 'naive') or that he was lying to King. There are good reasons for regarding the first alternative as the more likely, for we know that in several ways he was curiously imperceptive in his relations with the English ministers. He was certainly imperceptive in his failure to sense the rivalry between the two ministers, and naive in supposing that he could himself heal the rift. It surely is more in keeping with what we know of Swift's character that he was the unwitting dupe, rather than the accomplice, of Oxford and Bolingbroke. Lord Orrery, his first biographer, made one of his shrewder remarks when he described Swift as enjoying the 'shadow', not the 'substance' of the minister's confidence: 'He was employed, not trusted.'[77]

Even if not a Jacobite himself, it may seem absurd to suppose, as is implied by Bolingbroke's remark, that Swift could credibly have used the charge of Jacobitism against the whigs. It had always been the tories who had been suspected, since their support of the proposal for a regency in 1689, of being ill-affected to the Revolution settlement. It was a tory government that had been suspected of plotting to restore the Pretender in 1710-14. It was tories such as Bolingbroke and Ormonde who joined the Pretender in 1715. For all this, the charge of Jacobitism could be deployed against the whigs with great rhetorical advantage. Charles Davenant had made the accusation in *The True Picture of a Modern Whig* (1701), in which he had shown the whigs as willing to plunder the nation under whatever king happened to be on the throne. 'Do you think we care who Rules,' asks the typical whig Tom Double, 'so we can have the Places?'[78] In 1711 Joseph Trapp argued that 'the *Whigs themselves are Jacobites*, if there be any such thing as a *Jacobite* in Nature'. It was the

[77] John Boyle, Earl of Orrery, *Remarks on the Life and Writings of Dr Jonathan Swift* (1752), p. 47; reprinted in *Swiftiana XI* (New York, 1974).

[78] *The True Picture of a Modern Whig*, p. 45.

whigs, Trapp pointed out, who asserted the legitimacy of the Pretender and therefore accepted that he had a hereditary claim to the throne; and the whigs who asserted the lawfulness of resisting established governments.[79] Whig theory thus provided a perfect justification for Jacobitism. Swift made much the same points in the *Examiner* No. 40 (10 May 1711); and in the 'Index' that he compiled for the collected reprint of the *Examiner* (1712), he has this concise entry: '*Jacobites*, vide *Whigs*' (*PW* xiv.7). It was widely believed, and not without truth, that some prominent whigs had made overtures to the exiled James II and later to the Pretender. In 1692, admiral Russell (later Earl of Orford) had been suspected of deliberately failing to follow up his naval victory at Barfleur, a scandal that Swift perhaps alludes to in the passage in *Gulliver's Travels* where the magician exposes the dark secrets of modern history, one of which is the anecdote of the admiral who 'for want of proper Intelligence' was forced to 'beat the Enemy to whom he intended to betray the Fleet' (*PW* xi.199). Several very prominent whigs, among them the Duke of Shrewsbury, were accused of involvement in Jacobite intrigue by Sir John Fenwick at the time of his own arrest for Jacobite activities in 1696.[80] The charge (made earlier by Davenant and others) that the whigs would quite willingly fall in with the Pretender for a larger share of power than Queen Anne would allow them is dramatised in Swift's *Letter from the Pretender to a Whig Lord* (*PW* vi.145-6), a little squib published in 1712 to help discredit whig claims of concern about the danger to the protestant succession. In *The Public Spirit of the Whigs* (1714) Swift suggested that instead of raising the alarm about the tories, whig scaremongers like Burnet and Steele should examine which of the leading whigs 'engaged in a Plot to restore the late King *James*, and received Pardons under his Seal' (*PW* viii.39). Later in the same pamphlet, Swift accused Lord Chief Justice Parker, who had recently presided at the trial and conviction of Hilkiah Bedford (who, though not in fact its author, had accepted responsibility for the crypto-Jacobite treatise *The Hereditary Right of the Crown of England Asserted*, 1713), of having himself 'often drank the abdicated King's Health upon his Knees' (*PW*

---

[79] *The Character and Principles of the Present Set of Whigs* (1711), p. 20. Earlier in the same pamphlet, Trapp presents a typical tory caricature of the whig theory of government (p. 5).

[80] Horwitz, *Parliament, Policy, and Politics*, pp. 182-3.

viii.65).[81] With a history of such charges against the whigs in tory pamphlets, Bolingbroke's suggestion in his letter of 3 August 1714 marked out a perfectly feasible rhetorical strategy for Swift to adopt. This he did (not necessarily, of course, as a direct result of Bolingbroke's suggestion) in the first extended political essay that he wrote in his exile in Ireland, the *Enquiry into the Behaviour of the Queen's Last Ministry* (*PW* viii.131-80).[82]

This pamphlet was begun in June 1715, abandoned and taken up again about 1717 and finished some time before 1721. It was not, however, published until 1765. Despite its title, the *Enquiry* is by no means confined to an 'enquiry' into the politics of 1710-14. It has a great deal to say, usually through implication rather than direct statement, about the policies of the new whig government under George I. Running through the pamphlet is the theme that, while the tory government of Queen Anne was the true friend of the Hanoverian succession, negotiating the peace which allowed the unopposed accession of George I, the whigs are really the Pretender's best friends, not only (as they had been before 1714) in accepting his legitimacy and allowing resistance, but through the national discontent that their self-interested maladministration has created, a condition most favourable to the flourishing of Jacobite sentiment. The methods and arguments that Swift uses to exculpate Queen Anne and her tory ministry are calculated and deployed to reflect on George I and his whig government.

The *Enquiry* is divided into two unequal chapters. The first (which is twice the length of the second) was written in 1715; its subject is the destructive dissensions within the tory government of 1710-14. The second and shorter chapter, begun about 1717, attempts to clear the ministry from the charge of Jacobitism. Despite the time lag between the composition of the chapters, the subject matter of the second is adumbrated in the first, so that the whole seems to have been planned from the start in its present form. Nevertheless, the topic of each chapter had a specific contemporary relevance. In 1715, at the time of the impeachments of the tory leaders and before the outbreak of the Jacobite rising, the most urgent polemical need was the provision of a defence of the old ministry not so much against its enemies as against the internecine feud of pamphlets that had

---

[81] For the Bedford case, see Kenyon, *Revolution Principles*, p. 158.

[82] There is a separate edition of the *Enquiry*, ed. Irvin Ehrenpreis (Bloomington, 1956), with a substantial historical introduction and full notes.

broken out following the publication of Defoe's *Secret History of the White Staff* (September 1714).[83] This pamphlet was intended as a defence of Oxford's part in the tory government, and it provoked replies on behalf of the faction opposed to Oxford, principally of course Bolingbroke. By 1717, however, the unsuccessful Jacobite rising and the Swedo-Jacobite plot, with both of which too many tories had been implicated or associated, had given a new urgency to the need to defend the tory ministry against the old charges of having plotted to restore the Pretender. A theme common to both chapters is the implied contrast between the conduct of the government that Swift is defending and the policies of the current government that he is attacking.

In Chapter 1, Swift describes the tory government as the subject of two opposite and mutually exclusive charges. The ministry, and especially its leader Oxford, had been charged by the more extreme tories of playing a too conciliatory part, of not going far or fast enough with purging the whigs and establishing a thoroughly tory regime. The whigs, on the other hand, accused it of moving only too fast towards the restoration of the Pretender. Swift evidently intended these opposite charges to cancel each other out, with the net result that the Oxford ministry would be seen to have pursued a moderating policy between two extremes (Swift's own favourite rhetorical pose). The implied contrast is with the post-1714 government, which had been dominated by the whigs and which had been pursuing single-mindedly the consolidation of power in exclusively whig hands. Thus when Queen Anne's reluctance to dispense entirely with the whigs is mentioned (*PW* viii.144, 163), the apparent criticism of the queen serves two ulterior purposes. One is that it helps to create a rhetorical impression of impartiality. The second and more important is that it makes an implied criticism of George I for playing so entirely into the hands of the whigs. Swift suggests that, if the queen's last ministry became a tory one, the fault was not with the queen but with the factious whig ministers who refused to continue to serve in it. Queen Anne pressed Somers and Cowper 'somewhat more than became her Dignity to continue in their Stations' (p. 167). George I, by contrast, wilfully neglected the 'glorious Opportunity then in his Majesty's Hands of putting and End to Party Distinctions for the

---

[83] For the pamphlet skirmishes, see Ehrenpreis, introduction to the *Enquiry*, pp. xv-xxi.

time to come' (p. 140) when he came to the throne. Swift ignores, of course, the inconvenient fact that such tories who were offered (admittedly minor) offices refused them. Similarly, what appear at first sight to be accusations that Queen Anne was obstinate and stubborn (pp. 140, 146) are really disguised commendations of her continuing firm to her ideal of non-party government (which, whatever his real views on this subject in 1710-14, it suited Swift in 1715-17 to approve) and underhand criticisms of George I's weakly allowing himself to become the prisoner of the whigs.

The offensive against the whigs is carried on more openly in Chapter 2. Here Swift seeks to undercut the whole charge of Jacobitism by asserting that even the whigs themselves do not really believe it, but only exploit it for party advantage (*PW* viii. 164). His second line of defence is the observation that to have turned national opinion towards the Pretender would, in 1710, have been difficult and would have been a work of time. Since the whigs came to power in 1714, by contrast, 'several Millions are said to have changed their Sentiments' (p. 165). Later Swift links the 'prodigious Disaffection at present' (meaning 1715) with the national disenchantment with the post-Revolution regime in 1690-1. The easiest way to make people favourably disposed towards the Pretender would have been by comparing him with someone worse 'of whom we have had Experience, which was not *then* the Case' (p. 173). The accession of George I has done more for the Jacobite cause, Swift hints, than anything else could have done. A few pages later he again makes a similar insinuation that it would have required 'the visible Prospect of a generall Defection, which (then at least) was not to be hoped for' (p. 177) to have made the restoration of the Pretender practicable. The cumulative effect of these and other hints is to develop a contrast between Queen Anne, who tried hard to act as the monarch of the whole of her people, and George I, who had allowed himself to be used as the tool of a faction; and also between the tories, who were foolish enough to neglect the opportunities they had of perpetuating themselves in power (pp. 174-6), and the whigs, who have entrenched themselves in power by betraying their principles. The theme of the whigs' desertion of their principles is taken up later in Swift's 'Letter to Mr Pope' (1721). In the *Enquiry* it is clearly the whigs who are meant by the description of a party 'acting in Opposition to the true Interest of their Country' who despite their pretence of liberal principles are quite happy to 'chaffer publick Liberty for

Personall Power, or for an Opportunity of gratifying their Revenge' (p. 174). As an example, Swift cites the Septennial Act of 1716 as a notable instance of the sacrifice of supposed whig principle to their hunger for power (p. 176). In all these various ways, then, it is the whigs, not the tories, who are the true Jacobites, for they have done more to make the Pretender and his cause attractive and popular, by rendering George I and his government odious to the people, than ever the Pretender's supposed friends were able to accomplish.

Hatred of George I for his employment of the whigs, and of the whigs for betraying their country for party power, are thus the dominating feelings behind the *Enquiry*. Bold as are some of the reflections in the pamphlet (too bold, it seems for contemporary publication to be considered), none are so outspoken as an apparently rejected paragraph which is found, in Swift's hand but crossed out, in one of the manuscripts. It comes so close to an endorsement of the 1715 rebellion that it is worth quoting at length the first sentence:

> If the King of a free People will chuse to govern by a Faction inferior in Number and Property to the rest and suspected of Principles destructive to the Religious or Civil part of the Constitution, I do not see how a civil War can be avoided. (*PW* viii.218)

It is not clear just where in the *Enquiry* this paragraph would have been placed, but it is obviously a comment on George I and it is not surprising that Swift deleted it as too inflammatory, even for a pamphlet itself about as critical of the government as it well could be. His hatred of George I can also be seen in another bold move that he contemplated in 1718-19, although here again (this time perhaps not entirely from prudential motives) he thought better of it. As early as the 1690s, Swift had contemplated preparing an outline digest of English history. The need for a good brief history of England had long been felt, and Sir William Temple had tried to promote the publication of one. Temple himself wrote an *Introduction to the History of England* (1695), devoted mainly to the reign of William I. Swift evidently thought of his own work as a continuation of Temple's; he began with William II and reached (without completing) the reign of Henry II. In 1718 he evidently had some thought of bringing this fragmentary work to a conclusion for he wrote a dedication to Count Gyllenborg, who had been Swedish ambassador in

London from 1703 until his arrest in 1717 at the time of the scare about the Swedo-Jacobite plot. Gyllenborg was clearly implicated in a plot to use Swedish forces to effect the restoration of the Pretender. Swift says that he had originally intended to dedicate his history to Gyllenborg's master, King Charles XII of Sweden, who had been killed in 1718. Since Charles XII was, at the time of his death, George I's principal antagonist on the international scene, it is hard to think of a more provocative choice of dedicatee for a *History of England*, passing over the more obvious candidate, the present British king. Swift's admiration for Charles XII was perfectly genuine, and can be traced back at least as far as 1709. On 30 October 1709 he wrote to Ambrose Philips that 'My Heart is absolutely broke with the Misfortunes' of the king: his defeat by Peter the Great at Poltava and his flight to Turkey. Swift added, with reference to the hopes he had about this time of securing a diplomatic post, that 'nothing pleased me more in the Thoughts of going abroad than some hopes I had of being sent to that Court' (*Corr*.i.153). Yet this admiration was certainly sharpened by his intense dislike of George I. Swift presumably got to know Gyllenborg reasonably well during his residence in London in 1710-14 (he may have met the count on an earlier visit), and it may have been Gyllenborg who gave him a manuscript containing a Latin character (or rather eulogy) of Charles XII and a Latin poem on the king's defeat at Poltava. Swift valued this manuscript enough to keep it in his possession until his death.[84] In 1712 he certainly made a close acquaintance with the Marquis de Monteleon, the Spanish ambassador, the only diplomat to register a protest at Gyllenborg's arrest in 1717. As late as 1725 Swift would single out Gyllenborg and Monteleon as among the few foreign diplomats whom his young friend James Stopford might meet on his travels in Europe and who would be glad to meet a friend of his (*Corr*. iii.63).

A second pamphlet in which Swift tried to refute the charge of Jacobitism by transferring it to the whigs themselves was his 'Letter from Dr Swift to Mr. Pope', a piece cast in an epistolary

---

[84] It is now in the Henry E. Huntington Library (MS. HM 14366). Its provenance can be traced back to Deane Swift, Swift's editor and biographer, and I therefore assume it passed to him either directly or through Mrs Whiteway; see George P. Mayhew, *Rage or Raillery; The Swift Manuscripts at the Huntington Library* (San Marino, 1967), p. 4. Mayhew describes the manuscript (p. 174), but does not discuss it. For Swift's admiration of Charles XII, see F.P. Lock, *The Politics of 'Gulliver's Travels'* (Oxford, 1980), pp. 56-65.

form and dated 10 January 1721 (*PW* ix.25-34; also in
Corr.ii.365-74). It seems most unlikely that this 'letter' was ever
really sent through the post. It was not published until 1741,
when it appeared in the collection of letters (mainly between
himself and Swift) of which Pope engineered the printing and
publication.[85] There is no reason, however, to doubt that Swift's
date is at least approximately correct, for the piece is closely
related in theme to the *Enquiry into the Behaviour of the
Queen's Last Ministry* (which was completed in 1720 at the
latest) and in occasion to the *Proposal for the Universal Use of
Irish Manufacture* (1720; *PW* ix.15-22). The *Proposal* had been
prosecuted for its alleged subversive tendencies, Chief Justice
Whitshed (as Swift tells Pope in the 'Letter') trying to bully the
jury into a conviction, having 'protested solemnly that the
Author's design was to bring in the Pretender' (*PW* ix.27).
Swift's purpose in the 'Letter' is to clear himself of the charge of
Jacobitism which had now been regularly levelled at him for
several years. As at the beginning of the earlier *Enquiry* and in
the dedication of the 'History' to Gyllenborg, Swift is at pains to
emphasise his private station and also his ignorance of and lack
of interest in current events and personalities. He protests that
his only knowledge of 'the Family which now reigns' comes from
the prayer book; he is 'utterly ignorant' of the 'character and
person' of the new king, 'nor ever had once the curiosity to
enquire into either' (*PW* ix.26,28). Swift's strategy in the 'Letter'
(again as in the *Enquiry*) is to turn the tables on the whigs, this
time by asserting his own firmly-held 'whig' convictions, which
are patently opposite (though Swift does not make this point
explicitly) to those being followed by the present set of whigs in
the English government. This is the strategy that had been used
by Charles Davenant in his 'Tom Double' pamphlets (1701-10),
and more recently by bishop Atterbury in his election manifesto
for the 1715 election, *English Advice to the Freeholders of
England* (1714). In his pamphlet Atterbury had predicted that
the whigs would proceed to break most of their supposed
principles, sacrificing them to their desire to retain and
consolidate their power. In several important respects, such as
the Septennial Act and the maintenance of the standing army,

---

[85] For the complex story of the printing and publication of this volume, see
A.C. Elias, Jr., 'The Pope-Swift *Letters* (1740-41): notes on the first state of the
first impression', *Papers of the Bibliographical Society of America*, lxix (1975),
323-43.

Atterbury's predictions were soon fulfilled.[86]

In the 'Letter to Mr Pope', before setting out his 'whig' principles, Swift makes the important statement that 'I always declared my self against a Popish Successor to the Crown' (*PW* ix.31). This is, at first sight, an endorsement of the Revolution, and written in 1721 it must surely be taken primarily to refer to the question of who should have succeeded Queen Anne. But it may have a secondary reference back to the Exclusion Crisis of 1680-1, and may possibly bear a more equivocal interpretation in relation to the Revolution of 1688. In a very interesting marginal comment in his copy of William Howell's *Medulla Historiae Anglicanae* (9th ed., 1734), Swift says of the Exclusion Bill: 'Wd to God it had passed' (*PW* v.264). His approval of this very whiggish measure is also seen in a marginal comment on Burnet's *History*, where he says of the alternative proposal to place limitations on the power of a popish successor to the crown that 'it was the wisest, because it would be less opposd, and the King would consent to it. otherwise an Exclusion would have done better' (*PW* v.279). Some exclusionists did become tories, usually passing through the 'country' party in the 1690s.[87] But the principal opposition to exclusion came from the church party or tories, and it seems most likely that a mature Swift would, in 1680-1, have taken the side of the church, against exclusion. Yet it is easy to see why, in retrospect, Swift might have wished that the Exclusion Bill had passed. It would have been legal and parliamentary, as Swift notes in another marginal comment on Burnet (*PW* v.279). Excluding an heir would also have involved a much lesser break with the hereditary principle than deposing a reigning king. The exclusion of James in favour of his anglican daughter Mary might have preserved the alliance of church and state more nearly intact. As it was, Danby, who in 1675-9 had tried to implement pro-anglican policies at the head of a conservative ministry, proposed at the Convention in 1689 the

[86] Atterbury's *English Advice* is reprinted in *Somers Tracts*, xiii.521-41, together with a whig reply of the same title (xiii.542-59). Atterbury's pamphlet was published in January 1715, and the government offered a reward of £1000 for information leading to the arrest of its author; G.V. Bennett, *The Tory Crisis in Church and State, 1688-1730: The Career of Francis Atterbury, Bishop of Rochester* (Oxford, 1975), pp. 192-4.

[87] Examples are Edward Harvey of Combe, Sir Eliab Harvey, and Morgan Randyll; see David Hayton, 'The "country" interest and the party system, 1689-c.1720', *Parties and Management in Parliament, 1660-1780*, ed. Clyve Jones (Leicester, forthcoming). I am grateful to Dr Hayton for allowing me to read his paper in typescript.

crowning of Mary as the next heir as an expedient preferable to the tory conscience to declaring the throne vacant and thereby making the monarchy to a degree elective. If James had been excluded, there might have been no Revolution. This would have meant no problems about swearing new oaths, no non-juring separation from the established church, no undermining of the anglican monopoly or of the anglican principles of passive obedience and non-resistance, no special favours for the dissenters. What an attractive prospect this must have seemed to Swift in 1721. Such a slight dynastic change need not seriously have weakened the traditional structures of power and authority. Nothing had done more to establish the right of the dissenters to a legal toleration than James II's ill-advised pursuit of recognition of the rights of his fellow-catholics. So we need not suppose that Swift would have been a whig in 1681 (which he certainly would not have been) to understand why, from the perspective of the 1720s, he might wish that an Exclusion Bill had passed. As elsewhere, Swift was willing to sacrifice the monarch, and even to an extent monarchy itself, to the interests of the church, which had been the real loser in the Revolution settlement. At the Convention in 1689, a motion declaring a popish king inconsistent with the safety of a protestant kingdom passed without opposition in both houses, in sharp contrast to the deep divisions that were revealed by the various particular proposals that came up for discussion. To have been against a 'Popish Successor' was no very radical opinion in 1689 or later.

Outlining his principles after this initial declaration against a popish successor, Swift makes four major points. Three of these refer to important 'old whig' or 'country' principles savouring of the 1690s: his opposition to a standing army (a perennial issue, but one which reached a peak of topical interest in 1697-8); his desire to see annual parliaments (a particularly controversial issue at the time of the agitation about the triennial bills in 1692-4); and his dislike of the expedient of suspending the Habeas Corpus Act (which had happened at the time of the Assassination Plot in 1696). The fourth principle, his 'abomination of the setting up of a moneyed interest', was never an 'old whig' problem, but it can be linked with the old 'country' concern with the problem of corruption and placemen in the Commons. Despite Swift's solemn disclaimer of any knowledge of modern (post-1714) politics, all four of these principles can be directly related to developments since 1714, and together they amount to a comprehensive indictment of the new whig regime and in particular its shameless betrayal or abandonment of true 'whig' principles.[88]

The Habeas Corpus Act had been suspended in 1715 for six months in response to the threat posed by the Jacobite rebellion in Scotland. It permitted the government to arrest and detain without trial such prominent suspected Jacobites as Sir William Wyndham. Many people, some whigs as well as many tories, regarded this suspension as unnecessary, at best an alarmist over-reaction on the part of the government and at worst the setting of a bad constitutional precedent to help it discredit its political opponents. Sir Richard Steele (who had been knighted for his service to the Hanoverian cause), Swift's arch-enemy in 1713-14, had his doubts about the wisdom of the measure and began to write a pamphlet against it. He seems, however, to have been persuaded of the justice of the government's policy, perhaps by his friend Addison, the very type of the new oligarchic, establishment whig.[89] Addison devoted one of his *Freeholder* papers (No. 16, 13 February 1716) to the subject. Swift's comments in the 'Letter to Mr Pope' may have been written in direct opposition to this paper, for he there refutes the analogy with the Roman institution of a temporary dictator which Addison alleged as an historical parallel to justify the suspension. Later in 1716 the whig government passed the Septennial Act, which extended the maximum term of the existing and of all future parliaments from three to seven years. The official reasons given were the unquiet state of the nation in the aftermath of the 1715-16 rebellion and the excessive heats of party rivalries that frequent elections had generated. The real reason behing the measure was obviously that the government was not confident of winning an election fought in 1718. The act had the effect of entrenching the whig government in power until other means could be manipulated to give it greater control of elections. Swift had already commented unfavourably on this expedient in the *Enquiry* (*PW* viii.176) before he came to write the 'Letter'. His belief in short parliaments was genuine and longstanding; his first political mission had been his

---

[88] Kenyon, *Revolution Principles*, pp. 173-99, shows how far the whigs abandoned their principles after 1714.

[89] For the draft pamphlet or periodical essay, see *Steele's Periodical Journalism, 1714-16*, ed. Rae Blanchard (Oxford, 1959), pp. 330-2. Calhoun Winton, *Sir Richard Steele, M.P.: The Later Career* (Baltimore, 1970), suggests that it may have been Addison who persuaded Steele in the bill's favour; Steele spoke for it in parliament (pp. 82-3).

unsuccessful attempt to persuade William III and the Earl of Portland of the virtues of the Triennial Bill that William vetoed in 1693 (*PW* v.193-4).

Opposition to the idea of a 'standing army' was perennial, and nominally at least was voiced by practically everyone. In 1717-18, however, it was an especially controversial and sensitive issue with definite Jacobite overtones and implications. No one was willing to come out openly in favour of the idea of a standing army. Government apologists had instead to explain why (though they were very much against a standing army in principle) it would be unwise and premature to disband the army at this particular moment of great danger from at home and abroad. The rebellion of 1715 had provided such a pretext, as did the Swedo-Jacobite plot of 1716-17. In reality, the government wanted (in 1717-18) to keep up large standing forces (a substantial navy as well as the army) in order to support George I's expansionist foreign policy (principally conceived on behalf of his electorate) in northern Europe. George had acquired Bremen and Verden (formerly Swedish possessions) from Denmark and wished to add them permanently to the electorate of Hanover. To prevent Charles XII (who naturally wished to regain his German dominions) attacking Hanoverian territory by land, George needed a navy (which, as elector, he did not possess) to operate in the Baltic. Under the terms of the Act of Settlement, of course, Britain was not obliged to defend George's continental dominions, and it would have been most unpopular to have admitted that the Baltic fleet was doing just that. Instead, the pretence had to be maintained that they were principally there for the defence of British trade (it was true that vital naval supplies came from the Baltic). In this conflict Swift's sympathies were naturally more with his hero, Charles XII, than with the self-aggrandising George I. In a major and much-publicised speech in the House of Commons on 4 December 1717, the prominent Jacobite William Shippen virtually accused the king of wanting to establish absolutism on the model of his German territories, a reflection with which Swift would certainly have agreed and for which Shippen was committed to the Tower. Much the same issues, with the standing army identified as a symbol of absolutism, were canvassed both in the Commons and the Lords during debates on the Mutiny Bill (an annually-renewed measure designed to protect the fiction that the army was not a 'standing' one) in February 1718. An illustration of the way in which 'old whig' principles were used to attack the government is recorded in the debate on 4 February, when auditor Harley (Lord Oxford's younger brother) quoted from Lord Molesworth's *Account of Denmark* (1694; long established as a classic statement of whig attitudes) on the dangers of standing armies. Molesworth himself (an Irish peer and a member of the English Commons) was in the house at the time and had to try to refute the implied parallels between absolutist Denmark and contemporary England. Thus the 'standing army' was by no means an academic issue when Swift wrote his 'Letter to Mr Pope'; and he would return to the subject in *Gulliver's Travels* (*PW* xi.131, 138).[90]

The attack on the 'moneyed interest', though not strictly an 'old whig' issue, was certainly an old Swiftian theme. It was really a characteristically country-tory concern, and as such had been exploited by Charles Davenant and also by Swift himself in his tory pamphlets and in the *Examiner*. Since the death of Queen Anne, the most important occasion on which the question of the bad effects of 'money' and especially 'credit' had been the centre of controversy was the South Sea speculative fever of 1720. The South Sea Bubble came to epitomise irresponsible financial speculation. Although the South Sea Company had been founded by Harley in 1711, in a move designed to weaken the near-monopoly position of the whig-dominated Bank of England, the Bubble was the result of the company's assumption of a much larger share of the national debt in a scheme sponsored by the whig government in 1720.[91] Swift wrote a ballad on *The Bubble* (*Poems* i.250-9), which he sent to Charles Ford in December 1720 to have printed in London (where it was published on 3 January 1721). The writing of this poem at about the time of the composition of the 'Letter to Mr Pope' shows that Swift was by no means pre-occupied with Irish politics but that he was taking a great deal of interest in contemporary events in England.

The Bubble expresses Swift's dislike of whig financial

[90] For a general study of the issue, see Lois G. Schwoerer, *'No Standing Armies!': The Antiarmy Ideology in Seventeenth Century England* (Baltimore, 1974). For the theoretical objections to standing armies, which go back to Machiavelli, see Pocock, *Politics, Language, and Time*, pp. 118-26, and *The Machiavellian Moment*, especially pp. 411-20. Defoe, unlike Swift, was always in favour of a standing army; see Jean Béranger, 'Defoe et les forces armées dans la nation', *Hommage à Emile Gasquet (1920-1977)*, Annales de la Faculté des Lettres et Sciences Humaines de Nice, No. 34 (Paris, 1978), pp. 119-31.

[91] Plumb, *Sir Robert Walpole*, pp. 293-328; and more generally, John Carswell, *The South Sea Bubble* (1960), and Dickson, *The Financial Revolution*.

chicanery, but with so much popular feeling against the South Sea Company it was hardly a very dangerous poem to print. The 'Letter to Mr Pope', like the earlier *Enquiry into the Behaviour of the Queen's Last Ministry*, is an altogether more subversive pamphlet, although its subversiveness is partially concealed under an appearance of talking about non-current events and issues. But there is no mistaking the contemptuous way the 'Letter' refers to 'the Family which now reigns', nor the ostentatious disclaimer of the panegyric on George I in Thomas Gordon's *Dedication to a Great Man, concerning Dedications* (1719), a pamphlet which had (rather vexingly for him) been attributed to Swift (*PW* ix.28). In the 'Letter' Swift presents himself as so far from being a Jacobite that he is a much better whig (in what he chooses to regard as the true sense of the term) than any so-called whig now in power. He tells how, during his years of influence in Queen Anne's reign, he had often interceded on behalf of whig writers; he implies that no one among the venal whigs will do the same for the now unfortunately-placed tories. Just as he had earlier thought that the Revolution of 1688 had been, on balance, marginally beneficial, so now in the 'Letter' Swift concedes that the balance is still (just) in favour of the Hanoverian regime. In 1716 he had written to archbishop King that 'I look upon the coming of the Pretender as a greater Evil than any we are like to suffer under the worst Whig ministry that can be found' (*Corr*.ii.239). In the 'Letter' he certainly describes about the 'worst Whig ministry' that could be found, and in repeating his belief that Revolution was only justified when present evils are greater than those 'which usually attend and follow a violent change of Government' (*PW* ix.31), Swift implies that the same balance holds in favour of the present government. He never made any secret of his connections and sympathies with known and suspected Jacobites, and was quite willing to write about political themes in ways that would have been recognised as crypto-Jacobite. This was imprudent, for it exposed him to suspicions of being a Jacobite himself. This he never was (indeed he liked to think, and here again he was wrong, that because he was innocent he could act as though he was above suspicion), but he liked to show that he could understand why honourable and thoughtful men, provoked beyond endurance by the corruptions of the whig ministry, were forced (perhaps against their better judgements) to embrace the Pretender as offering the only hope for an end to whig maladministration.

CHAPTER THREE

Swift's Political Values

Swift has often been charged with political inconsistency, with being a political turncoat. His enemies accused him of deserting the whigs and joining the tories in 1710 because, disappointed of preferment by his old party, he hoped to get it from his new one.[1] That Swift regarded himself as in some sense a 'whig' in 1710 and even later is beyond doubt, and he was certainly so regarded by contemporaries. Even after he began to write in support of the new tory government, on several occasions he described himself as still a whig. Writing to his ex-friend Steele in May 1713 he professed himself 'in politics, to be what we formerly called a Whig' (*Corr*.i.359). Swift implied that it was not he, but the whigs who had deserted their principles. Other contemporaries made such claims, and the parties had shifted their ground sufficiently since the 1680s to give them some plausibility. Modern commentators, more sympathetic than Swift's enemies, have generally allowed that Swift was justified in claiming an underlying consistency behind his change of party allegiance. Yet as with many other important questions in Swift studies, opposite interpretations have been advanced. He has been seen as a natural whig driven by circumstances into the tory camp; as a natural tory whose background and connections kept him in the whig fold until he realised his true political home; and as a temperamental moderate who deplored party extremes and looked for a middle way between them.[2] While each of these

---

[1] *An Hue and Cry after Dr S—t* (3rd ed., 1714), p. 8; *Dr S——'s Real Diary* (1715), pp. 3-4; both reprinted in *Swiftiana II: Bickerstaffiana and Other Early Materials on Swift*, 1708-1715 (New York, 1975). Oldmixon accused Swift of having offered his services to Godolphin, and of having turned to the tories in spite at their being refused; *The Life and Posthumous Works of Arthur Maynwaring* (1715), pp. 158, 168, 200.

[2] Ricardo Quintana, *Two Augustans: John Locke, Jonathan Swift* (Madison, 1978), p. 76; Richard I. Cook, *Jonathan Swift as a Tory Pamphleteer* (Seattle,

views contains some element of truth, it is the second that comes closest to expressing the whole truth. Swift was a natural tory.

The terms 'whig' and 'tory' carried precise enough meanings and connotations at any particular juncture, but their significance changed markedly over the course of Swift's involvement in English politics. Contemporaries were fond of pointing this out, and it became a peculiarly tory theme to accuse the whigs of having deserted their principles.[3] Swift offers an account of the history of the two parties in the *Examiner* No. 43 (31 May 1711). Its theme is the moral degeneration of whiggism, and making some allowance for partisan bias it is substantially true. Swift begins by identifying the tories as the upholders of traditional monarchical government, while presenting the whigs as disguised republicans. He notes approvingly that at the Convention in 1689 the tories had supported the regency proposal (which Swift himself favoured). During the course of William's reign, the whigs became the 'court' party through their stronger support of the war effort, while the tories (disenchanted with the new regime and its innovatory tendencies) became the 'country' party of natural opposition. In this way Swift implies that the tories remained firm to their principles, but the whigs changed with the times. In the reign of Queen Anne, the alliance between Marlborough and Godolphin and the whigs is described in terms of a simple conspiracy to monopolise as much power and profit as possible. Swift's is an oversimplified and hardly impartial account; yet it is true that the whigs, who began as an opposition party, had become by 1716 the natural party of government and establishment.

As the parties gravitated between natural opposition and government, they took most of their members with them. There was always, of course, a small group of 'court' supporters without strong party ties, but those politicians who were attached to a party usually remained with it. The only really major politician who can be said to have changed sides was the Earl of Nottingham, who deserted the tories on the question of the peace terms in 1711. Yet he had advocated his policy of 'No Peace without Spain' as early as 1704, when he had been Secretary of

---

1967), pp. x, xvii; Kathleen Williams, *Jonathan Swift and the Age of Compromise* (Lawrence, Kansas, 1958), pp. 100-1.

[3] See for example Simon Clement, *Faults on Both Sides* (1710), reprinted in *Somers Tracts*, xii.678-707, especially pp. 685-6. See also above, pp. 23-4, 127.

State; he could quite plausibly argue that he was remaining true to his principles, and that it was the tories who were reneging on the national war objectives.[4] If sudden changes of allegiance such as Nottingham's were quite exceptional, gradual shifts over a long period were somewhat commoner. Robert Harley entered parliament as a sufficiently extreme whig to vote for the Sacheverell Clause (intended to disqualify most tories from taking part in local politics) in 1689, but he soon moved away from extremism towards moderation, at first in the 'country' party and then as a mild tory. It can certainly be argued that, after first experiencing the evils of extreme partisanship, Harley thereafter remained loyal to the idea of moderate, preferably nonparty government.[5] Those writers who are found in different company at different times may also, like Harley, have seen themselves as loyal to principles rather than party. Defoe, for example, by any test of ideas or principles, was a convinced whig; yet his periodical the *Review* subtly changed its complexion to suit the colour of the government of the day. His motives were, of course, partly prudential, since his finances were precarious and he looked to the government for money for various kinds of service.[6] But he was also a constructive and pragmatic thinker whose natural bent was towards the government because only through the government could plans be translated into action. Swift put principle above party in an almost opposite way. His basic political values were always the same: order, stability, and hierarchy. His loyalties were to the defenders of these values, whoever they might be, and he attacked whoever and whatever he saw as posing the most serious and immediate threat to them. Always a natural tory, for he was by temperament authoritarian, he would stick to his tory values even when these seemed to have been deserted by the tory party of the day. This led him, in 1701, to espouse the cause of the whig lords, impeached by the irresponsible actions of the tory-dominated Commons. In 1710 he supported the tories when

[4] Henry Horwitz, *Revolution Politicks: The Career of Daniel Finch, Second Earl of Nottingham, 1647-1730* (Cambridge, 1968), pp. 172-7, 230-4.

[5] Angus McInnes, 'The political ideas of Robert Harley', *History*, L (1965), 309-22; see also below, note 17.

[6] In *The Machiavellian Moment* (Princeton, 1975), J.G.A. Pocock argues that writers like Davenant, Defoe, and Swift were to some extent 'entrapped' in a 'highly ambivalent rhetoric', and that this makes it unprofitable to ask questions about their sincerity and motivation (p. 446). In my view, Pocock seriously underestimates the relevance of biography to an understanding of political ideas and their development.

they seemed to promise a government conducted in the national interest and not for the benefit of a few individuals. These values would ultimately become embodied in *Gulliver's Travels*, where a wild caricature of whiggism is recognisable in the make-up of the detestably individualistic yahoos; and where the social organisation of the Houyhnhnms expresses the spirit of Swift's toryism.

i

Two difficulties confront any attempt to give a coherent account of the early development of Swift's political thought, from the 'Ode to Sancroft' of 1692 to the *Discourse* of 1701. One is the poverty of the surviving biographical material, with hardly any letters extant. There are a few tantalising glimpses of Swift's political activities: his mission to the king to explain the merits of the Triennial Bill in 1693, his expectation of patronage from Lord Sunderland in 1697. But only surmise can link these isolated facts. The second difficulty has to do with the nature of English politics in the 1690s, when the political world was more complex and less stable than it became under Queen Anne. William III disliked the idea of government dominated by party as much as Queen Anne would, and he was more successful in avoiding it. None of his ministries had so pronounced a party character as did all those from 1705 to the end of the reign of Queen Anne. William was helped by the fact that, in his reign, the parties themselves (even the whigs) were less cohesive; and there was a strong polarity (much weakened after 1700) between 'court' and 'country' that cut across party lines and helped to neutralise strong party loyalties. The 'country party' drew support from both whigs and tories, and although it was never a 'party' in the same sense as the whigs and the tories formed 'parties', it developed its own rhetoric and it enjoyed a range of favourite issues on which it could attract bipartisan support.[7]

---

[7] For an analysis of the 'country' party, see Geoffrey Holmes, *British Politics in the Age of Anne* (1967), pp. 116-47. Much can be learned from Dennis Rubini, *Court and Country, 1688-1702* (1967), but his interpretations should be treated with caution; for more persuasive treatments of the 'country' party, see Henry Horwitz, *Parliament, Policy, and Politics in the Reign of William III* (Manchester, 1977); and David Hayton, 'The "country" interest and the party system, 1689-c.1720', *Parties and Management in Parliament, 1660-1780*, ed. Clyve Jones (Leicester, forthcoming).

Swift's political ideas and attitudes in the 1690s can best be understood as combining the natural toryism of a churchman with the undoubted intellectual appeal of certain 'country' ideas, some of which would later find their place among his political ideals as embodied in *Gulliver's Travels*.

When Swift left the household of Sir William Temple in 1694 to seek ordination, it was in something of a fit of pique.[8] But there is no reason to doubt the genuineness of his vocation for the priesthood, even though external circumstances may have decided the occasion of his seeking it. He had previously decided to enter the church, and had been waiting for a promised sinecure. His leaving Temple may have been linked to Temple's failure to press Swift's claims to an English prebend strongly enough. In January 1695, soon after his ordination as a priest, Swift was presented to the living of Kilroot, near Belfast, where he resided for less than a year. He seems to have left Ireland in mid May 1696, and to have been back with Temple at Moor Park in June. Swift would later describe his task as a clergyman as that of 'defending a post assigned me' (*PW* ix.262), and it may seem bathetic that he should so soon have abandoned his first outpost. Yet his seeking ordination was undoubtedly an act of faith in an institution that seemed to be threatened both from outside and from within. The church was no longer the spiritual arm of the state, as it had been in the golden days of Clarendon and Sheldon. Yet to many Englishmen, including Swift, it still seemed to offer the best bulwark against anarchy and atheism. As a churchman, Swift would always have been a tory. Under William III the church's equivocal relationship with the civil establishment meant that a churchman could also espouse 'country' politics, for the genesis of the new 'country party' was post-Revolution dissatisfaction with the settlement worked out in 1689. No institution of interest had emerged so badly from the Revolution as the church.

There were two directions in which a tory who, like Swift, had favoured the 'regency' proposal at the Convention in 1689, might move politically: towards Jacobitism, or towards the 'country' party. Swift (like his mentor Sir William Temple) was by temperament a conservative, and would naturally take the 'country' alternative, from a real conviction that the Revolution

---

[8] For Swift's ordination and the Kilroot interlude, see Irvin Ehrenpreis, *Swift: The Man, his Works, and the Age* (1962-7), i.145-68. For the condition of the Irish church in Swift's time, see Louis A. Landa, *Swift and the Church of Ireland* (Oxford, 1954).

had gone as least as far as was necessary in constitutional change. As we have seen, he never regarded Jacobitism as practical politics. In 1693 he had his first introduction to the realities of political life at the highest levels when Temple sent him to the king to expound the merits of the Triennial Bill, which had passed both houses of parliament but which the king was reluctant to pass and which in the end he vetoed.[9] Swift's own account of this episode, in his autobiographical fragment 'Family of Swift' (*PW* v.193-4) was written much later (about 1727-9) and is coloured by party prejudice; but the incident is too important to pass over merely because there is no contemporary source for the details of Swift's part and opinions. The bill had been introduced into the House of Lords by the Earl of Shrewsbury; it provided for triennial parliaments for the future, and set a date for the maximum duration of the existing parliament. It was a popular 'country' measure, and it also attracted support (for selfish tactical reasons) from many whigs in the government. William sent his confidential adviser, the Earl of Portland, to seek Temple's opinion. Temple was in favour of the bill, and he subsequently sent Swift to explain his reasons, briefly to the king and at greater length to Portland. The existing parliament, known as the 'Officers' Parliament' from the large number of army officers and other placemen who were members, might become (so country party members feared) as corrupt and compliant as the 'Cavalier Parliament' that Charles II had retained from 1661 to 1679. So the court wanted to keep it, while the country party wanted a dissolution with future parliaments limited to three years. It is easy to see why the bill had Temple's support: it was the same kind of highminded constitutional reform as his scheme for a remodelled privy council that had briefly been tried in 1679.[10] Swift's support of the bill, to the extent that he was not merely repeating Temple's arguments, was also for constitutional reasons. In his 'Letter to Mr Pope' Swift would later say that he 'adored the wisdom of that Gothic

[9] For the Triennial Bill, see Anchitell Grey, *Debates in the House of Commons from the Year 1667 to the Year 1694* (1769), x.299-308; and Narcissus Luttrell, *Parliamentary Diary, 1691-1693*, ed. Henry Horwitz (Oxford, 1972), pp. 390-416 (and also the biographical appendix summarising the political affiliations of M.P.s). For a modern account, see Dennis Rubini, *Court and Country*, pp. 104-14. Swift's future patron, the Earl of Sunderland, may have advised the king to veto the bill; J.P. Kenyon, *Robert Spencer, Earl of Sunderland, 1641-1702* (1958), p. 254.

[10] For Temple's reform of the Privy Council, see Homer E. Woodbridge, *Sir William Temple: The Man and his Work* (New York, 1940), pp. 193-7.

Institution', the annually elected parliament (*PW* ix.32). So drastic a reform was never seriously proposed in the 1690s; triennial parliaments seem to have been regarded as an acceptable substitute.

We do not know in what terms Swift tried to justify the bill to William and Portland. In his later account he cites only one argument, and that a negative one: he claims to have refuted the argument (put forward by opponents of the bill) that Charles I owed his ruin to his passing an earlier triennial bill in 1640. He argued that it was not the triennial bill, but another bill 'which put it out of his power to dissolve the Parliament then in being, without the Consent of the House' (*PW* v.194). We may surely assume that this was at least one of Swift's more important arguments in 1693, if he remembered it thirty years later. Fairly full accounts of the debates in the House of Commons survive, and at least three speakers are recorded as having referred to the precedent of Charles I's triennial bill. Sir John Lowther (a court whig) spoke of 'such a Law as this' as having been 'the ruin of the Nation'. Lowther seems to have confused the triennial with the perpetuating bill, but this does not really make any difference, because two other speakers (Heneage Finch, an opposition tory; and Lord Coningsby, an opposition whig) used the argument that the former triennial bill led naturally to the later and more destructive measure.[11] The different political associations of the three members who are known to have used the precedent of 1640 (other members may, of course, have done so too) is evidence of how confused attitudes to the question were in terms of normal political loyalties. It also seems to be the case that Swift's point about the really mischievous bill having been the perpetuating one had already been made, since both Finch and Coningsby used the 'thin end of the wedge' kind of argument to get round it. William would surely have heard of this argument, and Swift must have had more to say if he hoped to convince the king. Unfortunately the only other comment that Swift makes in his autobiography is that the king's veto of the bill 'put that Prince under a necessity of introducing those People called Whigs into power and Employments, in order to pacify them' (*PW* v.194). This remark (if it is not just later prejudice) shows, as does the reference to Charles I, that Swift supported the bill as a country-

[11] Grey, *Debates*, x.305 (Lowther); Luttrell, *Diary*, p. 393 (Finch), p. 414 (Coningsby).

tory, not as a whig measure. This is important since the bill was both supported and opposed across party lines. There had of course been whigs in the government since 1689, but the demonstration of the government's weakness without them (many whigs having supported the bill in order to embarrass the court) forced William to increase their representation. William did not want to employ them, but the tories had shown themselves too unreliable to be the government's main source of support in the Commons.[12]

Some time between 1693 and 1697 Swift's sympathy for 'country' politics had waned sufficiently for him to seek and hope for patronage from that very personification of the corrupt politics of the 'court', the second Earl of Sunderland. From a modern historical perspective, the last phase of Sunderland's career, as a (mainly unofficial) adviser to William III, can be seen as the most constructive chapter in his political life. That was by no means how his role in the post-Revolution world appeared to his contemporaries. They could not easily forget his sponsorship of pro-French policies under Charles II, or his subservience to James II's despotic ambitions, or his opportunistic conversion to catholicism. Few politicians were so universally mistrusted and unpopular. His influence on William III appeared sinister. When in 1697 he accepted the office of Lord Chamberlain, fear of his enemies and awareness of his vulnerability made him resign it after only a few months, despite William's willingness, indeed strong desire, that he should continue. In 1697 it made very good sense to look to Sunderland as a source of patronage; in April 1697 his influence was stronger than it had ever been. On 1 December 1697 Sir William Trumbull, one of the Secretaries of State, resigned in disgust (he had been unhappy in office for some time, and this was the last straw) when a coveted prebend of Windsor went not to his brother, for whom he had requested it, but to a rival nominee of Sunderland.[13] Such a prebend was exactly the kind of sinecure that Swift was looking for, and for which (he would later claim) Temple had secured the king's promise.[14] If Sunderland had

[12] Horwitz, *Parliament, Policy, and Politics*, pp. 114-18; Kenyon, *Sunderland*, pp. 250-1.

[13] Kenyon, *Sunderland*, pp. 290, 295-6; my account of Sunderland is based on Kenyon's biography.

[14] Since Sunderland's resignation came as a surprise to many (the king even refusing to accept it at first), Swift's looking for patronage from him may not have been the mistake that Ehrenpreis supposes (*Swift*, i.262). The king's promise of a prebend is mentioned in Swift's letter to his uncle William Swift of 6

remained in power, Swift might have been rewarded (for a pamphlet in the minister's defence?) with a prebend or some other ecclesiastical plum. But it may still appear strange that a man of Swift's integrity should seek preferment from an unprincipled rogue, such as most contemporaries regarded Sunderland.

The most obvious source from which Swift could have obtained a more favourable estimate of Sunderland was of course the earl himself. Sunderland had known Temple since the reign of Charles II and Temple's diplomatic days, and we know of at least two occasions during Swift's residence when Sunderland stayed at Moor Park: in September 1694, and in July 1697 when he brought the terms of the peace to show Temple. Swift regarded the connection as important, for in his preface to the third part of Temple's *Memoirs*, which he edited and published in 1709, he went out of his way to speak respectfully of Sunderland, who had died in 1702 (*PW* i.268); and he sent an inscribed copy to his son, the third earl, from whom he may have retained some hopes of patronage.[15] As late as 1731 Swift would recall Sunderland's visits to Moor Park with an affectionate amusement (*Corr*.iii.458). Sunderland's cynicism, shocking to his more conventional contemporaries, would more likely have endeared him to Swift. Some bond of personal sympathy is certainly suggested by the tone in which Swift announced: 'My Ld Sunderland fell and I fell with Him' (*Corr*.i.26). This was on the occasion of Sunderland's resignation. The two men certainly shared many political ideas and principles. Sunderland was not a 'party' man but a 'royal servant' (in other words, a natural tory) in the ministerial tradition of Clarendon and Danby, and subsequently of Godolphin and Harley. He was a political elitist, contemptuous of representative institutions; like Swift, a temperamental extremist. He was a francophile, and a man of culture; Dryden had chosen to flatter him (in the dedication to *Troilus and Cressida*) by supposing him capable of founding an English academy, just as Swift would later flatter Harley. There is

---

December 1693 (*Corr*.i.12), and later in his autobiographical fragment, where Canterbury and Westminster are specifically mentioned (*PW* v.195). A prebend of Windsor was a very desirable preferment; in 1713 it still seemed a suitable reward for Swift's services to the tories (*JS* ii.661-2; *Poems*, i.173).

[15] For Sunderland's visits to Moor Park, see Kenyon, *Sunderland*, pp. 268, 285, 292. The presentation copy of Temple's *Memoirs*, Part III, to the third earl is now at Trinity College, Cambridge; see *The Rothschild Library* (Cambridge, 1954), ii.649 (No. 2408).

evidence that Sunderland would, in the later 1690s, have liked to have increased tory representation in the government as a counterweight to the excessive power of the whig Junto. He was on good terms with Harley, and in 1700 he tried to induce Harley to join a moderate tory ministry. Sunderland had shown a sympathetic understanding of Irish problems, and he had supported that favourite of the backbench tories, the land bank.[16] These are some of the ways in which Swift, who had not known Sunderland in the more disreputable periods of his career, might well have formed a sympathetic attitude to the earl that would have made it seem perfectly proper to use him as possible source of promotion without thinking that to do so might compromise his integrity or his principles.

Some parallels have already been suggested between Sunderland and Robert Harley. Both men saw their proper role as that of managers of a government above party, an ideal that (however impracticable in contemporary conditions) appealed to Swift, even if (in practice) what Swift meant by this was very close to a tory government. Harley entered parliament in 1689, and at first he was a committed whig. By 1692, however, he was on friendly terms with 'country' tories like Sir Christopher Musgrave, and in 1701 he was elected Speaker of the House of Commons as the 'country' as opposed to the 'court' candidate. Of all the tory ministers in Queen Anne's reign, he was always the most open to seeking support from the moderate whigs and the least keen to pursue high-flying tory policies.[17] Swift was never an extreme whig, but his political development over the course of the 1690s shows the same kind of movement towards a centre-tory position. Harley did not accept office until 1702; in 1701 indeed, he was a leader of the tory opposition that Swift attacked in his *Discourse*. Swift's conversion from 'country' to 'court' had been completed by 1697, when he sought patronage from Sunderland; Harley's took somewhat longer. In 1705 Harley would claim (although by then he had allied himself on different

[16] See Kenyon, *Sunderland*, especially pp. 85 (Dryden's dedication), 141 (Ireland), and 278 (the land bank). Bishop Burnet says that Sunderland claimed that the land bank would help reconcile the tories to the government; *History of his Own Time* (Oxford, 1833), iv.308.

[17] How far Harley's 'moderation' was a matter of genuine conviction, and how far it was mere opportunism is a difficult question; for a balanced appraisal, see Geoffrey Holmes, *British Politics in the Age of Anne*, pp. 265-8. Angus McInnes, 'The political ideas of Robert Harley', and *Robert Harley: Puritan Politician* (1970) is much more favourable to Harley.

occasions with practically every group in the House of Commons) that 'I have the same principles I came into the House of Commons with'.[18] Both Harley and Swift would have claimed that the consistency in their political principles had been their defence of what they saw as the true constitution of the country against the attempts of selfish minority groups to capture it and exploit it for their own ends. Under William III, Harley had seen this threat as coming from the court. Under Queen Anne he came to see the threat as emanating from the overmighty combination of the Marlborough-Godolphin alliance.

In 1693, when he wanted to persuade the king to pass the Triennial Bill, Swift thought that the royal prerogative might reasonably be curtailed. By 1697, when he allied himself with Sunderland, he had obviously adopted a 'court' perspective. The change cannot be dated precisely, but it can be associated with his experience in the presbyterian-dominated parish of Kilroot. The most immediate literary result of his period at Kilroot was *A Tale of a Tub*, which may have been begun there and which was certainly influenced by his experience there. Swift himself said that the 'greatest Part' of the *Tale* had been written in 1696 (*PW* i.1). This date has been generally accepted, at least for the religious satire; the digressions are thought to be somewhat later, probably 1697-8.[19] Politics do not feature very prominently in the *Tale*, at least not directly, but it is easy to perceive Swift's political values behind both the religious and the literary satire. The ideal order is equally subverted by the personal authoritarianism of Peter and by the rampant individualism of Jack; while the world of the 'modern' author of the digressions is a parody or inversion of normal values. Contemporary society, as it is depicted both in the adventures of the brothers and in the world of the Grub-Street hack, is a more vividly imagined version of the upside-down world of the pindaric odes, reminding one most of the 'Ode to the Athenian Society'. The ideal order is set against meaningless, frenetic activity; change can only be for the worse. There is some direct political comment. In the 'Digression concerning Madness' political extremism is presented as one of the forms of unsuspected madness, and Swift alludes (among more distinguished historical figures) to four

[18] Letter of 16 October 1705 to Sir Robert Davis; Historical Manuscripts Commission, *Portland Manuscripts*, iv (1897), 261.

[19] Ehrenpreis, *Swift*, i.186-7.

contemporary English politicians: Sir Edward Seymour, Sir Christopher Musgrave, Jack Howe, and Sir John Bolles (*PW* i.111). The first three of these were among the leading tory extremists, prominent members and frequent speakers in the House during the whole of the 1690s and beyond. They might have appeared in any list of tory hotheads drawn up in these years. Bolles, however, was a much less important politician, and his inclusion may yield a possible clue as to the occasion for Swift's disgust with the 'country' tories and his re-orientation towards the court. Bolles was widely regarded as half-mad. He achieved notoriety in 1701, when he was chosen to chair the committee appointed to draw up the Act of Settlement; according to bishop Burnet, the choice of Bolles was intended to express the tory party's contempt for the protestant succession, that they should entrust it to such a madman.[20] This cannot, however, be the occasion for Swift's allusion to Bolles, or at least it would be inconsistent with his attempts elsewhere in the *Tale* to maintain consistency in topicality, as with the two 'fine Gentlemen' in Section II (*PW* i.52). An occasion in 1696 can be suggested, though only tentatively. When the Assassination Plot was discovered in February, an association (modelled on the Elizabethan one) was drawn up in support of the king; its terms were much like those of the abjuration oath which had troubled tory consciences in 1695. When the association was introduced into the Commons on 25 February 1696, eighty-nine M.P.s (the hard-core tories) refused to sign it; they included all four of those listed by Swift in the *Tale*.[21] Swift returned from Kilroot in the spring of 1696. He would have abhorred the plot itself, and since he rejected the *de facto* theory he would not have had much sympathy with those who refused the association. He would certainly have disapproved of the actions of the more extreme tories who, when parliament reassembled in October, fought a factious battle against supply. This small group (of about fifty M.P.s) was led by Seymour, Musgrave, and Howe. Bolles is not referred to as a leader, but on two of the three crucial divisions he was one of the two tellers for the minority, which suggests a certain standing within the group.[22] Whether or not this was the occasion that gave rise to Swift's allusion in *A Tale of a Tub* is

[20] Burnet, *History of his Own Time*, iv.499-500 ('Sir John Bowles'); for other anecdotes of Bolles, see Geoffrey Holmes, *British Politics*, p. 89, note †.

[21] Horwitz, *Parliament, Policy, and Politics*, pp. 175, 338-57.

[22] Horwitz, *Parliament*, p. 184; *Journals of the House of Commons*, 26 October, 3 and 4 November 1696. Bolles was a teller on the first two occasions.

unprovable; it was certainly the kind of situation that could easily have given him a disgust at the merely factious tactics of the 'country' party. Even the limited degree of condonement of the plot implied by the refusals to sign the association might have shocked Swift into feeling that the real constitutional threat to order, stability, and hierarchy now came not from the hard-pressed king but from the selfish factiousness of the House of Commons. That such was his attitude in 1701 is amply demonstrated by the *Discourse* of that year. The turning point may well have been 1696.

ii

Swift described himself as a whig on occasion, and looked to whig ministers for patronage, but he was strangely reluctant to publish political pamphlets on the whig side of contemporary questions. Before he joined the tories as a propagandist in 1710 he published just two political pamphlets, each nominally 'whig' yet each actually revealing rather the limits of Swift's whiggishness than his wholehearted commitment to the cause. *A Letter from a Member of the House of Commons in Ireland, to a Member of the House of Commons in England, concerning the Sacramental Test* (*PW* ii.111-25; published December 1708, though dated 1709) is a warning to the anticlerical element in the whig party, and to those who favour the dissenters, not to attempt to repeal the Test Act. The fictive author of the pamphlet describes himself as a good whig, and one of Swift's aims is to show that (in Ireland at least) there is no inconsistency in being both a whig and a churchman. In English terms, however, the *Letter*'s defence of the church, the clergy, and the Test Act made it a distinctly tory-looking tract, whatever its Irish-whig guise. Archbishop King, guessing Swift's authorship, asked him 'pray by what artifice did you contrive to pass for a Whig?' (*Corr*.i.123).

The other pamphlet that Swift published before he joined the tories was the altogether more important *Discourse of the Contests and Dissensions between the Nobles and the Commons in Athens and Rome, with the Consequences They Had upon Both Those States* (*PW* i.195-236; 1701). This piece has the best credentials of any of Swift's pamphlets for being thought 'whiggish'. It was published in defence of the four recently-impeached lords, of whom three were leaders of the whigs. When

Swift returned to England in 1702, he revealed his authorship of the tract and this brought him into friendly contact with two of the impeached lords, Somers and Halifax (*PW* viii.119). Swift evidently expected them to aid his search for preferment, and it must be to the *Discourse* that he was referring when he reproached the whigs with ingratitude (*JS* i.13). Contemporary pamphleteers attributed the *Discourse* to the veteran whig champion, bishop Burnet. On the basis of the connections with the whig leaders that his authorship of the *Discourse* had helped to establish, Swift would later try to solicit the remission of the First Fruits and Twentieth Parts for the Irish church. While in London for this purpose in 1707-9 he became friendly with such whig wits as Addison, Steele, and Ambrose Philips. In November 1710 Swift had, in Ireland at least (news of his new intimacy with Harley not having reached there), the reputation of being so much 'a favourite of the late party in power' (*Corr*.i.189) that he was removed from his commission, ironically enough just as he had succeeded in it.

There are, however, certain other circumstances about the publication of the *Discourse* that (even without an examination of the text of the pamphlet itself) serve to qualify the idea (admittedly fostered by Swift himself) that it was a whig tract. In the dozen years since the Revolution, the two parties had been gradually reversing their traditional roles. The whigs had become courtiers and administrators, the tories increasingly identified with the 'country' party and opposition. This process reached a climax in 1701, in which year it was the tories who (in Swift's view) were acting as dangerous demagogues and the whigs who were defending the royal prerogative. Swift had lived in London for over ten years without writing a political pamphlet; if he had been 'watching for an opportunity to make himself useful to the Whigs', as has been suggested, it seems curious that he chose the moment when they were acting like old-fashioned tories.[23] In 1701 Swift had already written (in 1696-8) *A Tale of a Tub*, although he would not publish it until 1704. The 'Digression concerning Madness', although for topical reasons some of the contemporary politicians it uses as examples are tories, is a complete indictment of whiggism in a

[23] Frank H. Ellis, introduction to his edition of Swift's *Discourse* (Oxford, 1967), p. 15. Although I do not share Ellis's view that the *Discourse* is a whig tract, I am greatly indebted to his edition, which provides a full account of the pamphlet's historical context, full notes on the classical sources, and texts of the contemporary attacks.

broad sense. Elsewhere in the *Tale* Sir Humphrey Edwin, the Lord Mayor of London who (in 1697) attended dissenting services in full civic regalia, is singled out for attack (*PW* i.131). No 'whig' would have attacked the dissenting interest so strongly. In 1701, the same year as the publication of the *Discourse*, Swift also published his edition of a third volume of Sir William Temple's essays or *Miscellanea*. At the head of the collection he placed 'Of Popular Discontents', an essay which Temple had written at the time of the disorders and disturbances fomented by the demagogue Shaftesbury during the Popish Plot and Exclusion Crisis in 1679-81.[24] Swift evidently regarded this essay as apposite in the situation of 1701. As we shall see, the real purpose of the *Discourse* is not so much a defence of the four lords as an attack on popular participation in government in the conservative tradition that can be traced back through Temple's essay to classical antiquity.

There are important differences between the rhetorical strategy of the *Discourse* and the methods that Swift would use as a political pamphleteer in 1710-14. In the later pamphlets he appeals for agreement to the reader's common sense and prejudices, with less use of theory and appeals to authority (Swift tries to sound authoritative himself instead) and fewer citations of classical examples. Swift does use such devices as parallel history and allegory in the *Examiner*, but their role there is subordinate. This is as we would expect, for the *Discourse* was written when his reading was still 'fresh in his Head', as he would say of *A Tale of a Tub* (*PW* i.1). In 1701 Swift felt able to flatter his readers by supposing them capable of following quite recondite classical parallels and applying the examples to the contemporary situation. In his later pamphlets, writing for the government and not just for himself, he is heavier-handed and more concerned to make sure that his point is driven home. Yet there are similarities of technique between the early and the later works. The *Discourse*, like the later *Conduct of the Allies*, begins with a great question-begging statement of principle. Swift claims as self-evident and agreed on all sides an 'absolute unlimited Power' (*PW* i.195) in all government; this would certainly have been denied by both Locke and Hoadly.[25] Just as

---

[24] Woodbridge, *Sir William Temple*, pp. 248-53.

[25] Locke, *Two Treatises of Government*, II, 170-4; ed. Peter Laslett (Cambridge, 1960), pp. 399-400. Charles Leslie argued that an absolute power, wherever placed, overthrew the Locke-Hoadly theory of consent; the *Rehearsal*, Vol. III, No. 7 (24 April 1708).

in the *Conduct* Swift begins with a series of supposedly hypothetical situations, so the main body of the *Discourse* (Chapters II and III) is concerned with historical examples drawn from classical Greek and Roman history, with hardly a hint that they have any application to contemporary England. Thus by the time they reach Chapter IV, where Swift begins in earnest to make his applications, readers have been conditioned into accepting Swift's interpretations; for both the general principles and the historical examples have been presented as matters of fact rather than opinion. In its basic rhetorical strategy, then, the *Discourse* partly anticipates Swift's characteristic later methods, although (and here again its closeness in time to *A Tale of a Tub* is suggestive) it is a more intense and energetic piece of writing than most of the later tory pamphlets.

Several reasons can be suggested for Swift's decision (which he never repeated for any of the later pamphlets) to cast the *Discourse* in the form of 'parallel history' rather than as a direct commentary on contemporary events. One is that readers seem to have responded to indirect political comment with something of the excitement that attends the clandestine, a survival from the period when any political discussion might be attended with dangers. Another is the old hermeneutic principle that what is sought with difficulty is found and enjoyed with the greater pleasure.[26] Perhaps most important for Swift himself was the authority conferred by the historical parallels, at a time when no one doubted the value or the relevance of historical analogies. Parallels could be drawn from many sources: the Bible, classical antiquity, English or European history. In his *Introduction to the History of England* (1695), Sir William Temple had written a sympathetic account of the reign of William I as an indirect defence of William III. In his *Discourse upon Grants and Resumptions* (1700), a tory piece attacking the four impeached lords, Charles Davenant made much more detailed (though correspondingly harder to follow) use of medieval English history than Temple had; his purpose was to find parallels for the wicked and corrupt ministers. In his poem *The Dyet of Poland* (1705) Defoe used the chaotic political conditions of contemporary Poland for a thinly-disguised attack on the factious tories who opposed the whig policy of wholehearted

[26] This idea can be traced back through Petrarch to St Augustine; D.W. Robertson, Jr., *A Preface to Chaucer* (Princeton, 1962), p. 62.

prosecution of the war.[27] In this last case the 'parallels' are so attenuated as to be in effect little different from the creation of an imaginative allegory, as in the anonymous *Free State of Noland* (1701), where 'Noland' is transparently England under a new name.

There were good reasons for Swift's choice of classical rather than English or modern European parallels. His view of history was uniformitarian, in that he believed that human nature itself was a constant; but he also believed in historical cycles and recurrences, so that only parallels from comparable periods and countries would be valid. In practice, this excluded the middle ages and most of modern Europe, whose political systems were too different from England's. The favourite choices were naturally the city-states of Greece, and republican Rome, civilized societies which had enjoyed systems of mixed government (combining monarchic, aristocratic, and popular elements) similar to England's. There were other advantages in using these as sources. Those periods of classical history studied in the school texts would be familiar to the whole of the educated reading public. Everyone would have heard of Cato or the Gracchi, while very few would have been able to appreciate Davenant's allusions to obscure medieval ministers. The major characters of classical history also came, so to speak, ready moralised. The classical historians themselves had written their histories to teach moral and political lessons, and their characters belonged to (indeed they often defined) recognisable moral types. Thus parallels with classical history carried a kind of implicit moral authority. The character and achievements of a Cato or a Caesar were known, so that the establishment of a parallel would include the application of the common moral judgment. Thus when Addison's *Cato* was staged in 1713, Marlborough was identified either with Cato or with Caesar, according to political prejudices; but it occured to no one to interpret Caesar as the hero.[28]

It was not, however, altogether to Swift's advantage that Roman history and its interpretation was so familiar to his readers. For the standard reading of Roman history was an

[27] On Temple's history, see Woodbridge, *Sir William Temple*, pp. 254-61. For a brief account of Davenant's *Discourse* (actually published late 1699), see Ellis, introduction to Swift's *Discourse*, pp. 17-21. There is an annotated edition of Defoe's *Dyet of Poland* in *POAS*, vii.72-132.

[28] John Loftis regards the 'political meaning' of *Cato* as 'still enigmatic'; *Politics of Drama in Augustan England* (Oxford, 1963), p. 57.

unfortunately 'whig' one, in which it was usual to contrast the virtue and liberty of the republic with the luxury, slavery, and despotism of the empire.[29] Thomas Hobbes had complained in *Leviathan* that reading (or rather, mis-reading as he saw it) classical history tended to put subversive political notions into young men's heads; Sir Robert Filmer agreed with him on this point.[30] Swift records that such had been his own experience. He once told Lord Somers that being 'long conversant with the Greek and Roman authors, and therefore a lover of liberty' he was 'much inclined to be what they called a Whig in politics' (*PW* viii.120). Steele was thus exposing his ignorance both of the classics and of education when in 1714 he complained that the (mainly tory) clergy preached high-flying political ideas learned 'from the pompous Ideas of Imperial Greatness, and Submission to absolute Emperors, which they imbibed in their earlier Years'.[31] Nothing could be further from the truth, as Swift was quick to point out (citing Hobbes); the common school texts taught liberty, not despotism (*PW* viii.37). This 'whig' interpretation of Roman history is found at length in Algernon Sidney's *Discourses concerning Government* (1698), and it was not seriously challenged until the middle of the eighteenth century. It was a problem for Swift in writing his *Discourse* that the Gracchi, whom his plan required him to present as irresponsible demagogues, were widely regarded as popular heroes, as they were by Sir William Temple.[32] Fortunately there

[29] For modern studies, see Addison Ward, 'The tory view of Roman history', *Studies in English Literature*, iv (1964), 413-56; James William Johnson, *The Formation of English Neoclassical Thought* (Princeton, 1967), especially pp. 31-68; and Howard D. Weinbrot, *Augustus Caesar in 'Augustan' England: The Decline of a Classical Norm* (Princeton, 1978).

[30] Hobbes, *Leviathan*, Part II, Chapter 21; ed. Michael Oakeshott (Oxford, 1947), pp. 140-1. Filmer quotes this passage approvingly in his 'Observations upon Mr Hobbes's *Leviathan*', *Patriarcha and Other Political Works*, ed. Peter Laslett (Oxford, 1949), pp. 244-5. Hobbes himself (unlike Swift) escaped the pernicious effects that came too often from classical history; in his Latin verse autobiography he records that it was Thucydides who first taught him the folly of democracy and the superiority of government by one man or an oligarchy; 'Vita'; *Opera Philosophica quae Latine Scripsit Omnia*, ed. William Molesworth, i (1839), lxxxviii. Hobbes subsequently translated Thucydides in order to make available an adequate version of a good, anti-democratic historian. In 1698 Swift read and made an abstract of Hobbes's translation; *A Tale of a Tub*, ed. A.C. Guthkelch and D. Nichol Smith (2nd ed., Oxford, 1958), p. lvii.

[31] *The Crisis*, dedication 'To the Clergy of the Church of England'; *Tracts and Pamphlets*, ed. Rae Blanchard (Baltimore, 1944), p. 130.

[32] In 'Of Popular Discontents' (published in *Miscellanea*, Part III, 1701), Temple called the Gracchi 'the truest lovers of their country'; *Works* (1814), iii.33.

were alternative interpretations on which Swift could draw, such as Jean Bodin's in his *Six Livres de la République* (1576), from which Filmer had taken his examples from classical history.[33] In the *Discourse*, however, Swift does not confront the 'whig' interpretation directly. Instead he accepts the wisdom of Roman republican institutions, but attributes the downfall of the republic to the encroachment of popular power (*PW* i.221-2). In the *Republic* (VII, 544c-569c), Plato had argued that the tyranny of the many would inevitably lead to the tyranny of a single person; this is how Swift presents Roman history in the *Discourse*.

Swift's political theory in the *Discourse* is based on a distinction between power and its exercise. Thus he places an 'absolute unlimited Power' of last resort in the people as a whole (*PW* i.195). Yet the possibility of the actual exercise and abuse of this power was frightening. In the 'Sentiments of a Church-of-England Man' Swift would reject arbitrary power, whether in the hands of one man or many, as 'a greater Evil than *Anarchy* itself; as much as a *Savage* is in a happier State of Life, than a *Slave* at the Oar' (*PW* ii.15). The people's absolute power Swift places ordinarily in the legislature as a whole, and in cases of extreme necessity in the people themselves (*PW* ii.16-22). This division is very useful to him in the *Discourse*, for it means that when he dislikes the proceedings of the legislature he can appeal to the people, yet when popular opinion is running against him he can take refuge in legislative authority. To the extent that he makes absolute submission to constituted authority the rule, Swift is obviously much closer to Hobbes than he is to Locke. As we have already seen, he was unwilling to provide any theoretical justification of the Revolution of 1688, preferring to rely on tory arguments such as that from the necessity of events, or (as in the 'Sentiments') evading the issue through the use of a *reductio ad absurdum* (*PW* ii.22).[34] In practice, however, Swift modifies his theoretical absolutism by accepting the commonplace idea of a

---

[33] Swift's annotated copy of the Paris, 1579 edition was No. 591 in the sale catalogue of his library; Harold Williams, *Dean Swift's Library* (Cambridge, 1932). For Swift's marginalia on Bodin, see *PW* v.244-7; as with Hobbes, Swift's basic objection to Bodin is to his placing absolute power in the executive. I have used Jean Bodin, *The Six Bookes of a Commonweale*, ed. K.D. McRae (Cambridge, Mass., 1962), which reprints the 1606 English translation with notes on the variations between Bodin's different editions and texts. For Filmer's use of Bodin as a quarry for classical examples, see *Patriarcha*, ed. Laslett, pp. 86-8.

[34] See above, p. 98.

necessary 'balance of power' within the state, and this is his major concern in the *Discourse*.

A mixed government, Swift says, combining monarchic, aristocratic, and popular elements, is based on 'Nature and Reason', being found not only in the admired governments of the gothic past but also in the governments of classical antiquity, most especially in those of Sparta and republican Rome, which Polybius had singled out as the most stable and lasting (*PW* i.196-7). All this is commonplace, but Swift makes somewhat unscrupulous use of the idea of the 'balance' when he describes it as something held by the monarch, who deals 'the remaining Power with the utmost Exactness into each Scale' (*PW* i.197). This gives the monarch the really decisive role, for he is not (as might have been expected in a 'mixed' government) a king with fixed and limited powers but a free agent able to alter the balance of power at will. His part is analogous to that of the political 'trimmer' described by the Marquis of Halifax in his handbook of pragmatic toryism, *The Character of a Trimmer* (written in 1684, though not printed until 1688), an influential pamphlet which may have suggested to Swift the basic format of his 'Sentiments of a Church-of-England Man'. Halifax had suggested that the wise 'trimmer' would determine his course in the light of whatever posed the greatest current constitutional danger. Thus Halifax himself had opposed exclusion in 1680-1, but later opposed the policies of James II and accepted the Revolution.[35] From the birth of the two parties under Charles II, it had been traditional for the tories to regard popular power as the greater threat, and to uphold the royal prerogative as a guard against it; and for the whigs to seek to restrain the prerogative and to defend popular liberties. In practice, however, both parties used either argument as it suited their current aims. Thus in a speech in the House of Lords on 20 October 1675, the whig leader the Earl of Shaftesbury argued that the current threat to the constitution came from the attempt of the House of Commons to restrict the judicial functions of the House of Lords. He did this because the government (to which he was in opposition) had a majority in the lower house. Yet in 'A Letter from a Person of Quality', a pamphlet written in the same year either by Shaftesbury himself or under his close supervision, we

---

[35] The fullest study is still H.C. Foxcroft, *The Life and Letters of Sir George Savile, Bart., First Marquis of Halifax* (2 vols, 1898), which includes an edition of *The Character of a Trimmer* (ii.280-342).

find the more natural whig argument that the constitution was being undermined by the court party, with the support of the bishops and office-holders in the House of Lords. Here he shows no interest in preserving the powers of the Lords as a constitutional bulwark.[36] In 1701, the year of Swift's *Discourse*, the situation was even more complicated. The impeachments of the four lords were being pressed by a tory-dominated House of Commons; yet popular sentiment in the country as a whole was (or at least, it was successfully being manipulated so as to appear) strongly against the impeachments and in favour of making the legislature's first priority preparations for the inevitable war against France, not useless recriminations about the past.

This peculiar situation allowed Swift to manipulate the idea of the 'people' and their political power as it suited him. He lodges, as we have seen, a power of last resort in the people, though only to be exercised in great emergencies. This allows him to appeal over the heads of the House of Commons to the people as a whole, as when he defines the maxim 'Vox populi, vox dei' in terms of 'the Universal Bent and Current of a People; not the *bare Majority* of a few Representatives' (*PW* i.225). But he does not say how this 'Bent and Current' of the people is to be known, if not through their elected representatives; unless (which is the implication) the king is to be guided by it in dealing out 'the remaining Power' (*PW* i.197). Swift would always regard the actual exercise of power by the people or their representatives as likely to result in chaos and national decline, and his whole interpretation of Roman history in Chapter III of the *Discourse* is designed to show this. He thought that parliaments were indeed important, but the role he assigned to them was a strictly limited one. This was why he was in favour of annually elected parliaments (*PW* ix.32), a reform which would have considerably reduced the influence of individual M.P.s and reduced the legislature to what Swift thought it ought to be, a jealous check on the executive. Swift deplored the exercise of executive power by the parliament, as had happened at the time of the Civil War and as threatened to happen again in 1701. His idea of the proper role of parliaments is described in the *Discourse* in terms of the constitutional practice in Rome under Romulus: 'the *People* being only convoked upon such Occasions, as by this Institution

---

[36] *State Tracts* (1689), pp. 57-61 (Shafesbury's speech) and 41-56 ('A Letter'); see also above, pp. 115-17.

of *Romulus*, fell into their Cognizance: These were to constitute Magistrates, to give their Votes for making Laws, and to advise upon entering on a War' (*PW* i.212). Even upon such occasions, the voices of the people cannot overrule the decisions of the patricians or the king. By analogy, Swift implies that the same conditions were roughly true of England from the reign of William I to that of Henry III. Since then the power of parliament has gradually grown until it has become excessive. Swift followed Sir Robert Filmer and other conservative thinkers in regarding the tyranny of the many as likely to be far worse than that of any individual. So little faith does he have in the choices of the people that at the end of the *Discourse* he recommends bribery as a lesser evil than the election of those who win power by 'servile Flatteries of the People' (*PW* i.302). Employing a graphic image from the Old Testament, he describes '*The Raging of the Sea*, and *the Madness of the People*' (*PW* i.231) as two things that only God can control.[37]

By associating the king and the lords with popular opinion against the House of Commons, Swift deploys a distinction that Cicero had used in his *Pro Sestio*, where he defines the 'optimates', the 'best men', as those who have the true interests of the people at heart, against the so-called 'populares', who are really unscrupulous demagogues intent only on power and profit for themselves. Thus Swift, like Cicero, is able to identify his own party (as he does the tories in the pamphlets he wrote in 1710-14) with the national interest and his opponents with selfish factionalism. Towards the end of the *Pro Sestio*, Cicero returns to the theme of the 'optimates' to warn his audience that patriotism may require the sacrifice of popularity. He cites examples from the history of Athens to show that, even among that giddy and fickle people, there was never a lack of patriots ready to serve the state even against the foolishness of the populus at large. He names three men: Themistocles, Miltiades, and Aristides.[38] Such a list, a small roll-call of patrician heroes, became something of a commonplace. In a passage of his *Six*

---

[37] Ellis, in his edition of the *Discourse*, pp. 150, 162, suggests that Sir William Temple was the real source of this image. But it is surely a recollection of Psalm 65.7 in the metrical version in the 1662 *Book of Common Prayer*, which links 'the raging of the sea: and the noise of his waters, and the madness of the people'. Charles Leslie uses the same phrases as Swift in *Best of All* (1709), p. 29; see also below, p. 159.

[38] Cicero, *Pro Sestio*, xlv, lxvii. Swift used a passage from this speech (from lxv) as the epigraph for the *Examiner* No. 32 (15 March 1711); *PW* iii.106.

Livres making the same point as Cicero, Jean Bodin names the same three, with the addition of Socrates and Phocion. In his *Patriarcha*, again making the same point, Filmer repeats Bodin's list with the single omission of Socrates.[39] When Swift, for Chapter II of his *Discourse*, where he discusses the great men of Athens who were unjustly and ungratefully disgraced by the people, his list practically chose itself: Miltiades, Aristides, Themistocles, Pericles, Alcibiades, and Phocion. His choice of heroes was thus in a venerable tradition of conservative thought. In his later writings, and from his later experience, he would add such moderns as Sir Thomas More, Sir William Temple, and the Earl of Oxford, all men of integrity who suffered for not complying with the wickedness of the times.

Chapter II of the *Discourse* is devoted to the six major Athenian martyrs, and Swift suggests various parallels between them and the four impeached lords. The biographical organisation suited his purpose here, because the constitutional history of Athens did not follow the kind of neat pattern of gradual encroachments of popular power that he saw in English history. The early history of Rome, however, could be seen in such a way, as an originally wellbalanced state undermined by the excessive growth of popular power. For Chapter III, therefore, instead of a mainly biographical approach Swift gave a brief chronological account of Roman history. When he comes to the first impeachment in Roman history, that of Coriolanus, which he describes as 'like to have been so fatal to their State' (*PW* i.214), he seems to regret that his plan does not allow him to tell the story at the same length as his Athenian examples. Nothing is more indicative of his tory interpretation of Roman history than his evident sympathy with the haughty aristocrat Coriolanus. His major source for this period of Roman history was not Plutarch or Livy but Dionysius of Halicarnassus. Livy had little interest in Coriolanus, giving him only three chapters in all. Dionysius devotes most of a book to the episode of the impeachment of Coriolanus, and part of another to the story of his flight to the Volsci and attack on Rome. Plutarch (who parallels him with Alcibiades) tells his life at length, but dispassionately as a study of character, relatively free from political bias. Dionysius, who really deserves such epithets as 'copious and rhetorical' more than the 'exact and diligent' with which Swift praises him (*PW* i.216), gives the whole story of

[39] Bodin, *Six Bookes*, VI, iv; ed. McRae, p. 704; Filmer, *Patriarcha*, p. 88.

Coriolanus a decidedly aristocratic bias and treats it more from a political than a personal point of view.[40] His sympathies, like Swift's, are with the patricians against the selfish demagogues who stir up popular discontents for their own ends. In one of the public debates, for example, after Marcius has made a somewhat intemperate anti-popular speech, the consul Minucius effectively restates the aristocratic case in terms more moderate than Marcius had used but making essentially the same points (7.28-32). This speech clearly has the approval of Dionysius, and the people as a whole are pacified. At this moment Dionysius puts into the mouth of the tribune Bellutus a speech (7.34) deliberately intended to provoke Marcius into saying something rash, as it does. Dionysius is at pains to emphasise Bellutus's low birth and lack of personal qualities, and to suggest that Bellutus raises popular tumults because only through them can he expect to achieve a position of eminence as a demagogue (7.33). We might almost be reading Swift, who makes the same point about the leaders of the Commons in Chapter IV (*PW* i.227). Swift's argument that it is important to resist the first encroachments of popular power (*PW* i.226) is almost transcribed out of Marcius's first inflammatory speech in the senate as given by Dionysius (7.22-4). To this we may add a further piece of evidence that Swift, like Dionysius, approved of Marcius's intransigence: he thought his withdrawal from Rome at his mother's entreaty a pusillanimous act, placing it among the notable instances of mean-spiritedness in his list 'Of Mean and Great Figures' (*PW* v.86).

The really tory, authoritarian nature of Swift's political thought and historical analysis in the *Discourse* is apparent from his agreement with Filmer and Leslie against Sidney. In 1683, at the height of the tory reaction, Algernon Sidney, a whig aristocrat, was executed for the republican views expressed in his unpublished manuscript on political theory. This made him into a whig martyr. His *Discourses concerning Government*, posthumously published in 1698, is an elequent book that combines historical examples with political theory in a classic exposition of whig thought. It seems at first to have exercised greater influence than Locke's *Two Treatises*.[41] Three points essential to Swift's argument in the *Discourse* will serve to

[40] Livy, *History of Rome*, 2.34-5, 40; Plutarch, 'Coriolanus'; Dionysius of Halicarnassus, *Roman Antiquities*, 7.19-65, 8.1-61.

[41] J.P. Kenyon, *Revolution Principles* (Cambridge, 1977), p. 51.

illustrate the comparison: the ways in which popular states treat their 'best' men; the results of internal political disputes; and the comparative dangers of the tyranny of one man and the tyranny of the many. Filmer had argued (in a long tradition of conservative thought) that in a democracy the worst men thrive, while the best are kept under or actually punished for their eminent services to the state. Sidney is sceptical of the parts played by these so-called 'best men', arguing for example that whatever Scipio's services to the state he should have been willing to stand trial like any other citizen. In general Sidney regards impeachment as a necessary and indeed healthy exercise of popular power against the excessive 'greatness' of too-powerful individuals.[42] Swift's whole *Discourse* is based on the same premise as Filmer accepted, that popular power can only lead to political chaos and disaster, and it is a theme to which he returns in his later writings. In the *Examiner* No. 24 he describes the effect of great political changes as 'making the *Dregs* fly up to the Top' (*PW* iii.65). Swift was followed by Charles Leslie, who in his right-wing periodical the *Rehearsal* cites Alcibiades and Coriolanus as examples of 'the Brutality and *Ingratitude* of *Common-Wealth Mobbs*' (No. 70, 3 November 1705) and more sweepingly asserts of democracies (as Swift does) 'there being hardly any of their *Deliverers* who have not been Ruin'd and *Undone* by the *People* whom they had *Sav'd*' (No. 111, 8 June 1706). Swift says in the *Discourse* that 'almost every great Man they had among them' was impeached by the Athenians (*PW* i.206).

Filmer had argued that 'the dissensions which were daily between the nobles and the commons' (the very theme of Swift's title) often 'shed an ocean of blood within Italy and the streets of Rome'. Sidney took an opposite view, arguing that such quarrels 'as arise between the Nobles and Commons frequently produce good Laws for the maintenance of Liberty, as they did in *Rome* for above three hundred years after the expulsion of *Tarquin*, and almost ever terminated with little or no blood'.[43] Swift might have been writing with Sidney in mind when, in the *Discourse*, he admits that 'no Blood was ever drawn' until the time of the Gracchi; but he qualifies this admission by saying that, although the balance had long since become weighted too heavily on the

---

[42] Filmer, *Patriarcha*, pp. 88-90; Sidney, *Discourses concerning Government* (1698), II,xviii, pp. 138-45.

[43] Filmer, p. 87; Sidney, II, xxiv, p. 198.

side of the people, this was in some measure counterbalanced by the frequent wars and the consequent great credit won by the commanders (*PW* i.216-17). Swift is rarely very favourable to the idea of generals winning political influence and power, but here he clearly sees it as preferable to unrestrained popular power. Filmer had headed one of his chapters 'Popular Government more Bloody than a Tyranny'; Sidney had argued that more is to be feared from the hatred and power of a tyrant than from those of a multitude.[44] Here again Swift follows Filmer, and again he seems to be replying to Sidney when he argues that it is a fallacy to suppose that power is more safely lodged in many hands than in one. A large number is 'as capable of enslaving the Nation, and of acting all Manner of *Tyranny* and *Oppression*, as it is possible for a single Person to be' (*PW* i.200). In the *Rehearsal* Leslie would argue that 'to cure the *Tyranny* of a *King*, by setting up the *People*, is setting 10000 *Tyrants* over us, instead of *One*'. To reinforce the point he uses powerful biblical imagery: 'The Wrath of a *King* is said to be like the *Roaring* of a *Lion*: But that of the *People* is like the *Roaring* of the *Sea*. It is an *Inundation* which Sweeps all before it' (No. 51, 21 July 1705). Swift had used the same biblical image in the *Discourse* to compare '*The Raging of the Sea*, and *the Madness of the People*' (*PW* i.231).[45]

The incongruity, the result of the peculiar political situation of 1701, of Swift's writing apparently on behalf of the whigs is further illustrated by the interesting fact that two of his nominal opponents in the immediate controversy of 1701 were actually writers whose general political philosophy he shared, however little he might agree with their interpretation of the immediate political situation. Charles Davenant's *Discourse upon Grants and Resumptions* (1700) was a major statement of the tory case to which Swift was replying in his *Discourse*. Yet as political thinkers Swift and Davenant shared the same 'old whig' (which meant, in 1700, almost neo-tory) or Harringtonian analysis of and attitude towards the post-1688 political and economic developments. Davenant's 'Tom Double' pamphlets anticipate in many ways the charges that Swift would bring against the whigs in the *Examiner* and in the *Conduct of the Allies*.[46] Charles Leslie, whom we have just seen as the ally of Filmer and

---

[44] Filmer, pp. 90-2; Sidney, II,xxix, p. 228.
[45] See above, note 37.
[46] See above, pp. 22, 111-12.

Swift against Sidney in the interpretation of Roman history and on the question of the dangers of popular power, actually wrote against Swift's *Discourse* in *The New Association of those Called Moderate-Men with the Modern-Whigs and Fanaticks* (1702).[47] Yet Swift would certainly have agreed with the substance of Leslie's pamphlet; he disliked moderate men, modern whigs, and fanatics as much as Leslie did. It is significant that the way Leslie chose to attack Swift was to accuse him of being unwhiggish; it proved surprisingly easy to quote the *Discourse* to show this. In his first discussion of the *Discourse*, Leslie selects and puts together a number of decidedly 'undemocratic' sentiments (all of which, of course, reveal the really tory thinking that lies behind Swift's tract) and uses them to show that the whigs are not consistent in their pretence of appealing to the people and of placing political power in the people's hands. In a second discussion, in his 'Supplement' (which is dated 1703), Leslie returns to the attack, singling out Swift's description of the puritans (*PW* i.230) as coming very oddly from an author (Leslie evidently assumes that it is bishop Burnet) sympathetic to the dissenters. More generally, he again exposes the way Swift plays fast and loose with the idea of 'popular' power, according as it suits his rhetorical convenience. Another critic, the anonymous author of *The Source of Our Present Fears Discovered* (1703), who also attributes Swift's tract to Burnet, makes the same kind of points as Leslie. He exposes Swift's convenient lack of definition of the terms 'executive power' and 'last resort', and the despotic implications of the way Swift uses the metaphor of the 'balance of power'; and concludes (quite rightly) that the 'drift' of the *Discourse* 'is to shew the Preferrableness of a Government by one or a few Persons'.[48] This really is the 'drift' of the piece. The author of *The Source of Our Present Fears Discovered*, like Leslie, had no difficulty in identifying the weakness of the *Discourse* as a whig tract: that its political assumptions and ideas are really tory, authoritarian ones, though temporarily pressed into the service of oligarchs, three of whom happen to be whigs. The defence of the four lords, though it was the occasion of the tract, does not play a very prominent part in the *Discourse* as a whole. Only in Chapter II are they the focus of attention. Elsewhere, the institution of impeachment

---

[47] The relevant portions are printed in the *Discourse*, ed. Ellis, pp. 242-51.

[48] The Swiftian portions are printed in the *Discourse*, ed. Ellis, pp. 228-42; the quotation is from p. 233.

serves as a convenient focus for Swift's real interest, which is in the dangers that follow the growth of popular power. The most powerful and deeply felt passages in the *Discourse*, which share in some measure the intensity more characteristic of *A Tale of a Tub* than of Swift's political writings, are those that express Swift's fear and loathing of the irrational activities of a mob out of control. The madness of the people, whether the 'people' are a real mob or a House of Commons that ought to know better, is uncomfortably reminiscent of the madmen and enthusiasts of *A Tale of a Tub*. In its emphasis on the usual Swiftian values of order, authority, and stability, the *Discourse* anticipates Swift's later tory tracts. When, while he was writing the *Examiner*, Swift completed the collection of a volume of his shorter pieces (published in 1711 as *Miscellanies in Prose and Verse*) he felt no awkwardness in placing the 'whig' *Discourse* at the head of the collection, much as he had put Temple's 'Of Popular Discontents' at the head of the third volume of *Miscellanea* in 1701. Only one major change was required to fit the *Discourse* to its new place. In 1711, the 'people' had recently elected a tory House of Commons of which Swift approved; he therefore cancelled the *Discourse*'s final paragraph in praise of bribery, being more sanguine (for the moment at least) about the ability of the 'people' to elect the right men without needing to be bribed into following their own best interests.[49]

iii

Swift's reputation, in his own day and since, as an Irish patriot and more generally as the 'vindicator libertatis' (in his own phrase from his epitaph), rests more on the *Drapier's Letters* than on any other of his works. It is easy to see why the 'Drapier' should be more popular than the 'Examiner', and why anthologies of Swift's writings represent his pamphleteering more often and more extensively from the *Drapier's Letters* than from the tory tracts of 1710-14. The issues involved seem to be simpler, morally and politically, and they appear to require less

---

[49] The cancelled paragraph is printed in the text in Ellis's edition, pp. 126-7; in Davis it is relegated to the textual notes (*PW* i.301-2). The omission of this paragraph was a very late decision. A copy of *Miscellanies in Prose and Verse* (1711) now in the British Library contains both the paragraph as originally printed (pp.91-4) and also p. 91 as reprinted for substitutuion; this copy has been reproduced in facsimile, with an introduction by C.P. Daw (Menston, 1972).

'background' knowledge than do the tory pamphlets. Swift's presentation of the issues in the *Drapier's Letters* is designedly simplistic (he was writing for a wider and less highly-educated audience than had been the case in 1710-14), and his rhetoric is easier to follow than the subtler manipulations of the Queen Anne pamphlets. In the *Drapier's Letters* the sentiments in favour of 'liberty', in conjunction with the appealing 'David and Goliath' theme, are irresistible to readers and critics schooled in modern liberal-democratic traditions. Yet Swift was by no means, in the *Drapier's Letters* or elsewhere, the disinterested champion of 'liberty' in any unrestricted sense. He distrusted the way in which 'liberty' tended to lead to anarchy. In the mixed motives that prompted him to write the *Drapier's Letters*, libertarian sentiments are likely to have played only a small part. That he had a perfectly genuine belief in the moral right of Ireland to be legislatively independent of the English government of the day is beyond doubt. But at least as powerful as a motivating force, and probably rather more so, was his hatred of the whig regime in London, and of George I and Walpole in particular.

Swift never concealed his contempt for Ireland, the Irish, and Irish politics. He regarded his residence there as an exile, and he regarded it as a great disappointment that instead of receiving the dignity in the English church that he coveted he was rewarded for his political services only with the deanery of St Patrick's, Dublin. When he returned to Ireland after the death of Queen Anne, his initial resolution was not to meddle in local politics (*Corr*.ii.127). For several years he kept this resolution, remaining obsessed with the past, and his literary efforts were devoted partly to his justifications of the queen's last ministry and partly to covert attacks on the policies of the new whig government in London.[50] When Swift's attention was finally captured by local issues, they were not purely Irish ones but concerned with Anglo-Irish relations and therefore involved the detested English ministry. Not content with impeaching Swift's old friends the tory leaders, the whig government in London continued to give fresh sources of irritation. It was English influence that procured the passing of a Toleration Act for Ireland in 1719. This provided a real boost for the dissenting interest, and one that was highly unpalatable to Swift, who hated any legal recognition of the rights of dissenters.[51] Before

[50] See above, pp. 122-33.
[51] J.C. Beckett, *Protestant Dissent in Ireland, 1687-1780* (1947), pp. 71-81.

the 1719 act, as Swift had written to Sir Arthur Langford in 1714, in a vain effort to have him close a dissenting conventicle that he had provocatively established in Swift's own parish of Laracor, the protestant dissenters had been 'suffered to have their conventicles only by connivance, and that only in places where they formerly used to meet' (*Corr*.ii.141). In 1720 the Declaratory Act 'for the better securing the Dependency' of Ireland, passed by the British parliament, had removed the function of the Irish House of Lords as a court of appeal. Swift refers to this indignity and grievance in the *Drapier's Letters* (*PW* x.35, 55). Other iniquities of the English whig government are obliquely catalogued in the 'Letter to Mr Pope' (1721). But it was the case of Wood's halfpence that brought together many abuses and corruptions into a single cause, involving not only the dependent state of Ireland but the financial and other mismanagements of the English government.

In July 1722 William Wood had been granted a patent to coin copper farthings and halfpence for use in Ireland. He seems to have obtained the favour through a bribe of £10,000 paid to the king's morganatic wife, the Duchess of Kendal. The patent was objectionable to the Irish on several grounds. It seemed a national affront that no one in Ireland, and not even the (English) Lord Lieutenant had been consulted about it, and that the coins were to be minted in England. It was claimed that Wood was being allowed to coin far more money than was really required (his patent specified £108,000 worth of the copper money, against an estimated need of perhaps £20,000), and that the terms of the patent were too favourable to Wood: there were insufficient safeguards against debasement, counterfeiting, and overcoining; and Wood was not obliged (as had been the case with earlier patents of this kind) to redeem his coins with legal tender. As early as 1722 the Irish Commissioners of Revenue had protested against the patent, but it did not really become an important public issue until both houses of the Irish parliament made similar protests in September 1723. The handling of the issue by the English government was inept and insensitive, with the result that a formidable coalition against the patent was built up in Ireland, including groups and interests normally antagonistic to each other.[52]

Swift had broken his self-imposed silence as a pamphleteer in 1720 with *A Proposal for the Universal Use of Irish Manufacture*

[52] For the political context of the *Drapier's Letters*, see Oliver W. Ferguson, *Jonathan Swift and Ireland* (Urbana, 1962), pp. 83-138.

(*PW* ix.15-22), in which local patriotism had been fuelled by his anti-English sentiments inspired by his hatred of the whig government. In March 1724 appeared a much more important pamphlet, the first of the *Drapier's Letters*. Four others had followed before the end of the year; two others were written (one in 1724 and one in 1725) but not published until 1735.[53] As in the case of his tory writings in 1710-12, Swift was rhetorically fortunate in that he had no need to argue with or to convert his audience. Everyone agreed in detesting Wood's patent and what it stood for. Swift's task was to confirm and encourage his readers in their opposition to Wood, and through him to the whig government in London. His pamphlets enjoyed a spectacular success. As is well known, their influence on public opinion helped force the English government to withdraw the patent. Swift had once again scored a great propaganda victory. This time there was the additional reward of a lasting reputation as a patriot and a champion of liberty. In one very important respect the *Drapier's Letters* are quite different from Swift's English pamphlets of 1710-14. Swift did not, of course, write under his own name. But there was no need to pretend impartiality; the Drapier very frankly takes a side. Swift rarely used a pseudonym in 1710-14, and never for important pamphlets. But writing for the smaller political world of Ireland, and Dublin in particular, Swift wished to keep the issues at a level that could be understood by the ordinary man. It was easy to visualise 'M.B., Drapier' as an individual tradesman with a shop at an address in a real Dublin street. As a perfectly ordinary shopkeeper, he symbolises the need for everyone to become involved in the fight against Wood. Swift went to unusual pains to create the Drapier as a credible fictive author. Sometimes the Drapier is self-consciously deferential, excusing his presumption in meddling with matters above his proper sphere. He pretends to little or no Latin, and when Swift uses an anecdote from a classical source the fact is disguised. Biblical references and imagery, however, are commonly employed (whereas they are uncommon in the earlier political pamphlets) to great effect.[54] Yet the mask of the

---

[53] The letters were originally published under various, usually cumbersome titles; I refer to them as Letters I-VII. There is a separate edition of the *Drapier's Letters* by Herbert Davis (Oxford, 1935), which has notes ·and a substantial introduction; for convenience, however, I have given references to the edition in *PW* x.

[54] Charles Allen Beaumont, *Swift's Use of the Bible* (Athens, Georgia, 1965), pp. 36-44. Although Swift uses many biblical allusions in the *Examiner*, they

Drapier is always patently a mask. The tone of the pamphlets is peremptory, even scolding, as in the earlier *Proposal for the Universal Use of Irish Manufacture*. Except for the deliberate moments of self-conscience deference, the voice is an authoritative one addressing inferiors. There are, of course, some differences of tone and technique between the letters. Letter III, addressed to 'the Nobility and Gentry of the Kingdom of Ireland', is more deferential in tone than the others, and also makes greater use of statistical evidence and arguments.[55]

One of the important advantages that Swift derived from the use of a humble fictive author like the Drapier is the appearance of being a David fighting the Goliath of the English Philistines (the Drapier himself makes this comparison; (*PW* x.48). For although the nominal antagonist is the insignificant William Wood, Swift's readers are never in any doubt that the real enemy is the English government. Another advantage is the use of the Drapier as a 'naive' narrator (much as Swift would use Gulliver on occasion) who sometimes pretends not to understand the workings of high politics, for example how it comes about that an important man like a Lord Lieutenant could possibly be sent to do the bidding of a William Wood (*PW* x.57). The use of a humble figure like the Drapier, rather than the anonymous but obviously authoritative fictive speakers of the tory tracts of 1710-14, also fits in with Swift's general strategy. This is to attack the whigs for appealing to 'whig' principles; and who better to remind the whigs how far they have deserted their old principles than someone like the Drapier, one of the small urban merchants who were traditionally mainly whig supporters. Swift had already used a similar strategy in his 'Letter to Mr Pope', where he describes how he had 'passed for a disaffected person' by trying 'to make my court to some people on the prevailing side, by advancing certain old whiggish principles, which it seems had been exploded about a month before' (*PW* ix.33).[56] There are several different ways in which Swift uses whig principles against the whigs in the *Drapier's Letters*: through the citation of precedents, through the discussions of the royal prerogative and its limitations, and through arguments from general principles.

---

appear less prominent among the classical allusions and the generally more literary and allusive style.

[55] For a discussion of the imagery and rhetoric of the *Drapier's Letters*, see C.J. Rawson, 'The Injured Lady and the Drapier: a reading of Swift's Irish tracts', *Prose Studies*, iii (1980), 15-43.

[56] See above, p. 127.

In each case Swift's aim is to convict his English whig opponents of having deserted their principles, and to capture for himself and his own side the supposedly whig virtue of the defence of liberty.

There was nothing specifically whig or tory about the search for and the use of precedents as historical arguments. From the chequered course of English history precedents could generally be found without much difficulty to support most arguments. In his classic statement of the case for Irish legislative independence, *The Case of Ireland's Being Bound by Acts of Parliament in England, Stated* (Dublin, 1698), William Molyneux had devoted much more space to arguments from precedent than to arguments from general principles.[57] Although he put his case most vigorously, his precedents were vulnerable and were challenged at once and at length. Swift, too, would find precedents something of a two-edged weapon. He makes most use of them in Letter I, where he uses them to define the royal prerogative as it relates to the legal tender of currency (*PW* x.9-10). In Letter III he has to argue against the precedents alleged by the other side, and to do this effectively he develops a distinction between precedents declarative of the 'ancient constitution' (or those that support his own case) and the legalistic use of bad precedents drawn from bad reigns and the advice of worse ministers (or those that make against him). This is a most ingenious strategy. It allows Swift to associate himself with John Hampden (an earlier David against a royal Goliath) and his principled opposition to Charles I's illegal exactions (*PW* x.20). At the same time, he contrives to make the whigs appear to rest their case on the evil precedents furnished by the Stuarts. This in turn ties in with his treatment of the subject of the royal prerogative, of which the tories were the traditional defenders and the whigs as traditionally jealous of its tendencies to encroach on popular liberties. In the *Drapier's Letters* Swift makes the whigs appear to be trying to push the royal prerogative beyond its legally-defined limits. He had done this already in the *Proposal for the Universal Use of Irish Manufacture*, where the whig Earl of Wharton is quoted as claiming a dispensing power for the crown, when it suited his party to use it (*PW* ix.20-1). The dispensing power had been condemned by the Bill of Rights in 1689. In the *Drapier's Letters*,

[57] There is a modern edition of *The Case of Ireland Stated*, with an introduction by J.G. Simms (Dublin, 1977).

and particularly in Letter II, Wood is described in terms of an absolute despotic monarch, and in these passages he is clearly intended to stand as a surrogate for the king himself (*PW* x.18-19). More generally, Swift deploys whiggish arguments to suggest how far the 'modern' whigs have degenerated. In Letter III he argues from '*Reason* and *Justice*' against pettifogging legalism (*PW* x.36). In Letter IV he draws an implied contrast between a typical self-seeking modern whig like Lord Wharton (who is not named, but whose administration of Ireland is clearly the object of attack; *PW* x.58-9) and 'several of the greatest Patriots, and *best Whigs* in *England*', exemplified by the Irish patriot Molyneux (*PW* x.61-2). In Letter V, addressed to Lord Molesworth (himself a prominent whig), Swift refers to 'dangerous Authors, who talk of *Liberty as a Blessing, to which the whole Race of Mankind hath an Original Title*'. These 'dangerous Authors' are all impeccable whigs: Molesworth himself, Locke, Molyneux, and Sidney (*PW* x.86). Later he speaks of having hidden these subversive writings at the bottom of a chest, covered from sight by the works of the absolutist theorists Bodin, Filmer, and Hobbes (*PW* x.94).

It would be wrong to regard all this as mere cant, trumped up by Swift to serve the present turn, even though we know that in 1701 his political theory was aligned with Bodin and Filmer against Sidney. For by 1724 the political condition of England made several traditional sources of whig arguments of more use to the opposition tories. This is true of Sidney's interpretation of Roman history, and of Molesworth's account of how Denmark had become absolutist in 1660.[58] But even apart from this shift and its effect on political polemic, which dictated the deployment of 'whig' arguments against the whigs, Swift also used themes that reflected perfectly genuine and long-standing concerns of his own, not just his desire to turn the tables on the whigs. For example, the objection that Wood (unlike earlier patentees) was not obliged to redeem his coins for legal tender leads in the *Drapier's Letters* to a vividly imagined nightmare of runaway inflation. Since Wood's coins will be minted in almost infinite quantities, of such poor quality as to be practically

---

[58] Molesworth, *An Account of Denmark as it Was in the Year 1692* (1694); Swift owned a copy at some time, although it does not appear in the sale catalogue of his books. It is now at Trinity College, Cambridge (*Rothschild Library*, i.383; No. 1444). The way Molesworth's book could be used against the 'modern' whigs is seen in auditor Harley's speech in the Commons in 1718; see above, p. 132.

valueless, they will only be accepted at the very low intrinsic value of the metal content. Vast quantities will be required for the simplest transactions, like buying a pot of ale. Once debasement and counterfeiting have set in, the currency will collapse and the economy will be forced to return to barter as a means of exchange (*PW* x.6-7). Behind this nightmare vision we sense Swift's tory fear of an economy based on money rather than land, and especially the likely results of any debasement of the coinage, the almost inevitable result of the large-scale use of a fiduciary medium of exchange instead of one of intrinsic value. Inflation would afflict particularly those whose incomes were fixed, such as landed proprietors (whose lands might be set for very long leases) and most especially the church, whose money income had already been very seriously eroded by past inflation and whose landed income was all too often irresponsibly leased for low rents and high fines.[59] For all his espousal of what had once been distinctively 'whig' ideas and doctrines, Swift's political values remained tory in their essence. The whigs, in 1714, had captured the establishment, and he was driven into lifelong opposition, but he remained true to his old values of order, stability, and hierarchy. In the *Drapier's Letters* he might approve Molyneux's assertion on Ireland's behalf of certain Lockean political ideas, but his own world view remained a conservative, backward-looking one fundamentally opposed to Locke's.[60]

iv

Gulliver's Travels is Swift's most extensive and considered commentary on man's political follies and vices.[61] It was written between 1721 and 1725, a period when his deepest political hatred was directed against the corrupt whig oligarchy that seemed firmly entrenched in power in London. The danger to the

[59] Landa, *Swift and the Church of Ireland*, pp. 96-150, discusses Swift's ideas and fears about church temporalities.

[60] Ricardo Quintana, *Two Augustans*, pp. 71-82, tries (not, in my view, successfully) to find common ground between Locke and Swift. The fact is that Swift was hostile to all the major ideas we associate with Locke: to psychological relativism, to religious toleration, and to political liberalism.

[61] No study of Swift's politics could omit *Gulliver's Travels*, but since I have written about it (though in a different context and from a different perspective) in *The Politics of 'Gulliver's Travels'* (Oxford, 1980), I have kept my discussion here to a necessary minimum.

constitution, as Swift saw it at this time, came from this oligarchy; and in 1724, in the *Drapier's Letters*, Swift had himself tried to mobilise public opinion against it. It is therefore hardly surprising that in *Gulliver's Travels* (which was published in 1726) we find little of the fear and distrust of the encroachments of popular power that were so prominent in Swift's first political pamphlet, the *Discourse* of 1701. Swift's political ideals remained remarkably constant throughout his long involvement in politics, and in *Gulliver's Travels* these ideals are embodied in the imaginary societies (Brobdingnag, Houyhnhnmland, and old Lilliput) that Swift asks us to admire. Where there is a difference is that the objects of political satire in the *Travels* are more characteristic of Swift after 1714 than before. If at the time of writing *Gulliver* Swift had happened (as he was in 1710-14) to be on the side of a government confronting a factious opposition, the book would hardly have paid so much attention to the abuses of political power and authority by those invested with it. (Of course, it may be suggested that in such circumstances Swift would never have written such a book at all.) Since it was in fact written in the 1720s, *Gulliver's Travels* presents a rather more 'liberal' idea of Swift's politics than is really warranted. This is not to suggest that in *Gulliver's Travels* Swift says anything contrary to his real beliefs, or that his ideals are not fully and explicitly set out in the book. It is rather a question of emphasis, and of the fact that the book is a satire. To avoid misreading it, we need to view the satire (which is naturally the most prominent and most memorable part) in focus with the positive values expressed (which are often less memorably or appealingly put).

One theme that remains constant in Swift's political writings is his dislike of arbitrary power. In the *Discourse* it was popular power that threatened to become arbitrary, in *Gulliver's Travels* the object of attack is personal despotism. Arbitrary power, he wrote in one of his 'Thoughts on Various Subjects', 'is the natural Object of Temptation to a Prince; as Wine or Women to a young Fellow' (*PW* iv.244). Nominally, of course, the abhorrence of arbitrary power was bipartisan. Hardly anyone (Charles Leslie was a notable exception) was prepared to write openly in its favour.[62] Before 1688 it had been a whig theme, and

---

[62] Leslie consistently argues that the tyranny of one man is better than the tyranny of many; see the *Rehearsal*, No. 51 (21 July 1705); *The Finishing Stroke* (1709), p. 143; and *Best of All* (1709), p. 29.

the whigs had traditionally accused the tories of favouring it. After 1714 it became as naturally a tory theme, with the whigs accused of playing up to the despotic tendencies of George I and later George II (who were absolute monarchs in their German territories). Addison tried to counter accusations of this kind in the *Freeholder* No. 10 (23 January 1716), where he shows what true despotism is really like through a portrait of the rule of Muley Ishmael, the late Emperor of Morocco. Addison connects his arbitrary sway with that of Louis XIV in France, and contrasts it with the mild, constitutional rule of George I in Great Britain.[63] In the tory view, of course, George I was (or at least, would like to be) as arbitrary as any French or Moroccan monarch; as we have seen, Swift attacked his absolutist tendencies in the *Drapier's Letters*. Some features of the Emperor of Lilliput have been taken to suggest George I: his patronage of a faction at home, his ambitious foreign policies. But Swift's attack on absolutism in *Gulliver's Travels* goes well beyond George I (though he must have been in Swift's mind). The Emperor of Lilliput illustrates the European, and the King of Luggnagg the oriental style of despotism; it is the institution of arbitrary monarchy, not particular kings or emperors, which is the object of Swift's satire. In the description of Luggnagg, indeed, Swift underlines this point by the contrast between the casual way in which 'a young Lord of great Hopes' is accidentally poisoned, and the personal affability of the king (*PW* xi.205-6).

Kings possessed of arbitrary power are naturally willing to extend their exercise of it, as the Emperor of Lilliput is keen to follow up Gulliver's naval victory by enslaving Blefuscu and reducing it to the status of a province to be governed by a viceroy (*PW* xi.53). This was in effect Ireland's situation, but Swift's protest against imperialism and colonialism goes well beyond the Anglo-Irish situation. Listing the just causes of war, Gulliver tells his Houyhnhnm master that it is looked upon as very justifiable for a prince to 'send Forces into a Nation, where the People are poor and ignorant, he may lawfully put half of them to Death, and make Slaves of the rest, in order to civilize and reduce them from their barbarous Way of Living' (*PW* xi.246). Later Gulliver is even more outspoken about colonialism, condemning the 'Pyrates' whose activities result in the sending of a colony 'to convert and civilize an idolatrous and barbarous

---

[63] *The Freeholder*, ed. James Leheny (Oxford, 1979), pp. 82-7; and for the account of George I, No. 2 (26 December 1715), pp. 43-6.

People' (*PW* xi.294), or rather to exploit them for the purposes of economic imperialism. Swift shows himself a typical tory in his isolationist foreign policy, and he is enough of a true conservative to be on the side of barbarism where that happens to be the present establishment. His view of European man and civilisation is too pessimistic for him to share the smug self-satisfaction of an Addison contemplating the Royal Exchange and idealising a Britain at the hub of a world network of trade (and exploitation).[64] Swift associates trade with superfluous luxuries, and Gulliver's Houyhnhnm master wonders how a country could be so barren as not to afford its inhabitants the necessities of life (*PW* xi.252).

Brobdingnag is a limited monarchy, fortunately cut off from contact with the rest of the world. Its king represents Swift's ideal monarch, and he is contrasted with the Emperor of Lilliput whose arbitrary despotism was supported by a standing army. The King of Brobdingnag's only forces are a citizen militia, but he is secure in the love and respect of his people.|The tradition of describing an ideal or exemplary monarch can be traced back through such renaissance-humanist works as Erasmus's *Education of a Christian Prince* (1516) to Xenophon and Plato. Swift's king clearly belongs in this tradition, as he also anticipates many aspects of the ideal depicted in Bolingbroke's *The Idea of a Patriot King* (written about 1738, although not published until 1749).[65] Swift's king combines some features that had long been commonplace with others that reflect more particularly the political conditions of early eighteenth-century England. The king is presented in two different ways, through direct description of his character and habits and through his comments (mainly in Part II, Chapter vi) on Gulliver's account of Europe. The character of the king is firmly traditional. From Plato to Erasmus great stress had been placed on the need for the ideal prince to be well-educated.ʲThe King of Brobdingnag is 'as learned a Person as any in his Dominions', though without any trace of pedantry, which appears by contrast in the scholars who attend the court and who conceal their ignorance of what Gulliver is with jargon and empty speculation (*PW* xi.103-4).

[64] *The Spectator*, No. 69 (19 May 1711); ed. Donald F. Bond (Oxford, 1965), i.292-6.

[65] For an historical survey of the genre, see the introduction to Erasmus, *The Education of a Christian Prince*, ed. and trans. Lester K. Born (New York, 1936); and for Bolingbroke's *Idea*, see Isaac Kramnick, *Bolingbroke and his Circle* (Cambridge, Mass., 1968), especially pp. 33-5, 210, 214.

The king prefers national peace and prosperity to personal power, and rejects with indignation Gulliver's offer of the secret of gunpowder (*PW* xi.119). His personal qualities make him a dignified figure of authority, respected for his merits as well as his position. Although his character is very much in the traditional mould, there are a number of comments that the king makes that reveal a strong tory outlook. Although he laughs at the party distinctions as Gulliver describes them (*PW* xi.107), in 1726 to argue against the importance of the old party divisions was a distinctively tory position. It was Walpole and the whigs who insisted on the continued importance of party labels and who used the association between the tories and Jacobitism as a means of ensuring that only whigs would be employed by the king. In 1727, shortly after the death of George I, Swift seems to have briefly entertained some hopes that George II would approve 'a moderating Scheme, wherein no-body shall be used the Worse or Better for being call'd Whig or Tory' (*Corr*.iii.219). However little he had liked such schemes in 1710-14, it was clearly now in his and the tory interest to encourage them, just as it was in the whig interest to press for a continued whig monopoly of power based on the party's superior loyalty to Hanover.[66]

Swift also gives the King of Brobdingnag a tory view of religious conformity. He knows no reason why those with minority opinions (the dissenters) 'should be obliged to change, or should not be obliged to conceal them' (*PW* xi.131). It is characteristic of Swift to describe the spreading of heterodox opinions as comparable to selling poisons as cordials. A similar dislike of pluralism is seen in the king's amusement at the way Gulliver calculates the population of England by reckoning up the numbers in the various sects and parties. Brobdingnag itself is saved by its isolation from the need to have a foreign policy, but the king's comments on Gulliver's account of Europe shows that he approves of the tory naval strategy of minimal involvement in Europe: 'He asked, what Business we had out of our own Islands, unless upon the Score of Trade or Treaty, or to defend the Coasts with our Fleet' (*PW* xi.131, where the king's other 'tory' comments will be found). Bolingbroke's *The Idea of a Patriot King* was written several years later than *Gulliver's*

---

[66] Bolingbroke tried to minimise party differences in order to unite tories and opposition whigs into an alliance against Walpole; H.T. Dickinson, *Bolingbroke* (1970), pp. 194-7.

Travels, but it was inspired by the same disgust at the exclusive employment by George I (and later too by George II) of the whigs. Bolingbroke's book contains some unswiftian themes (such as his attack on priestcraft), but in important respects he follows Swift and the classical tradition: he emphasises the important example given by the personal morality and integrity of the monarch (Swift had made this point as early as his 1709 *Project for the Advancement of Religion*), and he stresses the need for the monarch to be properly educated. It was not easy to find a well-read philosopher-king in contemporary Europe; for Swift, Charles XII of Sweden had earlier at least partly fulfilled the role. Most real monarchs, or so at least it seemed to humanist commentators, were deplorably ill-educated. In *The Idea of a Patriot King* Bolingbroke laments the inadequate education of Louis XIV.[67] In the *Intelligencer* No. 9, a notable exposition of his views on education, Swift speculates that the son of a universal monarch would probably be the worst-educated person in the world (*PW* xii.46).

The most thoroughgoing presentation of Swift's ideal of political order is seen in Part IV of *Gulliver's Travels*, particularly in the contrast between the rationality of the Houyhnhnms, among whom debate (except on a single academic subject) is prevented by immediate unanimity, and the unruly yahoos, who will fight among themselves even when there is nothing to fight about. But Houyhnhnm rationality and order are not to be expected in human life. The best substitute for it is found in the political order of Brobdingnag. That system is far from perfect. There are beggars and malefactors, but at least there is no political strife or factionalism, nor (apparently) religious nonconformity. Stability in Brobdingnag has been achieved through a 'general Composition' (of which no details are given) between the main competitors for political power, the king, the nobility, and the people (*PW* xi.138). Although we do not learn very much about Brobdingnag's political system beyond the king's role, the important part played by the monarch is significant. Compared with the Athens or Rome of the *Discourse*, Brobdingnag obviously enjoys a strongly authoritarian form of government. Its stability is of course appreciably aided by its freedom from any external threats or rivalries, another reflection of Swift's tory isolationism. The

[67] *The Idea of a Patriot King,* in *Works* (1844), ii.372-429; for the reference to priestcraft, see p. 377, and for the importance of royal education, pp. 384-5.

Houyhnhnms, too, are free from foreign entanglements, and with them, freed from the constraints of reality, Swift is able to give his ideal of order and stability a more utopian twist. Their society is maintained at an optimal size by the strict practice of birth control (*PW* xi.268). Swift knew that this kind of permanent political stability was impossible in real societies. The best that could be hoped for was the slowing down of the rate of decline. Even the Sparta of Lycurgus had become corrupted by the import of money and luxury. In *Gulliver's Travels* the evils of social change, especially rapid social change, are seen in the relatively 'open' societies depicted in Parts I and III, in Lilliput and (especially) in Balnibarbi, where the people are starving and in rags as the result of their mania for 'projects' of every kind.

Swift's ideal political order is hierarchical, based on the exercise of power and influence by a mainly hereditary class whose inherited wealth and social position gives them a natural right to determine public policies. 'Law in a free Country,' he wrote in one of his 'Thoughts on Various Subjects', 'is, or ought to be the Determination of the Majority of those who have Property in Land' (*PW* iv.245). Swift's own social origins were modest, so that he could have claimed (like Dr Johnson) that his upholding the privileges of birth was free of any self-interested motive.[68] He does on one occasion refer to birth as an 'accidental advantage' (*PW* viii.135). This is in a passage in the *Enquiry into the Behaviour of the Queen's Last Ministry* where he is trying to construct a balanced character of Lord Oxford. To achieve credibility he has to impute some small faults, and to complain that Oxford valued his birth more than such things really merited was a good choice of 'fault' from Swift's point of view. It makes the point that Oxford (unlike, Swift wants us to think, many of the low-born whig leaders) did come from an old family, and yet at the same time it helps to create the impression that the author is a man of independent thought who is not impressed or awed easily. Elsewhere Swift speaks more favourably of the advantages of birth. In the *Examiner* he is fond of contrasting the upstart whigs with their natural social superiors the recently-restored tories. The most extended treatment of this theme is found in No. 40 (10 May 1711), where 'a Contempt for *Birth, Family,* and ancient Nobility' is identified as one of the most

---

[68] Boswell, *Life of Johnson*, ed. G.B. Hill, rev. L.F. Powell (Oxford, 1934), ii.153, 261.

pernicious of the 'Heresies in Politicks' propagated by the 'Partisans of the *late Administration*' (*PW* iii.150). Swift admits that there may be nothing more than popular opinion in favour of the supposed superiority of the claims of heredity; but he argues that even if this were so, it would still be a good enough reason for respecting it. Later, in the 'Letter to Mr Pope', he uses a similar argument in favour of hereditary monarchy. The 'right line' is to be preferred as 'established by law' and 'as it hath much weight in the opinions of the people'. The second is the more important, because while 'necessity may abolish any Law' it 'cannot alter the sentiments of the vulgar; Right of inheritance being perhaps the most popular of all topicks' (*PW* ix.31). Thus hierarchy, hereditary right, and the preservation of the establishment are made to seem part of the natural order of things which only the levelling whigs would attempt to destroy. Not that Swift is content to let hereditary right stand only on the basis of popular opinion. He advances several reasons for believing that nobility confers real benefits and advantages. These are the superior education and culture to which it gives (or ought to give) access; the examples of noble ancestors to emulate; and the political virtue that comes from having property to defend. In the tradition of the classical republicans, Swift thought that political power was best entrusted to those who had a real stake in their country. For, being already wealthy, they would not easily be bribed to betray the national interest which was also their own. Thus the King of Laputa is prevented from becoming absolute by his inability to corrupt a ministry to join with him in this design, his ministers all having their estates on the continent below (*PW* xi.171). As against these positive advantages of inherited nobility, there are the negative qualifications of the 'new men'. They are likely to have contracted, and to retain in their high stations, 'some sordid Vices of their *Parentage* or *Education*' (*PW* xi.198-200). In likely to have a whiggish contempt for whatever is established; and they will be exposed to the temptation of making their fortunes through corruption, either being bribed from above to betray the liberties of their country or by enriching themselves from the public purse, or by both methods. Swift admits that 'a Pearl holds its Value although it be found in a Dunghill; but however, that is not the most probable Place to search for it' (*PW* iii.151).

It was unfortunate that the scarcity of pearls made it indeed necessary to look for them even in the dunghills. In 1719 the whig government introduced a Peerage Bill, designed to stabilise the number of peers by limiting the royal prerogative in the creation of new ones.[69] In defence of the measure, Queen Anne's creation of twelve new peers at the end of 1711 (to give the tory government a majority in the House of Lords for its peace policy) was often cited as a bad example. Swift had been unhappy with this expedient at the time, although he thought it justified by necessity; nevertheless, he was firmly opposed to the 1719 measure. Writing to his friend Charles Ford to give his reasons, he noted that 'the Lords degenerate by Luxury Idleness etc and the Crown is always forced to govern by new Men' (*Corr.* ii.331). He later elaborated on this theme in the *Intelligencer* No. 9 (1728), where he laments the decay in the education of the natural leaders of society since the happy reigns of James I and Charles I. He identifies the two prime sources of corruption as fanticism during the Civil War and the interregnum, and the dissolute character of the court during the reign of Charles II. He adds that a more recent cause had been the bad influence of the army officers during the reign of Queen Anne (*PW* xii.47, 49). Only a thorough reform of the education of the nobility could end the need for these continual recruits from the lower ranks of the gentry (or from even lower down the social scale) and enable the nobility once again to take the part in public life that their rank required of them. Swift does cite one positive example in his *Intelligencer* paper on education: Viscount Mountcashel, a young Irish peer whom he thought was being properly educated. By this Swift meant that the lord was being educated as though he were not a peer (*PW* xii.51). It was the flattery of servants and boon-companions and the excessive fondness of doting parents that spoiled the typical nobleman's education. In the idealised educational system that Swift devised for the Lilliputians, the schools are indeed segregated by social rank, but care is taken to prevent the abuses complained of in the *Intelligencer*. Instead of receiving no training at all, the Lilliputian nobles receive a more careful and thorough education than their inferiors (*PW* xi.60-3).

This tendency to degeneration among the nobility was exacerbated in troubled times, for 'all great Changes have the same Effect upon Commonwealths that Thunder hath upon Liquors; making the *Dregs* fly up to the Top' (*PW* iii.65). Here Swift was thinking particularly of the type of 'new man' who had

---

[69] For a collection of sources and documents, see John F. Naylor, *The British Aristocracy and the Peerage Bill of 1719* (New York, 1968).

been introduced into public business since the Revolution and
the consequent great expansion of the civil and military services.
In part this simply reflected Swift's nostalgic belief that things
had been better in the good old days, for there had always been
'new men'. But the specialised skills needed in the more complex
kinds of government business (particularly credit and finance)
did mean that men were increasingly employed for particular
skills rather than for their birth or moral qualifications. This
newer type of civil servant did not, of course, emerge at the
Revolution; the career of Samuel Pepys is an example. But it
became more common after 1688.[70] In his account of Lilliput
Swift contrasts the original institutions of the country, which
paid most regard to moral qualifications, and the 'scandalous
Corruptions' that have crept in over the last three generations,
since the present emperor's grandfather began to choose
ministers by their dexterity in leaping, creeping, and rope-
dancing (*PW* xi.60). Modern candidates for public employments
are trained in these skills from their youth, 'and are not always of
noble Birth, or liberal Education' (*PW* xi.38). The theme of the
degeneration of the nobility is repeated in all four parts of
Gulliver's Travels. In Parts II and IV, Gulliver's accounts of
Europe include idealised images of nobility which are heavily
undercut (*PW* xi.128-9, 256). In Part III Gulliver sees many of
the secrets of modern history, which reveal the interruptions of
royal and noble lines and their degeneration (*PW* xi.198-200). In
isolation such passages could be read as attacks on the idea of an
hereditary aristocracy, but in the context of what we know of
Swift's political values they are clearly laments for the
degeneration of an ideal.

Swift could see perfectly well that his hierarchical ideal was
very far from being embodied in the peerage of early eighteenth-
century England. Just as he believed in episcopacy, but had a
low opinion of most contemporary bishops, so he respected the
idea of nobility, without having much regard for the House of
Lords of his day. A particular cirumstance that probably
influenced his attitude to the lords was that, during his period of
close involvement in English politics, the tory government often
had difficulty in managing the whiggish House of Lords. At the
end of 1711 Queen Anne had been forced to create twelve new
peers to give the government a majority, a most controversial

---

[70] On the expansion of the public service, see J.H. Plumb, *The Growth of
Political Stability in England* (1967), pp. 98-128.

measure. Swift disliked the expedient; in the *Journal to Stella* he described it as a 'strange unhappy necessity' which he blamed on the queen's 'confounded trimming and moderation' (*JS* ii.451). In his *History of the Four Last Years*, however, he offers a rather sophistical justification of the measure which reveals (if not his real opinion of it) at least his genuine concern with the whiggish degeneration of the House of Lords. He claims that almost a quarter of the peers were 'New Men', and what was worse, 'all Clients or Proselytes to the Leaders of the opposite Party' who had been 'above Twenty Years corrupting the Nobility with Republican Principles' (*PW* vii.19, 21). He therefore excuses the new creations as an attempt, in some measure, to correct this corruption.[71] Swift could regard noble promotions with a very partisan eye. In the *Examiner* No. 40 (10 May 1711) he describes the recently deceased tory Earl of Rochester as an ornament to the nobility, and compares him to Scipio (*PW* iii.152). Yet Rochester was the first earl of that creation, the second son of the first Earl of Clarendon, who was himself a country gentleman by birth and a lawyer by profession. Clarendon was a 'new man', but he was a tory by adoption. By contrast, the fortunes of the Cavendish family had been made under Henry VIII, partly from the dissolution of the monasteries (which itself would have been enough to have secured Swift's hostility), and they had been earls since 1618. But they were whigs, and Swift was therefore disposed to regard them as upstarts. In a marginal note in his copy of Robert Parsons' *Conference about the Next Succession to the Crown of England* (1594; Swift owned the 1681 edition) against Parsons' remark that the Cavendishes are 'but a mean Family' he commented 'yet now they are Dukes of Devonshire' (*PW* v.242). Since Swift could not feel much confidence in the whig peerage of his day, he turned instead to a more certain source of tory support and strength, the lesser country gentry. The Houyhnhnms have a hierarchical caste system, but nothing corresponding to a peerage. Instead they embody the tory ideal of small independent landowners to whom tory ministers like Danby and Oxford turned for support against the corrupt and self-seeking great nobles of the day.

*

[71] In *The Political State of Great Britain*, xvii (1719), 236-40, Abel Boyer published a list of peers and a table of creations since 1603; of the 178 current peerages listed by Boyer, only 35 enjoyed titles going back as far as 1603. In the same issue Boyer printed abstracts of several pamphlets on the peerage controversy.

The Revolution of 1688 achieved a permanent and successful settlement because most Englishmen (willingly) and even tories like Swift (grudgingly) preferred it, with all its faults, to popery and absolutism on the French model, which seemed the most likely results of a Jacobite restoration. James II had destroyed the possibility of reviving that semi-mythical alliance between royalism and anglicanism with which Clarendon and later Danby had sought to resist the levelling forces in English society. Yet most tories remained attached to it, and were reluctant to admit that it was beyond revival. In 1688-9 it was the Revolution itself that had seemed to threaten the fabric of society, and this feeling is evident in Swift's 'Ode to Sancroft'. But by 1700 it seemed to the conservative observer that an even more dangerous threat came from an irresponsible parliamentary opposition, ignoring national security in its selfish pursuit of factional goals. This provided the occasion for Swift's first political pamphlet, the *Discourse* of 1701, which by the accident of its occasion made him look more like a whig than he ever was. It was not until 1710 that a government was formed that could command his wholehearted loyalty to its pursuit of reactionary anglican policies that tried to reverse the post-1688 direction of social and religious trends. This was the only such government in Swift's lifetime, and he remained loyal to its memory. The accession of George I meant the triumph of the whigs, ending the possibility of the kind of alliance between church and state for which Swift had hoped. Yet he did not become a Jacobite, tempting as it must have been for him, because his overrriding belief in political order and stability told him that a Jacobite restoration would be worse than the worst possible whig government (*Corr*.ii.239). If he had died in 1715, Swift would have been remembered for *A Tale of a Tub* and as a 'furious high-Church man' in his politics, the fellow of Atterbury and Sacheverell. It was the capture and continued occupation of the establishment by the whigs that produced the *Drapier's Letters* and *Gulliver's Travels* and gave him a different reputation. By temperament and conviction he was conservative and authoritarian; an accident of history made him a patron and champion of liberty.

Index